Redefining Ancient Borders

The Jewish Scribal Framework of Matthew's Gospel

AARON M. GALE

t&t clark

NEW YORK • LONDON

T & T Clark International, Madison Square Park, 15 East 26th Street, New York, NY 10010

T & T Clark International, The Tower Building, 11 York Road, London SE1 7NX

T & T Clark International is a Continuum imprint.

Cover design: Brenda Klinger

Gale, Aaron M.
  Redefining ancient borders : the Jewish scribal framework of Matthew's Gospel / Aaron M. Gale.
    p. cm.
  Includes bibliographical references and index.
  ISBN 0-567-02511-X — ISBN 0-567-02521-7 (pbk.)
  1. Bible. N.T. Matthew—Social scientific criticism. 2. Sepphoris (Extinct city) 3. Scribes, Jewish. I. Title.
  BS2575.52.G35 2005
  226.2'066—dc22

                                                                    2005006787

Printed in the United States of America

05 06 07 08 09 10   10 9 8 7 6 5 4 3 2 1

This book is dedicated to my parents,
Morton and Miriam Gale,
of blessed memory,
to whom I am eternally grateful

Contents

Preface

THIS BOOK REPRESENTS THE CULMINATION OF YEARS of research that began on the campus of Northwestern University and Garrett-Evangelical Theological Seminary in Evanston, Illinois. In particular, I was inspired by one person, the late William Richard Stegner. Dr. Stegner, a senior scholar of New Testament studies at Garrett-Evangelical (and a well-respected Matthean scholar in his own right), served in many capacities as my doctoral adviser, mentor, and friend for a number of years until his untimely death in January 2003. Much of the research contained in these pages was gathered under his watchful eye. I owe much to his tutelage. He will be missed greatly.

When I began this work as a doctoral student, my initial thesis centered on the Matthean community's level of literacy. Yet as I compiled the various strands of evidence concerning the Gospel, many other intriguing issues came to the surface. Many foci of study seemed unresolved and/or debated by scholars. This resulted in the study taking on new life as a multidisciplinary examination. Hence, in this book I discuss a number of issues related to Matthew's Gospel, including the community's basic religious inclination, their location, wealth, as well as the issue of the group's literacy. Although I in no way claim to have all the answers, I hope this volume serves as a launching pad for continued dialogue among Matthean scholars.

Many fine people have contributed to the completion of this project, both directly and indirectly. I have had the luxury of not just one, but two fine mentors throughout my short career. In addition to Dr. Stegner, I owe a great deal to Dr. Sheila E. McGinn, Professor of Religious Studies at John Carroll University in Cleveland, Ohio. For many years Dr. McGinn has been a source of admiration and inspiration. Since my days as an undergraduate student at John Carroll, she (along with other members of the John Carroll University religious studies faculty) more than adequately prepared me for the rigors that this discipline entails. I am grateful for her wisdom and friendship.

More directly, I am deeply indebted to my exceptional undergraduate research assistant, Lauren Quattro. Lauren has worked tirelessly gathering information, typing, proofreading, and editing. Without her assistance this book would not have been possible. Her cheery, positive attitude was essential, and not only contributed to the completion of this book but to the sanity of its author. In addition, many others have volunteered their time and effort. I am encouraged as well as blessed to know so many kind and caring people. The list is endless: Stefanie Graczyk, Jim Barker, Stephanie Foutty, the fine people at the university, including Dr. Sharon Ryan, Ken Enoch, Phyllis Calhoun, and my religion students. Only one name may appear as the author of this book, but many people have, in fact, left their signature upon the cover. To all I am grateful.

Aaron M. Gale
West Virginia University, 2004

Introduction

Research Topics and Presuppositions

IN THIS BOOK I EXPLORE FOUR PRIMARY ISSUES RELATED to Matthean scholarship. I focus on the Matthean community's location, economic status, scribal nature, and level of literacy. These four areas are all predicated upon an original thesis, that the Matthean community was a conservative Jewish Christian group. This work began with my doctoral research at Northwestern University and Garrett-Evangelical Theological Seminary in Evanston, Illinois, from 1997–2001. Over the years, as I continued to add the latest scholarly perspectives to the text, I realized that this work had taken on a new dimension. It was now, in addition to a scholarly study, a survey of the diverse contemporary strands of Matthean scholarship present on the eve of, and into, the twenty-first century. Hence, for this book I have attempted to provide a variety of scholarly perspectives up to and including the most recent research.

I realize that some fine articles and books may have been omitted from this study, and for that I apologize. I also acknowledge that some methodologies may not be fully used. I also want to make clear that I provide my own conclusions based upon what I consider the best evidence available. Often, I realize that the "best" evidence itself may be sparse, and I try to point that out whenever possible. Often, I might agree with the vast majority of scholars; in other places my conclusions represent a minority view. In sum, I intend to provide the reader with a clear picture regarding the direction and nature of contemporary Matthean scholarship. The scope of this field is evolving, old theories are being tested and questioned, and it is my intention to reflect this change in the current study.

Matthew as a Jewish Christian Church

In this study I am assuming that the Matthean community was of Jewish Christian derivation. I make the case that the leaders of the congregation, as well as many of the community members, still adhered to the laws in the Torah.[1] This topic is addressed in chapter 1. The religious composition of the church is important, and the Jewish nature of the community sets the stage for the other conclusions drawn in this book.

Scholars have debated the Matthean community's religious practices. Some contend that the church was mostly Gentile, while others, myself among them, argue that the community was Jewish Christian. This study attempts to address both sides of the debate and offers a conclusion based upon historical and textual evidence.

---

1. By "Jewish Christian," I mean that Matthew's community was thoroughly Jewish, yet accepted Jesus of Nazareth as the Messiah. This, of course, differed from the "traditional" Jewish groups, who obviously did not recognize Jesus as any sort of authoritative religious figure. This group also differs from the Gentile Christian followers of Jesus who were not familiar with Judaism and kept none of the laws of the Torah. For a recent summary regarding the current debate surrounding Matthew's Jewish or Gentile nature, see Douglas R. A. Hare, "Current Trends in Matthean Scholarship," *Word and World* 18 (1998): 408–10. For many decades some scholars such as Samuel Sandmel have maintained that Matthew was a Gentile. See Samuel Sandmel, *A Jewish Understanding of the New Testament* (Cincinnati, Ohio: Hebrew Union College Press, 1956), 167. Yet in recent years many scholars believe that Matthew was a Jewish Christian. For instance, see Daniel J. Harrington, *God's People in Christ* (Philadelphia: Fortress, 1980), 96, and L. Michael White, "Crisis Management and Boundary Maintenance: The Social Location of the Matthean Community," in *Social History of the Matthean Community: Cross-Disciplinary Approaches* (ed. David L. Balch; Minneapolis: Fortress, 1991), 224. Also, regarding Matthew's audience, consult Rudolf Schnackenburg, *The Church in the New Testament* (New York: Herder and Herder, 1965), 70, and more recently, Jack Dean Kingsbury, *Matthew as Story* (Philadelphia: Fortress, 1986), 148–52.

Establishing the Matthean community's religion increases the validity of the conclusions concerning location, economic status, and literacy.

The Matthean Community's Location

The Matthean community has traditionally been placed in the city of Antioch, in Syria. In chapter 2, I refute the assertion and provide an alternative location (as some other scholars do)—Sepphoris in Galilee. The placement of the community is important, due to the varying economic, social, and religious situations that existed in the first-century Roman Empire. For example, a Galilean Jewish Christian congregation would have faced different forms of opposition than a Syrian Gentile group. Galilee, on one hand, had a fervent, competing Jewish population late in the first century C.E. Jews closer to Jerusalem practiced a religion more focused on the Temple and its cult. Syria, on the other hand, contained a mixed population of Gentiles and Jews. Jews in Syria practiced differently, due to interaction with Gentiles as well as their distance from the holy Temple in Jerusalem. Therefore, just as the Pauline Epistles were written to individual groups, the Gospels were created by geographically specific churches. In other words, each church created a gospel that addressed the particular concerns of its congregation. Although the Gospels would come to enlighten churches worldwide, they began as unique documents. The community's location is therefore crucial to this study.

The Matthean Community's Economic Status

The third chapter explores the economic status of the Matthean community. If the congregation produced a major work such as a Gospel, must it follow that the church was wealthy? Is there any textual and/or archaeological evidence available which supports the claim that the church had access to a large amount of funds? Scholars have debated the issue. Some claim that the community was poor and itinerant, while others argue that the group was wealthy and urban. This study seeks to clarify the matter by pro-

viding a survey of opinions as well as suggesting a plausible resolution. In the course of this examination, some of the latest archaeological and textual evidence is presented.

Scribal Authorship and Literacy

Initially, my work began as a study regarding the literacy of the
Matthean community. But after a fair amount of research I realized
that the authors of the Gospel seemed to be scholarly. Furthermore,
it seemed the authors were thoroughly versed in Jewish law and the
corresponding methods of rabbinic argumentation. I concluded
that those responsible for the production of Matthew's Gospel
were literate Jewish scholars. The scribal aspect of the Gospel is
addressed directly in chapter 4. Chapter 5 is an exegetical analysis
of various passages from the text. This will clarify my contention
that the authors of the Gospel, as well as the community itself,
must have been learned and well-educated.

I acknowledge that the topic of literacy in the ancient world is a
complicated and somewhat tenuous issue. The concept of literacy
is difficult to define.[2] One may interpret literacy as the ability to
read or write at any level.[3] This definition is problematic. For
example, does the ability to read or write indicate literacy, if one is
incapable of writing a sentence? Furthermore, if a person could
copy from an existing text, does this mean that he or she was literate enough to edit a Gospel?

The issue becomes more confusing when terms such as "scribe"
are brought into the discussion. Some scholars contend that the
New Testament world of the first century could be characterized as
a "scribal culture."[4] This phrase may refer only to a culture in

---

2. Rosamond McKitterick, *The Uses of Literacy in Early Mediaeval Europe*
(Cambridge: Cambridge University Press, 1990), 2.

3. William V. Harris, *Ancient Literacy* (Cambridge: Harvard University Press,
1989), 1–5.

4. John D. Harvey, "Orality and Literacy in the First Century," in *Listening to
the Text: Oral Patterning in Paul's Letters* (Grand Rapids: Baker, 1998), 39.

which reading was largely oral, while most of the population remained illiterate.[5] Remember, oral traditions were important in the New Testament era. Judaism was rich in oral law. Other scholars, however, emphasize the written word. For example, Vernon Robbins argues that first-century culture emphasized both written as well as oral concepts.[6] This debate between oral and written abilities is problematic.

In addition, statistics themselves make studying literacy difficult. In particular, the Matthean community existed within the larger scope of the Roman Empire, which probably had a low literacy rate. William Harris concludes that for most of the Roman world, the basic literacy rate was somewhere around 10 percent, and probably never exceeded 15 to 20 percent.[7] If this is the case, how can one make claims regarding literacy since the majority of people could not read or write? This is the task ahead of me. In essence, I make the case that the Matthean community, rooted in Judaism, indeed possessed the resources (money and scribes) necessary to place it among the elite few who educated communities.

Presuppositions, Limitations, and a Note Regarding Ancient Sources

Most scholars date the composition of Matthew's Gospel to around the year 85 C.E.[8] I accept this approximate date. Markan

---

5. P. J. J. Botha, "Mute Manuscripts: Analysing a Neglected Aspect of Ancient Communication," *Theologica Evangelica* 23 (1990): 42.

6. Vernon K. Robbins, "Progymnastic Rhetorical Composition and Pre-Gospel Traditions: A New Approach," in *The Synoptic Gospels: Source Criticism and the New Literary Criticism* (BETL 110; ed. C. Focant; Louvain: Louvain University Press, 1993), 116.

7. Harris, *Ancient Literacy*, 328.

8. This is a generally accepted view today. See Kingsbury, *Matthew as Story*, 121. I agree with Kingsbury. In fact, by the early twentieth century scholars such as Johannes Weiss already were narrowing down the date to somewhere in the final thirty years of the first century. See Johannes Weiss, *Earliest Christianity: A History of the Period A.D. 30–150* (trans. Frederick C. Grant; Gloucester, Mass.: Peter Smith, 1970), 2:752. Later scholars such as Harrington agree that the

priority, which presumes that Mark's Gospel was completed first, is also accepted. I do not attempt to prove that the Matthean Gospel was written first. Furthermore, the word "Matthew," when used here, refers either to the Gospel itself or to the group of scribal authors (not an individual), whoever they may be, responsible for the production of the Gospel. I am not maintaining that the disciple Matthew actually wrote the text himself.

I use various ancient works such as those written by the first-century historian Josephus, despite the fact that such accounts are not always accurate.[9] Josephus, in particular, had the reputation for glorifying his own deeds, as well as distorting historical events. Yet writers such as Josephus represent the sparse primary sources available for the period, so my only other alternative would have been to rely entirely on secondary or tertiary sources. The current study uses as many primary sources as possible. This adds to the authenticity of the scholarship. Therefore, I cautiously engage the numerous ancient sources relevant to the task at hand.[10]

A Final Note: The Case for Utilizing Rabbinic Sources in New Testament Study

Before proceeding, I wish to justify my usage of anachronistic Jewish rabbinic texts within this New Testament study. This methodology has been criticized by scholars who claim that texts dating

---

Gospel was recorded sometime after 70 C.E. See Daniel J. Harrington, *The Gospel of Matthew* (Sacra pagina 1; Collegeville, Minn.: Liturgical Press, 1991), 10–11. I am not concerned about an exact date. I am content to use 85 C.E. for the purposes of this study.

9. Unless otherwise noted, all passages from Josephus are taken from the following text: Flavius Josephus, *The Complete Works of Josephus* (trans. William Whiston; Grand Rapids: Kregel, 1981).

10. All Hebrew passages are from *The JPS Hebrew-English Tanaka: The Traditional Hebrew Text and the New JPS Translation* (2nd ed.; Philadelphia: The Jewish Publication Society, 1999). All Greek passages are from Kurt Aland and Barbara Aland, eds., *The Nestle-Aland Greek-English New Testament* (8th rev. ed.; Stuttgart: Deutsche-Bibelgesellschaft, 1994). All Septuagint passages are from Sir Lancelot C. L. Brenton, trans., *The Septuagint with Apocrypha: Greek and English* (Peabody, Mass.: Hendrickson, 1999).

from the second century or later are not valid for the study of first-century matters. Scholars also contend that such Jewish texts are biased against Christian principles. On the basis of these arguments, many have asked the question: can one utilize later Jewish texts to study the New Testament?

The Convincing Work of Geza Vermes

Much work has been done in this field by Geza Vermes. Vermes has addressed the problem of how the New Testament and Judaism can be studied in the same breath. I follow his work closely here. Keep in mind that with the possible exception of Luke, the other Gospels exhibit profound Jewish influence. This is especially true in the case of Matthew's Gospel. The problem with New Testament scholarship, according to Vermes, is that the Gentile Church (especially later on) actively sought to divorce itself fundamentally from the Judaism from which its literature derived.[11] Vermes contends that "expertise in the Jewish background to the New Testament is not an optional extra, but . . . , on the contrary, no adequate understanding of Christian sources is conceivable without it."[12] In sum, when studying the New Testament, one should not view Jesus or the Gospel writers as opponents of Judaism. Instead, for the most part they were themselves Jews. Therefore, the authors of the Gospels would have been familiar with first-century Jewish traditions and writings.

There are few first-century Jewish texts comparable to the Gospels. How then is one to study the Jewish nature of the New Testament? Vermes proposes the application of rabbinic literary sources as tools for the interpretation of New Testament texts (such as Matthew's Gospel). Specifically, the sources may be put to use within the context of a historical and comparative study.

There is a problem, however. Rabbinic texts such as the Mish-

---

11. Geza Vermes, *Jesus and the World of Judaism* (Philadelphia: Fortress, 1984), 59.

12. Ibid., 69.

nah or Talmud date from as late as 200–500 C.E. Here Vermes gets
to the core of the issue. He argues that various Jewish traditions
existed and were in use at the time the New Testament was written
during the first century. They actually prove quite vital to its study.
That the texts were not formally recorded until decades later does
not, therefore, discredit them. In other words, oral traditions were
already in use by the first century, and texts such as the Mishnah
and Talmud accurately describe them.

Many scholars agree with Vermes' hypothesis. For instance,
Jacob Neusner states, "[T]he evidence of the Mishnah begins in the
period before 70."[13] Also, Anthony Saldarini has observed, "We
take it for granted that Rabbinic literature, dating from 200 C.E. on,
cannot be used as evidence for Pharisaic thought in the time of Jesus
or for late first-century rabbinic thought at the time of Matthew. . . .
For the most part, the Mishnah and Talmuds are cited to show the
development of Jewish law over several centuries."[14] Bruce Metzger
offers his opinion on the matter: "Although the sixty-three tractates
of the Mishnah were not finally reduced to writing until about the
close of the second century, by the Patriarch Judah (died c. 219), it
is commonly allowed that their contents faithfully reproduce the
oral teaching of the generations of the Tannaim, who date from
about the beginning of the Christian era."[15]

Phillip Sigal concurs: "The view taken in this dissertation is that,
although the rabbinic texts are post-70 in the form in which we
have them, in many instances they represent older, pre-70 traditions."[16] I agree with these scholars. The rabbinic texts represent

13. Jacob Neusner, *Judaism: The Evidence of the Mishnah* (Atlanta: Scholars
Press, 1988), 3.

14. Anthony J. Saldarini, *Matthew's Christian-Jewish Community* (Chicago:
University of Chicago Press, 1994), 269. See also Claudia J. Setzer, *Jewish
Responses to Early Christians: History and Polemics, 30–150 C.E.* (Minneapolis:
Fortress, 1994), 34.

15. Bruce M. Metzger, *Historical and Literary Studies: Pagan, Jewish, and
Christian* (New Testament Tools and Studies 8; ed. Bruce M. Metzger; Grand
Rapids: Eerdmans, 1968), 52.

16. Phillip Sigal, *The Halakah of Jesus of Nazareth according to the Gospel
of Matthew* (Lanham, Md.: University Press of America, 1986), 28.

teachings that were in existence centuries before they were formally recorded. Recall how much of Judaic law relied upon "oral" interpretation of the Torah. The New Testament writers merely used this existing compendium of Jewish knowledge and incorporated it into their own texts.

These rabbinic teachings, in addition to the existing Hebrew Scriptures, contained teachings contemporary to the New Testament texts. Therefore, they were incorporated into the Gospels by their Jewish authors. This is especially true in the case of Matthew, who undoubtedly adhered to the Torah more than the other Gospel writers. I maintain, then, that the Jewish exegetical traditions of the later rabbis must have been in use even in the first century, and it is upon such traditions that Vermes builds his methodology.

This methodology requires a few pertinent assumptions. First, Vermes emphasizes the importance of recognizing the New Testament's link to both the Hebrew Old Testament and postbiblical Judaism.[17] Obviously, if one cannot provide a common foundation between rabbinic Judaism and the New Testament, it would be impossible to compare the two genres. Vermes also notes that Jesus himself probably spoke within an Aramaic-Hebraic atmosphere, not just a Greek one.[18] It is true that Greek was widely spoken in Galilee, but Aramaic and Hebrew were also used for colloquial and liturgical purposes, respectively.

Finally, Vermes states that this type of methodology requires the assumption that Jesus' teachings indeed were true to the Torah.[19] I agree with Vermes here. Passages such as Matt 5:17 confirm this point. Matthew portrays a Jesus who fully upholds the laws of the Torah. They remain valid for his late-first-century contemporaries.

Vermes, then, proves how texts like the Mishnah and Talmud (which discuss Jewish traditions) are capable of aiding in the interpretation of the New Testament. An illustration may be the best way to introduce the method. Consider Matthew's story of the virgin birth (see 1:18–25). Instead of accepting the story at face value,

---

17. Vermes, *Jesus and the World*, 74.
18. Ibid.
19. Ibid., 81.

Vermes turns to the rabbinic sources of the Tosefta and the Talmud for further understanding regarding the word "virgin."[20] The rabbinic teachings lead him to conclude that a "virgin birth" was indeed possible if one considers that according to Jewish tradition (of which Matthew was a part) a "virgin" was one who had not yet menstruated. Was it possible that an ovulating girl, who had not menstruated, if impregnated, could have a "virgin birth"? Vermes indicates that this is feasible. Whether one agrees with Vermes' interpretation or not, the rabbinic sources prove helpful. This serves, therefore, as an example of how Jewish exegetical traditional teaching, already in place in first-century Palestine, provides insight into Matthew's Gospel.

Vermes diagrams four possibilities concerning the relationship among the New Testament, rabbinic literature, and Jewish tradition.[21] First, there is the possibility that any relation between rabbinic literature and the New Testament is pure coincidence. Based upon the above discussion, it is obvious that he does not support this view. In fact, Vermes believes this is unlikely. Second, it is possible that rabbinic literature borrowed from the New Testament. Vermes dismisses this avenue of thought since it is doubtful that the competing rabbis would have been willing to learn from heretical Jewish Christian texts. Third, it is possible that the New Testament utilized Jewish Midrash (early Jewish sources of interpretation). This is unlikely since recorded forms of this literature did not exist in the first century.

The fourth option appears to be the most plausible. Vermes states, "Here we have a theory that is certainly possible and even probable."[22] Thus, he asserts that traditional Jewish teaching must have provided the foundation for the New Testament as well as the rabbinic literature. Since rabbinic literature contains Jewish exegetical traditions, this hypothesis appears to be the most likely of the four models.

---

20. Geza Vermes, *Jesus the Jew: A Historian's Reading of the Gospels* (Philadelphia: Fortress, 1973), 218–19.

21. Vermes, *Jesus and the World*, 84–86. The information from this section comes from here unless otherwise noted.

22. Ibid., 85.

Critics of Vermes

I accept Vermes' conclusions. Yet I do concede that this method of interpretation is criticized by other scholars. Joseph Fitzmyer has been a critic of Vermes. With the discovery of the Dead Sea Scrolls in 1947, Fitzmyer has concluded that later rabbinic sources are shaky at best when it comes to reliable New Testament interpretation.[23] Vermes first observes that Fitzmyer's argument is primarily based upon linguistic proof.[24] The Aramaic evidence found at Qumran (dated around the second century B.C.E. through the first century C.E.) leads to Fitzmyer's contention that no later linguistic findings should be admissible when studying the New Testament. He makes the case (and Vermes acknowledges its validity to a point) that since the Qumran texts are closer to the date of the New Testament, they should serve as the primary sources for interpretation. The later Jewish texts, then, are invalid.

In response, Vermes points out the limitations of Fitzmyer's methodology. He points out that surely "Aramaic speakers of the New Testament times used many more words than those attested in the extant literary and inscriptional remains."[25] Simply stated, how can minuscule pieces of text found at Qumran provide the basis for a study of all New Testament documents, including Matthew's Gospel? Vermes indicates that the comparative literature available is so scarce that it is virtually impossible to base an entire field of study upon it.[26]

Likewise, Vermes feels that this mistake is compounded by what he terms the "handling of the evidence."[27] These flaws in method-

---

23. Vermes points out two key pieces authored by Fitzmyer that argue this view. See, for instance, Joseph A. Fitzmyer, *A Wandering Aramean: Collected Aramaic Essays* (Society of Biblical Literature Monograph Series 25; Missoula, Mont.: Scholars Press, 1979), as well as his article "The Aramaic Language and the Study of the New Testament," *Journal of Biblical Literature* 99 (1980): 5–21.

24. Vermes, *Jesus and the World*, 77.

25. Ibid., 78.

26. Ibid.

27. Ibid. Unless otherwise noted, Vermes' argument in this paragraph is taken from this page as well.

ology are exposed when one considers some of Fitzmyer's examples. Consider, for instance, Fitzmyer's analysis of the Aramaic *korban* ("gift," made to God; Mark 7:11) and its relation to the Greek *doron theou* ("gift of God"). Fitzmyer concludes that the later Talmud is useless (compared to earlier Aramaic inscriptions found in Palestine), since it uses the term *korban* differently. Vermes deems this conclusion flawed because in reality Fitzmyer is quoting results from the earlier Hebrew Mishnah instead.[28] Fitzmyer also ignores the first-century historian Josephus's usage of the term. On the basis of such fundamental errors, one can successfully dismiss as unfounded many of Fitzmyer's linguistic challenges. Finally, Vermes concludes that the primary utility of Aramaic Qumran texts lies only in their relation to other first-century Aramaic documents.[29]

The rabbinic texts certainly conveyed layers of oral Jewish tradition that were in existence by the first century. Much can be gained, then, from the use of these rabbinic texts, even if they were formally recorded at later times. This is especially true in Matthew's case, since I contend that the Gospel authors not only were aware of such Jewish teachings, but that they utilized them extensively. Therefore, I employ rabbinic texts within my study of Matthew's Gospel. I make the case that these rabbinic documents are essential, even if they were not recorded until some time after the Gospels.

The Use of Jewish Exegetical Techniques in the Analysis of a Gospel

The same argument may be made regarding the use of Jewish exegetical techniques as they relate to Matthew's Gospel. One could make the claim that Jewish exegetical techniques such as the *binyan av* and *gezerah shavah* have no place in the study of a first-century gospel. Such rabbinic techniques were not in use until cen-

---

28. Ibid., 78–79.
29. Ibid., 80.

turies later; hence, they are invalid within a textual study of earlier Christian writings.[30] Again, this claim is made by scholars who dismiss the rabbinic texts as anachronistic.

I uphold the validity of this methodology. I argue that the authors of Matthew indeed utilized rabbinic techniques. As Robert Shedinger indicates, "But some scholars have begun to see evidence that rabbinic exegetical practice developed not suddenly in the classical rabbinic period but gradually, meaning that at least some form of what would later become classical rabbinic exegetical practice should be found in earlier Jewish literature."[31] Robert Shedinger further points out that numerous scholars have already proven that techniques such as the *gezerah shavah* were indeed in use well before the Mishnah and Talmud were recorded. In fact, other Gospel authors like John may have been using the technique.[32] Although I discuss Jewish exegetical techniques in a later chapter, I am confident that using them within the study of Matthean scholarship is valid.

---

30. Robert F. Shedinger, "Must the Greek Text Always Be Preferred? Versional and Patristic Witnesses to the Text of Matthew 4:16," *Journal of Biblical Literature* 123 (2004): 455. Shedinger points out this tendency by scholars, although he appears to accept the possibility.

31. Ibid.

32. Ibid., 455–56.

1

The Matthean Community
and Formative Judaism

IN THIS CHAPTER I ESTABLISH THE NATURE OF JUDAISM following 70 C.E. Then I link this understanding to the Matthean community to see if one may ascertain the religious situation facing the group. I begin by examining the general relationship among early Jewish Christians and formative Jews. This gives the reader a better perspective regarding the crisis that existed following the Jewish War. First, it is pertinent to provide a brief historical sketch for the period immediately following the Jewish Revolt of 66–70 C.E. Many changes had taken place after the war that would influence both Jewish and Christian thought.

The State of Judaism following 70 C.E.

Subsequent to the Jewish War, Palestine became a Roman province. Jews in Israel were now considered equal with the Jews in the Diaspora territories.[1] Prior to the war, Jews in Jerusalem had enjoyed a privileged status. Now most of those Jews were exiled or killed. Bo Reicke notes that the majority of Jews now lived outside of Pales-

---

1. Bo Ivar Reicke, *The New Testament Era* (trans. David E. Green; Philadelphia: Fortress, 1964), 283.

tine, due to the fact that most of them either had left during and
after the destruction of Jerusalem or had been forcibly expelled by
Rome.[2] Furthermore, the emperor Vespasian imposed a tax replacing the former tax given to the Temple. This new δίδραχμον tax
was now to be paid directly to Rome.[3] In sum, the life of the Jewish people had been permanently changed. Without the Temple and
the court of the Sanhedrin, daily life was in a state of upheaval.[4]

Formerly, many Jews in Palestine had been able to maintain a
relatively high social status. Now, however, the Jewish upper class
was bereft of most of their possessions. This, Reicke contends, may
have led some of the formerly wealthy aristocratic Jews to take "an
attitude of solidarity with the Romans."[5] It seems that some Jews
(possibly the remnants of the Sadducees) sought friendly relations
with their Roman conquerors, in hopes of regaining their previous
way of life. But how exactly did the Romans view the Jews?

There are some surviving examples from Greco-Roman literature that address the issue.[6] The great Roman historian Tacitus
wrote considerably in his *Historiae* about the state of Judaism in
the first century. For the most part, Tacitus found the customs of
the Jews "perverse and disgusting."[7] He refers to the Jewish faith
as "tasteless and mean."[8] Juvenal, a late-first-century Italian, also

---

2. Ibid., 284.

3. See Josephus, *Jewish War* 7:6:6.

4. Emil Schürer, *The History of the Jewish People in the Age of Jesus Christ*
(vol. 1; ed. and trans. Geza Vermes and Fergus Millar; Edinburgh: T&T Clark,
1973), 521.

5. Reicke, *New Testament Era*, 286. For evidence, see also Bar 1:12 and 2:21,
which speak of a peaceful life under "Babylonian" rule. "Babylon" was a common euphemism for the Roman Empire. The book of Revelation supports this
claim.

6. In particular, I am following one such study on the matter. See Molly Whittaker, *Jews and Christians: Graeco-Roman Views* (Cambridge: Cambridge University Press, 1984). All passages from Tacitus and other ancient historians in this
paragraph have been pointed out by Whittaker.

7. *Historiae* 5:5. All quotations from Tacitus here are taken from *The Complete Works of Tacitus* (ed. Moses Hadas; trans. Alfred John Church and William
Jackson Brodribb; New York: Random House, 1942).

8. Ibid.

did not care for the Jewish faith. He states in his *Satires* that "Jews sell for small change any kind of dreams you like" (see 2:6:542–547). Yet Judaism was also admired. Josephus observes that some non-Jews displayed a desire "to follow our religious observances."[9] This was particularly true with respect to the Jewish law of Sabbath observance. Pliny the Elder compliments the Jewish sect of the Essenes. He calls their lifestyle "marvelous" (see *Natural History* 5:73:1–3). Generally, Judaism following 70 C.E. was probably looked upon with disdain by most Romans.

I do not wish to get involved in the debate regarding the validity of the post-70 Yavneh rabbinic movement. Scholars have debated whether or not Yavneh was the actual city where postwar Judaism was restored by protorabbinic founders such as Yohanan ben Zakkai. Some scholars support this view. Jacob Neusner, for instance, has observed that the Yavneh movement allowed Judaism to remain a living faith.[10] Others, however, believe that the story was created by the rabbis in order to defend themselves against the brutality of Rome while glorifying the figure of ben Zakkai.[11] In particular, Saldarini feels that the group that gathered at Yavneh in late 70 C.E. (he does acknowledge this event) had little authority regarding the leadership of Judaism, was probably an informal group, and was a myth created by the later rabbis to idealize ben Zakkai and his work.[12]

Many scholars feel otherwise; some Jews did escape to the coast and began the restructuring of Judaism (Saldarini even admits meetings took place there). This was necessary considering all of

---

9. *Against Apion* 2:1:40.

10. Jacob Neusner, *First-Century Judaism in Crisis* (Nashville: Abingdon, 1975), 157.

11. J. Andrew Overman, *Matthew's Gospel and Formative Judaism: The Social World of the Matthean Community* (Minneapolis: Fortress, 1990), 40. Overman points out how scholars such as P. Schäfer believe the tradition of the Yavneh movement is a mere foundation myth (*Grundungslegende*). See P. Schäfer, "Die Flucht Johanan b. Zakkai aus Jerusalem und die Gründnung des 'Lehrhauses' in Jabne," in *Principat* 19/2 (ed. Wolfgang Haase; Berlin: Walter de Gruyter, 1979), 78.

12. Anthony J. Saldarini, *Matthew's Christian-Jewish Community* (Chicago: University of Chicago Press, 1994), 14.

the damage done to the religion by Rome during the war. First-century Judaism had relied upon two cornerstones: Temple and Torah. Therefore, the rabbis felt the need to gather at Yavneh in order to restructure the endangered religion. Daniel Harrington puts it best:

> The rabbinic movement in its origins is best seen as a response to the events of A.D. 70. . . . After A.D. 70 the Temple laid in ruins and the land was even more clearly under Roman control. Only the Torah remained unscathed. The challenge facing the founders of the rabbinic movement was to shape a form of Judaism that remained faithful to the tradition.[13]

Shaye Cohen concurs, observing that the rabbis at Yavneh attempted to unify the Jewish religion. This was necessary, because after the war Judaism had become fragmented and sectarian in nature.[14] Although there were periods of calm following the war, at times the late-first-century Roman emperors would zealously and ruthlessly persecute Jews.[15] Eusebius points this out in *The Ecclesiastical History*, in which the emperors (Vespasian, Titus, or Domitian; one cannot be sure) seek out those from "the family of David" (see 3:12, 19–20). Overman states, "It is important to recognize the beginning of social order and construction within so-called formative Judaism. The story of Yavneh represents the beginning of that process, and by no means its conclusion."[16] Yet how did the rabbis implement their plan to save Judaism?

The rabbis at Yavneh began by instituting a number of reforms—whether this group was a minority or not is not ultimately important, since eventually their reforms would be adopted by "normative" Judaism. First, they debated the status of some

---

13. Daniel J. Harrington, *The Gospel of Matthew* (Sacra pagina 1; Collegeville, Minn.: Liturgical Press, 1991), 14.

14. Shaye J. D. Cohen, "The Significance of Yavneh: Pharisees, Rabbis, and the End of Jewish Sectarianism," *Hebrew Union College Annual* (1984): 42.

15. A. R. C. Leaney, *The Jewish and Christian World, 200 BC to AD 200* (Cambridge: Cambridge University Press, 1984), 7:121. Leaney points out passages from Eusebius.

16. Overman, *Matthew's Gospel and Formative Judaism*, 42.

books of the Jewish canon.[17] Second, the rabbis began to promote stricter observances of the Jewish festivals, since the Torah, not the Temple, was now the focal point of religious observance.[18] The rabbis emphasized serious analysis and study of the Torah, and developed interpretations to give the Jewish people guidance during this dark time.[19] Daily prayers were also structured more rigorously, and realizing the need for education, the rabbis levied a rabbinical school tax.[20] All of these changes were designed to codify and preserve the faith. This information is important because it illustrates the desperate and volatile atmosphere that existed in Palestine late in the first century.

The State of Judaism in Galilee

I want to sketch briefly the religious scope of Galilee in the first century C.E., since it is relevant to the Matthean community's beliefs and interactions with other groups. Also, as Sanders notes, much has changed regarding the evidence available concerning the religious preferences of Galilee.[21] Archaeology has played a large role in this shift of beliefs. I note much of this evidence in the

---

17. Cohen, *From the Maccabees to the Mishnah* (Philadelphia: Westminster, 1987), 228–29. Although some scholars still believe that the Yavnean rabbis formed the Jewish canon, most no longer follow this line of thinking. See also Saldarini, *Matthew's Christian-Jewish Community*, 14. I follow the view that the canon already had been formed, but I do believe that it was still debated by the rabbis after the war.

18. See *m. Rosh Hashanah* 4:1–4, for instance. For a brief discussion of some of these changes, see also Frederic Manns, *John and Jamnia: How the Break Occurred between Jews and Christians, c. 80–100 A.D.* (Jerusalem: Franciscan Printing, 1988), 15–18.

19. Harrington, *Gospel of Matthew*, 15.

20. Reicke, *New Testament Era*, 288. For a more detailed discussion of the work of ben Zakkai, Gamaliel II, and other Jewish leaders, see Alexander Guttmann, *Rabbinic Judaism in the Making: A Chapter in the History of the Halakhah from Ezra to Judah I* (Detroit: Wayne State University Press, 1970), 187–257.

21. E. P. Sanders, "Jesus' Galilee," in *Fair Play: Diversity and Conflicts in Early Christianity* (ed. Ismo Dunderberg et al.; Leiden: Brill, 2002), 3.

ensuing chapters. First, I examine the scholarly and textual evidence that clearly support my conclusion that Galilee was far more Jewish than earlier scholars concluded. In particular, as Sanders points out, Jewish literature from the time of Alexander the Great to the rabbinic era is extremely helpful in discerning Hellenistic influences on Judaism. And for the most part, little mention is made of Hellenism's impact on the faith.[22] I argue that this is especially the case when considering first-century Galilee.

Following the destruction of Jerusalem, Jews were forced to relocate to places such as Yavneh to ensure the faith's survival. Thus, Galilee became a major center of Jewish learning. Helmut Koester states, "Galilee (see Matt 28:10, 16), not Jerusalem, is the place for the beginning of a new epoch: the mission to all the nations—and Matthew must have known that Galilee was also the starting-point of the reorganization of Judaism."[23]

Koester's assessment is accurate. After 70 C.E., many rabbis journeyed from the South to Galilee.[24] Rabbinic literature describes rabbis such as Rabban Gamaliel traveling to cities like Sepphoris and Tiberias.[25] Furthermore, and most pertinent to this study, Galilean Jewish scribes and sages came to the forefront at that time. For instance, the Mishnah indicates that a Galilean teacher instituted a new policy regarding prayer.[26] Seán Freyne also points out those Galilean students of halakah appear more frequently in Galilee after the year 70.[27]

Aharon Oppenheimer notes that Galilee was a center of Torah and Jewish learning. Many sages active in Galilee both before and after the Jewish War were teaching the Torah.[28] Among them were

22. Ibid., 39.

23. Helmut Koester, *Introduction to the New Testament: History and Literature of Early Christianity* (Philadelphia: Fortress, 1982), 2:177.

24. Seán Freyne, *Galilee from Alexander the Great to Hadrian: A Study of Second Temple Judaism* (Edinburgh: T&T Clark, 1980), 324.

25. See *t. Shabbat* 15:8, which mentions Sepphoris, and *b. Shabbat* 115a and *m. Eruvin* 10:10, which mention Tiberias.

26. See *m. Ta'anit* 2:5.

27. Freyne, *Galilee from Alexander the Great to Hadrian*, 326–27.

28. Aharon Oppenheimer, *The 'Am Ha-Aretz: A Study in the Social History*

sages such as R. Jose the Galilean, R. Halafta (located in Sepphoris), R. Hanina ben Teradion, and others.[29] In fact, the Talmud itself mentions many sages who were actively teaching the Torah in Galilee. For example, in the Babylonian Talmud we find common phrases such as כבן עזאי בשוקי טבריאהריני, which means, "I am like Ben 'Azzai in the market places of Tiberias."[30] Ben 'Azzai was a well-known scholar. Stories of other sages active in Galilee are found as well.[31] This indicates that Torah observance was being emphasized in the region following 70 C.E.

Overall, then, there was a marked increase in Jewish activity and interest in halakah in Galilee, following the Jewish War. Nevertheless, some rabbis also seemed to be frustrated. The famous Yohanan ben Zakkai has been quoted as saying, "O Galilee, Galilee, thou hatest the law; thine end will be to have to deal with brigands."[32] If Torah observance among Jews was being stressed in Galilee, then one can assume that ben Zakkai was referring to those Jews who had strayed from it. The Jewish Christians were likely the guilty party. This suggests that Jewish Christianity had taken root in Galilee alongside formative Judaism. The rabbis were struggling with the foreign Jewish Christian views. Conflict was in the air.

I wish to make one final point regarding Galilean Judaism. I am assuming that there was not a great schism between the former Judaism of Jerusalem and the Judaism of Galilee following 70 C.E. I also propose that Judaism was unified and remained loyal to the foundation that had been constructed in Jerusalem earlier in the

---

of the Jewish People in the Hellenistic-Roman Period (ed. K. H. Rengstorf; trans. I. H. Levine; Arbeiten zur Literatur und Geschichte des hellenistischen Judentums 8; Leiden: Brill, 1977), 210–13. All information from Oppenheimer is found in this section.

29. See *t. Makhshirin* 1:3.

30. *b. Eruvin* 29a. Other examples are found throughout the Babylonian Talmud. See *Sotah* 45a; *Qiddushin* 20a; *Arakhin* 30b.

31. See also stories of Elisha ben Avuyah from *y. Hagigah* 2:77b, as well as R. Elizer ben Hyrcanus as listed in *b. Sukkah* 28a.

32. L. E. Elliott-Binns, *Galilean Christianity* (London: SCM Press, 1956), 74. Elliott-Binns points this out. See *y. Shabbat* 15d.

century. In other words, I believe that Galilean Judaism differed little from the established Palestinian faith.[33] Galilee, for the most
part, did not represent some "sectarian" form of Judaism; it upheld
the principles of the former leaders in Jerusalem. The Torah
remained as valid in Galilee as anywhere else.[34] The passages from
the Mishnah quoted above support this assertion. It may even be the
case that when differences existed, the Galileans took a more fervent approach to the laws of the Torah than the Judeans. Lawrence
Schiffman observes, "Our examination of the specific references in
tannaitic sources to differences between the Galileans and Judeans
has revealed that, in most cases, the Galileans were more stringent
in regard to the law than their Judean coreligionists."[35]

Yet some regional differences did exist. As Freyne, in his discussion on bandits in Galilee concludes, "[D]espite the fact that the
Galileans shared a common faith with their brothers in the south,
regional factors and a historico-political and socio-cultural character played a very important part in determining their understanding and expression of their beliefs."[36] This suggests that the
differences in Torah observance existed among specific individuals
or groups. This is not damaging to my assertion above. For the purposes of this study, the differences matter little, if at all.

Josephus seems to support this view, judging by his silence on
the matter. He does not mention any radical form of Judaism present in Galilee. Therefore, the Torah remained the sole authority

---

33. Support for this assertion comes from other scholars as well. See W. D.
Davies, *Christian Origins and Judaism* (Philadelphia: Westminster, 1961), 21. See
also Freyne, *Galilee from Alexander the Great to Hadrian*, 322. Finally, see
Oppenheimer, *'Am-Ha-Aretz*, 213–15.

34. Eric M. Meyers and James F. Strange, *Archaeology, the Rabbis, and Early
Christianity* (Nashville: Abingdon, 1981), 36–38.

35. Lawrence H. Schiffman, "Was There a Galilean Halakah?" in *The Galilee
in Late Antiquity* (ed. Lee I. Levine; Cambridge: Harvard University Press, 1992),
156. As the quote indicates, Schiffman bases his conclusion upon the study of rabbinic texts. Therefore, I have confidence in his findings.

36. Seán Freyne, "Bandits in Galilee: A Contribution to the Study of Social
Conditions in First-Century Palestine," in *The Social World of Formative Christianity and Judaism: Essays in Tribute to Howard Clark Kee* (ed. Jacob Neusner
et al.; Philadelphia: Fortress, 1988), 65.

following the destruction of the Temple. This love of the Torah would continue into the rabbinic period under the work of the Yavnean leaders such as ben Zakkai. If anything, during the Yavnean period, Galilee's zest for the Torah became more intense.[37]

In sum, following 70 C.E. the course of Judaism would be changed forever. The faith had become strictly a religion of the book. The Torah was now Judaism's compendium of law and ethics. This remains true today. Furthermore, Judaism was fighting for its very survival in light of the current social situation. Following the destruction of Jerusalem by Rome, much of the population was dead, exiled, or imprisoned. There was a pressing need for a unified Jewish faith, and this played a part in the Jews' attitude toward other threatening groups, including the Jewish Christian Matthean community.

Before describing the state of Christianity in the late first century, I must clarify what I mean by "Christianity." Unless noted otherwise, when I refer to Christianity I am describing a fledging religion that was still dependent upon its parent faith, Judaism. The permanent schism between Judaism and Christianity took centuries, not years. Some scholars argue that even by the time of the Bar Kochba Rebellion in the second century, there was still no definitive separation between Judaism and Christianity.[38] In fact, the notion that Christians participated in Jewish religious services was mentioned by later Church fathers such as Origen. In his *Homilies on Leviticus*, he admonishes those Christians who are listening to him on Sunday for bringing up what they had heard the day before in synagogue.[39] This suggests that many Christian groups

---

37. Freyne, *Galilee from Alexander the Great to Hadrian*, 323–29.

38. Steven T. Katz, "Issues in the Separation of Judaism and Christianity after 70 C.E.: A Reconsideration," *Journal of Biblical Literature* 103 (1984): 76.

39. See Judith Lieu, "History and Theology in Christian Views of Judaism," in *The Jews among Pagans and Christians in the Roman Empire* (ed. Judith Lieu et al.; London: Routledge, 1992), 89. She is referring here to Origen's *Homilies on Leviticus* V 8. Augustine, writing in the fourth century, even fits into this category. See his *Expositio in epistuluam ad Galatas*, 35, in which he mentions the riot that would occur if a Christian were to be found observing the Jewish Sabbath.

were not yet separated from Judaism, even in the century following the Gospel of Matthew.[40]

Furthermore, pertaining to the actual beginning of Christianity,
Hans Conzelmann has noted:

> The conflict between church and synagogue is inherent in the found-
> ing of the church itself, for it is inherently a missionary church. Since
> the church itself originally consisted only of Jews and carried on its
> missionary work only among Jews, it was essentially an internal
> conflict. It did not understand itself as a new religion but as the true
> Israel, which believed that the promise to Israel was now being ful-
> filled.[41]

The Matthean Gospel confirms this. Jesus, after all, tells his disciples not to missionize the Gentiles, only the Jews (see 10:6). Therefore it is likely that the majority of first generation Christians must
have been, in reality, Jewish Christians.[42] The Old Testament
remained valid as holy Scripture for these first followers of Jesus. I
believe this was the case for a long period of time, as the Matthean
Gospel indicates.

There were probably a wide variety of Jewish Christian groups
that existed at this time.[43] I do realize that there probably were
Greek Christian groups that quickly abandoned the Torah.[44] They
were known as Gentile Christians. By the time of Paul, Gentile
Christians did not seem required to keep the Torah at all (see Gal
2; Acts 15). For the purposes of this study, and due to the fact that

---

40. This holds true outside of Palestine as well. For instance, Colin H. Roberts
has pointed out that in Egypt early Christianity was quite reluctant to disconnect
itself from Judaism. See Colin H. Roberts, *Manuscript, Society, and Belief in Early
Christian Egypt* (London: Oxford University Press, 1979), 56–58.

41. Hans Conzelmann, *Gentiles-Jews-Christians: Polemics and Apologetics in
the Greco-Roman Era* (trans. M. Eugene Boring; Tübingen: J. C. B. Mohr, 1981),
251.

42. Koester, *Introduction to the New Testament*, 2:199.

43. Saldarini, *Matthew's Christian-Jewish Community*, 24. See also Stephen
G. Wilson, *Related Strangers: Jews and Christians, 70–170 C.E.* (Minneapolis:
Fortress, 1995), 143–68.

44. Conzelmann, *Gentiles-Jews-Christians*, 252.

the Matthean community itself was both Palestinian as well as *primarily* Jewish Christian, it is more appropriate to examine Christianity as it related to Judaism. Therefore, when I speak of "Christians" of the late first century, I am still referring to those believers in Jesus who observed at least a portion of the laws of the Torah. Had the Matthean community been Hellenistic and Gentile, this study would have pursued a different course.

The State of Christianity following the Jewish War

As with Judaism, there are many facts about first-century Christianity that are unavailable to the modern scholar. For instance, Koester states, "We do not know the name of a single Christian from the decades that followed the deaths of the apostles of the first Christian generation, from the period of about C.E. 60–90."[45] This statement includes literature, which similarly lacked a definitive author. Additionally, as with Judaism, there is some debate surrounding the authenticity of the earliest surviving Christian documents. For instance, can one say with certainty that the disciples actually saw Jesus after his death as the authors of Matthew claim in 28:9? One cannot know, since the earliest New Testament fragments date from around 200 C.E. or later, with the exception of one fragment from John's Gospel.[46] This is 170 years after the death of Jesus. However, some points regarding the nature of the faith can still be made. Whenever possible, I try to restrict my comments to the Christianity of Palestine, since that is the region I am examining.

There were probably both written and oral streams of Christian Gospel traditions in existence following 70 C.E.[47] The Gospels were

---

45. Koester, *Introduction to the New Testament*, 2:279.

46. Ibid., 15. Note here the similarity between Jewish textual problems and Christian textual problems. This is why studying either religion in the manner being attempted here is quite a difficult chore. However, the portrayals within this section reflect an attempt to provide information based upon the most reliable sources.

47. John P. Meier, "The Antiochene Church of the Second Christian Genera-

written between 65 and 100 C.E. Evidence for this is confirmed by second-century documents such as *The First Letter of Clement* (see 1:1a; 7:1b), which reveals some actions taken against practicing Christians. Like Judaism, the various Christian groups were able to exist without a great deal of persecution by late-first-century Roman emperors such as Vespasian and Titus.[48] Roman leadership began to view Jews and Christians as equals, with one notable exception. Jews had long established their ethnic identity, while Christians remained united only by their common faith.[49]

Yet the destruction of the Temple remained important to the first Christians. There seem to be indirect references to the tragedy, as Matt 12:6 and 26:61 imply. In 12:6 Jesus says, "I tell you, something greater than the temple is here," while in 26:61 two false witnesses against Jesus accuse him of saying that he can destroy and rebuild the Temple. Furthermore, Matt 24:1–25:46 seems to allude to the destruction of the Temple as well.[50] Specifically, 24:2 is central since here Jesus states, "Truly I tell you, not one stone will be left here upon another, all will be thrown down."These references indicate some knowledge of the event, but oddly enough no direct accounts are found, with the exception of one mention in the apocryphal Epistle of Barnabas (16:4). Nonetheless, the event affected Jewish Christian groups such as Matthew's, which chose to remain in Galilee. The absence of any textual evidence may suggest nothing more than Christianity's lack of organized apologetic against the Jews.[51]

---

tion," in *Antioch and Rome: New Testament Cradles of Christianity* (ed. Raymond E. Brown and John P. Meier; New York: Paulist, 1983), 51.

48. Reicke, *New Testament Era*, 292.

49. Ibid., 305.

50. Bo Reicke points out that 24:2 is especially important since the author "strengthens the realism" of this catastrophic event by utilizing the imagery of the "stones." For his discussion on the matter, see Reicke, "Synoptic Prophecies on the Destruction of Jerusalem," in *Studies in New Testament and Early Christian Literature: Essays in Honor of Allen P. Wikgren* (ed. David E. Aune; Supplements to Novum Testamentum 33; Leiden: Brill, 1972), 121–34.

51. W. H. Lampe, "A.D. 70 in Christian Reflection," in *Jesus and the Politics of His Day* (ed. Ernst Bammel and C. F. D. Moule; Cambridge: Cambridge University Press, 1984), 155.

Struggles between Judaism and
Jewish Christianity

Following the Jewish War, the leaders of formative Judaism were concerned about the divisions among the Jewish population.[52] Certainly the new movement of Jewish Christianity represented one of the so-called divisions.[53] Jewish Christianity at this time was still a part of Judaism, as noted previously.[54] As a result of the Jewish rebellion against Rome, Judaism was now fighting for its very survival. As Robert Wilken states, "During the first and second centuries the Jews suffered greatly at the hands of the Romans, and their members were significantly depleted, especially in the eastern provinces."[55] Surely, then, something had to be done to preserve the faith.

The tensions between Judaism and Jewish Christianity had expressed themselves by the late first century. One of the basic attacks leveled by Jews upon Christians was that the latter movement was mere "magic."[56] Matthew 12:22–28 illustrates this charge. Rabbinic works also provide examples of Judaism's disdain for Jewish Christianity. The Talmud warns against believing those who say that they are "God" or are going up to heaven.[57] Jesus fit

---

52. Katz, "Issues in the Separation of Judaism and Christianity," 50.

53. Saldarini, *Matthew's Christian-Jewish Community*, 14. Saldarini notes that many movements competed for power among Palestinian Jews of the first century. Jewish Christianity would have been one of those movements.

54. See the section above, as well as Craig A. Evans, "Faith and Polemic: The New Testament and First-Century Judaism," in *Anti-Semitism and Early Christianity* (ed. Craig A. Evans and Donald A. Hagner; Minneapolis: Fortress, 1993), 11. In particular, Evans states, "The New Testament Christianity was Judaism— that is, what was believed to be the true expression of Judaism."

55. Robert L. Wilken, *Judaism and the Early Christian Mind: A Study of Cyril of Alexandria's Exegesis and Theology* (New Haven: Yale University Press, 1971), 9.

56. Alan F. Segal, *Rebecca's Children: Judaism and Christianity in the Roman World* (Cambridge: Harvard University Press, 1986), 143. The "magic" that the Jews were alluding to was probably the result of hearing miracle stories about Jesus.

57. Ibid., 149. See *y. Ta'anit* 65b for the exact reference.

both criteria. Christians came to believe that Jesus was the son of God, and he ascended to be with his Father. Therefore, the references here seemed to be aimed at the claims of Jesus' followers. And the Church fathers speak of Jews cursing Christians.[58] Hence, I make the case that, to some degree, Jews intentionally singled out Jewish Christians for chastisement, in both practice and literature.

One piece of literature often cited as evidence of this persecution is the ברכת המינים, "the blessing of the heretics." Reportedly instituted by the Jewish leader Gamaliel II (at Yavneh) at the end of the first century C.E., this addition is still read today as the twelfth blessing in the Hebrew prayer, the שמונה עשרה, "the Eighteen Benedictions."[59] This curse was created to exclude heretics (those with incorrect Jewish beliefs) from "the book of the living."[60] The blessing was directed at heretics, and was important to the rabbis because it is mentioned by name in both the Tosefta as well as the Talmud.[61] In part, the blessing reads, "And for slanderers let there be no hope, and let all wickedness perish as in a moment; let all thine enemies be speedily cut off, and the dominion of arrogance do thou uproot and crush, cast down and humble speedily in our days."[62]

---

58. Segal, *Rebecca's Children*, 150.

59. Reicke, *New Testament Era*, 305. The theory that Gamaliel II wrote the blessing is somewhat controversial, though, since some scholars believe that the phrase dates from much later. See Saldarini, *Matthew's Christian-Jewish Community*, 14. For the purposes of this study, however, I stand with numerous other scholars who maintain that it was composed in the first century following the revolt against Rome. Evidence for this position is found in the Talmud. See *b. Berakhot* 28b, in which Gamaliel is involved in the process (although Samuel the Small actually wrote it). See also Overman, *Matthew's Gospel and Formative Judaism*, 50, as well as Cohen, *From the Maccabees to the Mishnah*, 227.

60. Overman, *Matthew's Gospel and Formative Judaism*, 50. See also Lawrence Schiffman, *From Text to Tradition: A History of Second Temple and Rabbinic Judaism* (Hoboken, N.J.: Ktav, 1991), 153. It is Schiffman's definition of "heretic" that I am following here.

61. R. Travers Herford, *Christianity in Talmud and Midrash* (New York: Ktav, 1903), 136. Herford points this out. See *t. Berakhot* 3:25 and *y. Berakhot* 8a.

62. W. D. Davies, *The Setting of the Sermon on the Mount* (Atlanta: Scholars Press, 1989), 275. I am using Davies' Hebrew translation.

This blessing was aimed at any Jewish group that did not follow the teachings of the rabbis.[63] Jewish Christian groups such as the Matthean community would have been included. Any Jewish group that did not obey the teachings of the rabbis was a threat to the faith and would not have been tolerated. Furthermore, Jewish Christian groups like the Matthean congregation may have misunderstood the blessing, believing it to be directed *only* at them. This would have led to more dissension among the groups, as the conflicting tone of Matthew's Gospel indicates. This also would have led to increased tension between Judaism and Jewish Christianity in general.

Cohen, in fact, believes that the blessing of the heretics was designed to eliminate Jewish sectarianism and to unite all Jews.[64] Unity was needed more than anything else following the Jewish revolt. Therefore, "heretics" represented any persons who tried to differentiate themselves from the larger rabbinic group. Judaism could not tolerate any group that sought to shatter the fragile faith, so this blessing was intended to eliminate even the thought of it. I agree, then, with Overman, who states, "The *Birkat ha-Minim* was directed against schismatics or dissenters. That is to say, the benediction in question was aimed at any person or group that would disrupt the coalition that formative Judaism was struggling to forge in this period."[65]

So where does that leave the state of Judaism's relation to Jewish Christianity? I think two central points emerge from this discussion. First, it is clear that formative Judaism was struggling for survival, so the rabbis implemented a blessing against the heretics in order to dissuade any Jews from breaking away from the emerging mainstream of Jewish thought. Second, I think that Jewish Christian groups like Matthew's may have misunderstood the blessing, believing it was aimed specifically at them (see Matt 9:35; "their synagogues"). Judaism and Jewish Christianity were still linked, but tension was increasing among the groups.

---

63. Katz, "Issues in the Separation of Judaism and Christianity," 73. See also Schiffman, *From Text to Tradition*, 153.

64. Cohen, *From the Maccabees to the Mishnah*, 228.

65. Overman, *Matthew's Gospel and Formative Judaism*, 51.

Although it was not intended for that purpose, I believe that the blessing serves as a gauge regarding the situation between Jews and Jewish Christians late in the first century. Conflict was on the rise among the Jews and Jewish Christians, and this was particularly true regarding the Matthean community. Formative Judaism was reacting liturgically (by making the blessing part of the daily prayer regimen) in order to keep its membership intact. Jewish Christianity was going to have to react as well. This reaction is evident in Matthew's Gospel.

Evidence of Tension in the Matthean Gospel

As Overman points out, "Matthew's church viewed those people [the formative Jews] not just as rivals, but as threats to their safety and way of life. The Matthean community vied with the Jewish scribes and Pharisees for position and voice in Matthew's city or town."[66] Evidence for this is found in Matt 13:30, in which Jesus states in the parable of the tares, "Let both of them grow together until the harvest."[67] Overman provides an organized way to assess the general nature of the situation in Galilee. He points to the issue of Jewish leadership. The Matthean Gospel seems to criticize the current leaders of the Jewish community for their incorrect interpretation of the Torah.[68]

The Matthean scribes were also fighting for legitimacy regarding Torah interpretation. The community was defending its point of view.[69] To the winner went the prize: a role in the leadership of the Jewish community in Galilee. The authors of Matthew had to convince two groups of this: their own skeptical church members, as well as the outside Jewish leaders.[70] After all, it is likely that the

---

66. J. Andrew Overman, *Church and Community in Crisis: The Gospel according to Matthew* (Valley Forge, Pa.: Trinity Press International, 1996), 20.

67. Kingsbury, *Matthew as Story*, 153.

68. Overman, *Church and Community in Crisis*, 20.

69. Overman, *Matthew's Gospel and Formative Judaism*, 89.

70. Overman, *Church and Community in Crisis*, 21.

authors faced some dissension within their own community.[71] If the Matthean scribes could prove that they alone were the correct Torah interpreters, the community could legitimize their roles as the forerunners of a "new" Judaism, based upon Jesus Christ.

Jesus represented the fulfillment of the Torah, in addition to being the true interpreter of its laws.[72] Jesus' role as the true interpreter of the Torah is emphasized in Matt 5:17–48; Matt 23. Recall that Matt 5:17–18 states, "Do not think that I have come to abolish the law or the prophets; I have come not to abolish but to fulfill. For truly I tell you, until heaven and earth pass away, not one letter, not one stroke of a letter, will pass from the law until all is accomplished." This passage is important, because both the Old Testament and the Talmud state that one is strictly prohibited from adding or subtracting a single word or law to or from the Torah.[73]

This is especially true of Matt 12, in which Jesus debates the Pharisees over Sabbath laws and over other matters of Jewish halakah. Matthew defends the apostles' plucking of grain on the Sabbath as lawful. Overman states, "Matthew, though, claimed that his community was the only one that truly understood and fulfilled the law [Torah]."[74] Jesus' teachings in no way contradict the Torah or its laws.[75] Simply put, Matthew and formative Judaism were fighting over the Torah.

As a result of the increasing pressure from the Jewish community, the Matthean scribes had to develop their own roles and standards for living.[76] The community probably felt that it was being more and more cut off from formative Judaism and had to

---

71. For example, Matt 18:15–20 discusses what to do if there is dissension among two members of the church. This suggests that some problems had arisen among members of the Matthean community.

72. Daniel J. Harrington, *God's People in Christ* (Philadelphia: Fortress, 1980), 96.

73. David E. Garland, *Reading Matthew: A Literary and Theological Commentary on the First Gospel* (New York: Crossroad, 1995), 61. The passages cited are Deut 4:2 and *b. Sanhedrin* 90a.

74. Overman, *Church and Community in Crisis*, 21.

75. Geza Vermes, *The Religion of Jesus the Jew* (Minneapolis: Fortress, 1993), 21.

76. Overman, *Matthew's Gospel and Formative Judaism*, 90.

respond. Therefore, the Matthean community had organized itself to help facilitate the response. In other words, the community probably had some semblance of structure to it.[77] In fact, the Sermon on the Mount may serve as Matthew's cornerstone statement of how the community should operate.[78] Matthew thus responds to the crises in an organized manner through Jesus' careful interpretation of the Torah.

The Matthean Gospel as a Jewish Text

I want to point out that the structure exhibited in the Gospel, even if it is relatively "loose" in nature, is Jewish. The nature of Matthew's Gospel has been debated. Some scholars emphasize its Jewish qualities, others do not. There are good reasons for the first position. First, all titles mentioned in the Gospel are Jewish, outside of ἀπόστολοι in 10:2.[79] Similarly, the "prophets" mentioned in the Gospel are Jewish (see Matt 7:15–23). Second, only Jewish characters refer to Jesus as "teacher," or διδάσκαλε.[80] Usually these characters are Jesus' opponents, the Pharisees or Sadducees. In contrast, Gentiles call Jesus by other terms, such as "Christ" or "Son of God." I argue, then, that the authors of the Gospel wanted to convince their audience that Jesus was the authoritative Jewish teacher of the Torah. Matthew wished to educate the community in order to inoculate them against the tainted teachings of the opposing Jewish leaders.

Third, Matt 12:38 states, "Then some of the scribes and Pharisees said to him, 'Teacher, we wish to see a sign from you.'" Note

---

77. Kingsbury, *Matthew as Story*, 157.

78. Overman, *Church and Community in Crisis*, 22.

79. Edgar Krentz, "Community and Character: Matthew's Vision of the Church," *Society of Biblical Literature Seminar Papers, 1987* (ed. Kent Harold Richards; Atlanta: Scholars Press, 1987), 570.

80. Janice Capel Anderson, *Matthew's Narrative Web Over, and Over, and Over Again* (Journal for the Study of the New Testament Supplement Series 91; Sheffield: Sheffield Academic, 1994), 118. See Matt 8:19; 12:38; 19:16; 22:16; 22:24, 36 for examples. In this paragraph I am following Anderson's argument.

here that the opposing group's scribes and Pharisees are speaking to Jesus. This implies that the Matthean community was in conflict with some opposing Jewish groups, as I contested earlier. In the next passage Jesus provides a clever answer by using a quote from the Old Testament. Matthew does this to prove how Jesus is the true Jewish educator in the Matthean community.

Finally, Jesus' usage of the Old Testament in Matthew is obvious. As J. C. Anderson attests, the Jesus of the Matthean Gospel quotes the Old Testament more than even the narrator does.[81] Consider Matt 23:8, in which the term "rabbi" is used. Though portrayed negatively, the term appears in Jesus' own instruction. In this pericope, Jesus, probably to discredit the neighboring formative Jewish leaders, warns his followers, "But you are not to be called rabbi, for you have one teacher, and you are all students." Notice how this passage also seems to establish Jesus as the authoritative teacher of Jewish law. The "rabbis" of the Pharisees are not to be accepted; only Matthew's teachers are correct.

All of these titles (scribe, prophet, and teacher) represent those members of the community capable of teaching the laws of the Torah. Deutsch points this out: "Matthew's teachers will retain Torah, which includes not only scripture but oral tradition. But, as the text implies, Matthew's teachers will interpret it according to the tradition handed down in Jesus' name."[82] The Matthean community alone felt that it was entitled to inherit the religious tradition of Israel.[83]

Matthew 5:19 and the Torah

A brief example illustrates the Jewish nature of Matthew's Gospel. Consider Matt 5:19, in which Jesus upholds the validity of the

---

81. Anderson, *Matthew's Narrative Web*, 60. See Matt 4:4, 7, 10; 11:10; 12:3, 5; 19:4; 21:36, 42; 26:31; 27:46.

82. Celia Deutsch, *Lady Wisdom, Jesus, and the Sages: Metaphor and Social Context in Matthew's Gospel* (Valley Forge, Pa.: Trinity Press International, 1996), 127.

83. Harrington, *God's People in Christ*, 101.

Torah. The passage in part reads, "Therefore, whoever breaks one of the least of these commandments, and teaches others to do the same, will be called least in the kingdom of heaven." What does Jesus mean by the phrase "least of these commandments"? Is he referring to the commandments of the Torah?

Some scholars contend that Matthew is here abrogating the Torah by having Jesus supersede its teachings. This is a common argument against the Jewish nature of Matthew. Jesus has now fulfilled the Torah; it is no longer central to the Matthean community. The Gospel, therefore, wishes to do away with the Torah as well as its laws.[84] The authors of Matthew had separated themselves from Judaism. The Jewish traditions and laws retained in the Gospel are only residual; they are no longer taken seriously by Matthew's community.

I disagree with this view. Alternatively, I suggest that the authors of Matthew, although Jewish *Christians*, were applying the rabbinic teachings of their time. Likewise, Matthew was showing reverence for the Torah. Evidence supports this view. First, there is no other passage in the Synoptic Gospels resembling 5:19, so Matthew could not have just been copying these words from another New Testament source. Second, in 5:17–18, Jesus is speaking about himself, while in 5:19–20 he is referring to the teaching of his disciples.[85] Consequently, the authors of Matthew add these unique passages (not found in Mark) in order to clarify their point regarding Jewish law and the Torah. They are not merely copying from Mark. On its own, therefore, 5:19 contains an important message.

The textual evidence is also convincing. To begin, Jack Dean Kingsbury states that Jesus (in 5:19) was indeed warning against

---

84. See Graham N. Stanton, *A Gospel for a New People* (Louisville: Westminster, 1993). He believes that the Matthean community had parted with Judaism. See pp. 158–59.

85. W. D. Davies and Dale C. Allison Jr., *The Gospel according to Saint Matthew* (International Critical Commentary 1; Edinburgh: T&T Clark, 1988), 1:496. Also, see John P. Meier, *Law and History in Matthew's Gospel: A Redactional Study of Mt. 5:17–48* (Analecta biblica 71; Rome: Biblical Institute Press, 1976), 100.

breaking even the most insignificant Torah commandment.[86] Furthermore, if Jesus was actually dismissing the Torah and proposing his own teachings, why would he not just say so? For example, Mark 1:27 discusses a "new teaching" of Jesus. But Matthew omits this phrase from the Gospel.[87] There is no mention of any "new teaching" here. Matthew remains true to the original authority: the Torah.

Let me make one linguistic clarification. The key phrase of this passage is "one of the least of these commandments," a rather awkward grouping of words. Yet Matthew is probably incorporating an Aramaic idiom, which could be translated as something like "one of the least commandments."[88] This clarifies the wording of the phrase. Matthew's audience, then, would not have viewed the text as inadequate or unclear.

Recently, Douglas Hare has suggested what I deem to be a compromise position concerning 5:19. He believes that Matthew was not specifically ordaining complete adherence to all laws of the Torah; he was rather stating a general precept condoning its observance.[89] Jesus, in fact, represented the proper filter through which the Torah was to be understood. After all, according to Hare, Jesus himself appeared to do away with certain Jewish laws (8:3; 9:10), and Matthew's community no doubt was admitting Gentiles, who would have had little use for the Torah.[90]

Donald Hagner seems to think along similar lines. He believes it somewhat obvious that Matthew's community, comprised of Jewish Christians, would still have esteemed the Torah. Matthew

---

86. Jack Dean Kingsbury, "The Place, Structure, and Meaning of the Sermon on the Mount within Matthew," *Interpretation* 41 (1987): 138.

87. J. Daryl Charles, "The Greatest or the Least in the Kingdom? The Disciple's Relationship to the Law (Matt. 5.17–20)," paper presented at the Annual Meeting of the Society of Biblical Literature, Nashville, Tennessee, 18 November 2000.

88. Robert M. Johnston, "'The Least of the Commandments': Deuteronomy 22:6–7 in Rabbinic Judaism and Early Christianity," *Andrews University Seminary Studies* 20 (1982): 206.

89. Douglas R. A. Hare, "How Jewish Is Matthew?" *Catholic Biblical Quarterly* 62 (2002): 270–71.

90. Ibid., 271, 277.

5:17–19 supports this assertion.[91] What Hagner feels is most important, however, is not the Torah itself, but Jesus the Messiah.[92] The Torah's authority is supplanted by the teachings of Jesus, who is the true, authoritative interpreter of the Torah. I am inclined in part to agree with Hare and Hagner. It is true that the Matthean community likely was admitting Gentiles and upheld at least some of the laws of the Torah, but I am willing to go one step further. I maintain, like David Sim, that the authors of the Gospel were devout Jews who themselves continued to uphold the Torah laws as valid.[93] This will become clearer in the subsequent chapters.

Deuteronomy 22:6–7 and the Torah

Consider Deut 22:6–7, often referred to as "the law of the bird's nest" in Jewish literature. It states, "If you come on a bird's nest, in any tree or on the ground, with fledglings or eggs and the mother sitting on the fledglings or on the eggs, you shall not take the mother with the young. Let the mother go, taking only the young for yourself that it may go well with you, and you may live long." On the surface it seems that the pericope and the ruling of Deuteronomy have nothing in common.

That is not necessarily the case. Upon closer inspection, one finds that the passages are quite similar. The Mishnah distinguishes between "light" commandments and "great" or "weighted" ones. For example, *m. Avot* 2:1 and 4:2 clearly state that these two terms represent the type of commandments accepted in the ancient Jewish world.[94] Regarding lesser commandments, in 4:2 Ben 'Azzai

---

91. Donald A. Hagner, "Matthew: Apostate, Reformer, Revolutionary?" *New Testament Studies* 49 (2003): 202.

92. Ibid.

93. David C. Sim, *The Gospel of Matthew and Christian Judaism: The History and Social Setting of the Matthean Community* (Edinburgh: T&T Clark International, 1998), 123.

94. J. Daryl Charles, "The Greatest or the Least in the Kingdom? The Disciple's Relationship to the Law," *Trinity Journal* 13 (1992): 155–56.

states, "Run after the most minor religious duty as after the most important, and flee from transgression." Similarly, Deut 22:6–7, the so-called law of the bird's nest, traditionally has served as the prime example of a light commandment.[95] Examples of both kinds of commandments are also found in Matthew. For instance, 23:23 has Jesus rebuking the scribes and Pharisees for tithing mint, dill, and cumin (a lesser duty), while neglecting "the weightier matters of the law: justice and mercy and faith." In contrast, 12:1–9 speaks of more important or "great" commandments, such as the keeping of the Sabbath.[96]

The law of the bird's nest from Deut 22:6–7 has traditionally been interpreted in rabbinic literature as teaching two primary things: the importance of the Torah and the importance of human beings. Robert Johnston states it best when he says, "If God is concerned about something so trivial, *a fortiori*, how much more is he particular about his weighty commandments. If God is concerned about little birds, *qal we-homer*, now much more important is man! The birds are not important in themselves; they are but a foil for more important things."[97] The rabbis wished to stress the gentle treatment of fellow human beings as well. Moreover, the law of the bird's nest teaches the importance of the Torah and the rewards one may garner in the world to come.[98]

Was that not also Jesus' concern in the Matthean Gospel? Certainly 5:17–20 emphasizes observance of the Torah, while passages such as 22:34–40 instruct the community regarding the respectful treatment of fellow human beings. Matthew 5:19 serves as the perfect example of Jesus' teaching on the Torah. The Torah is to be upheld in its entirety, regardless of how small or large the commandment may be. Both groups (Jews and Jewish Christians) recognize "light" and "great" commandments. The authors of

---

95. Johnston, "'Least of the Commandments,'" 207. The Mishnah also mentions that Torah means more than merely treating birds kindly (see *m. Berakhot* 5:3 and *m. Megillah* 4:9).

96. Charles, "Greatest or the Least?" 155–56.

97. Johnston, "'Least of the Commandments,'" 208–9.

98. Ibid., 210.

Matthew refer to this by using language familiar to their Jewish audience. They select the phrase "the least of these commandments," which is strikingly similar to the language utilized by the rabbis in the Mishnah.

This passage illustrates the Matthean Gospel's close connection to the rabbis. The Jewish Christian group, as well as the opposing formative Jewish group, stresses the importance of upholding the Torah, as well as the respectful treatment of fellow human beings. The famous story of Hillel the scholar supports this conclusion. Hillel states that the meaning of the Torah may be summed up in one law: what is hateful to yourself, do not do unto your neighbor. Jesus, of course, emphasizes the same thing in Matt 22:39. Matthew 5:19 also serves as an example of how Jesus supports all laws of the Torah. Nowhere is the Torah negated.

Finally, I offer one more piece of evidence confirming the Jewish nature of the Matthean Gospel. This concerns the Jewish prayer, the *shema*, cited by Jesus in 22:37 (citing Deut 6:5). For much of the twentieth century some scholars claimed that Matthew's seemingly incorrect alteration of the Markan text indicated Gentile authorship.[99] One of the best modern responses to this assertion is offered by Paul Foster in his recent article.[100] Foster argues that Matthew's alteration of the text reflects the author's Jewish learnedness. The text bears this out. For instance, Foster notes that Matthew's use of ἐν (rather than Mark's ἐξ) indicates the author's wish to remain true to the Hebrew version, which used ב.[101] Even in the places where Matthew does seem to deviate from the Hebrew version, he still seems to be supporting the version found in the LXX. Hence, Foster remains unconvinced, based upon such alterations of the Markan version of the prayer, that Matthew was a Gentile.

---

99. G. Strecker, *Der Weg der Gerechtigkeit: Untersuchung zur Theologie des Matthäus* (Göttingen: Vandenhoeck & Ruprecht, 1962), 26.

100. Paul Foster, "Why Did Matthew Get the Shema Wrong?" *Journal of Biblical Literature* 122 (2003): 309–33.

101. Ibid., 332–33.

The Role of Gentiles in a Jewish Gospel

Much work has been done in recent years concerning the role of the Gentiles in Matthew's Gospel. In essence, even assuming that Matthew's community was led by Jewish scribes, certainly there would have been a significant increase in the number of Gentiles entering the church. How were Jewish Christians to address this influx of converts? A fine contemporary study has been conducted by Donald Senior. He makes the case that Matthew, in fact, addresses the Gentile issue more than other Gospel authors, particularly Mark.[102] He cites several passages in Matthew that support this assertion (in particular, note 1:2–16; 2:1–12; 4:12–16; 4:23–26; 8:5–13; etc.). Senior comments that eighteen passages seem to refer to Gentiles in a positive manner. And twelve of them are unique to Matthew.[103] These largely favorable references indicate that Matthew was, at the very least, thinking about how to deal with Gentile converts.

In sum, Senior believes that the Matthean community would have accepted Gentiles, assuming that they were educated regarding the Jewish teachings of Jesus.[104] I am willing to agree with this assertion. I believe that even Gentiles entering the community would have had to follow the Jewish laws set forth by the scribal leaders. Yet I disagree with Senior regarding the motivations of the Gospel authors. Senior concludes that ultimately Matthew was more concerned with conveying Jesus' message to a Christian audience (comprised more and more of Gentiles) than with defending his brand of Judaism against other formative Jews such as the Pharisees. Nonetheless, one cannot simply dismiss the myriad of references to the Torah laws as mere instruction on Jesus' part. Clearly the authors of the Gospel were concerned with convincing others that they were the true Jews, even if they were accepting

---

102. Donald Senior, "Between Two Worlds: Gentiles and Jewish Christians in Matthew's Gospel," *Catholic Biblical Quarterly* 61 (1999): 14–18.

103. Ibid., 16.

104. Ibid.

Gentiles into the community. The Torah remained the authority, as interpreted through Jesus. This emphasis on the Jewish nature of the Matthean Gospel should not be overlooked or dismissed. The passage discussed above illustrates this point. Gentiles may have been on Matthew's mind, but the Torah remained in his heart. Matthew's zeal for the Torah will be made clearer via an exegetical analysis of the text in a later chapter.

2

Tradition in Transition, or Antioch vs. Sepphoris

Rethinking the Matthean Community's Location

Preliminary Observations: Matthew's Community as a City Church

IT IS LIKELY THAT CHRISTIANITY GREW WITHIN URBAN environments.[1] Therefore a plausible place to locate the Matthean community is in a major city. A brief survey of scholarship reveals that this is a reasonable premise. For example, Kingsbury states, "Indeed, there is good reason to believe that the Matthean community was a 'city church' that was materially well off."[2] Evidence for this position also comes from the text. For instance, Matthew

---

1. A good example of this theory is found in the work of Wayne A. Meeks. See *The First Urban Christians: The Social World of the Apostle Paul* (New Haven: Yale University Press, 1983), 10–11, and passim. Although Meeks concentrates mostly on Paul, he does note that the cities played a role in the development of Christianity beyond the apostle's work. On page 10 he states, "This preoccupation with the cities was not peculiar to Paul. Before Paul's conversion the believers in Messiah Jesus had already carried their new sectarian message into the Jewish communities of the Greco-Roman cities."

2. Jack Dean Kingsbury, "The Verb *Akolouthein* ('to follow') as an Index of Matthew's View of His Community," *Journal of Biblical Literature* 97 (1978): 66.

favors the word πόλις ("city"), in contrast to Mark's usage of the
term κώμη ("village").[3] Matthew uses the former term ("city")
twenty-six times, but "village" only four times. Matthew 11:1
states, "And when Jesus had finished instructing his twelve disciples, he went on from there to teach and preach in their *cities*."
Mark, however, uses πόλις only eight times, instead opting to use
κώμη seven times. Often Matthew omits Mark's mention of the
"village" altogether or changes the term to "city." For instance,
Mark 8:23 reads, "He took the blind man by the hand and led him
out of the village." This line is not found at all in the Matthean
Gospel.

In Mark's Gospel the use of "city" is often coupled with "village." Mark 6:56 states, "And wherever he went, into villages,
cities, or farms . . ." Matthew has no direct parallel; the author opts
instead for phrases incorporating πόλις or phrases such as "And he
went about all Galilee" (4:23, RSV) or "So his fame spread throughout all Syria" (4:24). Mark 6:6 also reads, "Then he went about
among the villages teaching." Matthew 9:35 reads, "Then Jesus
went about all the *cities* and villages . . ." This suggests that
Matthew incorporates a more urban tone into the text.

In addition, Matthew links the term οἶκος ("house") to πόλις at
least five times, again indicating that the community's permanent
dwellings were in or near the city.[4] For example, the magi travel to
a city (Bethlehem) and enter the house (2:8–11). Furthermore, in
Matt 10:11–12 Jesus instructs the disciples, "Whatever town or
village you enter, find out who in it is worthy, and stay there until
you leave. As you enter the house, greet it." Jesus resides in the city
of Bethany at the house of Simon the leper (26:6). This suggests
that the authors of the Matthean Gospel indicate their own community's location.

Yet scholars such as Eduard Schweizer have postulated that this
community was not metropolitan, but rather a wandering fringe

---

3. Jack Dean Kingsbury, *Matthew as Story* (Philadelphia: Fortress, 1986),
125. The following statistics come from here as well.

4. Michael H. Crosby, *House of Disciples* (New York: Orbis Books, 1988),
40.

group located somewhere near the border of Galilee and Syria.[5] In other words, the Matthean community paralleled the isolated Qumran community. Kingsbury points out this idea is quite similar to Gerd Theissen's view of the early Christians as "wandering charismatics" who gave up all of their goods in order to live and follow in the steps of Jesus.[6] Both Schweizer and Theissen seem to portray the Matthean community as wandering monastics, unconcerned with city life or permanent dwellings.

Schweizer cites Matt 8:20 as evidence of Jesus' wandering, rural nature.[7] In this passage Jesus states, "Foxes have holes, and birds of the air have nests; but the Son of man has nowhere to lay his head." However, this can easily be interpreted to mean that Jesus himself was peripatetic.[8] Since the passage in no way indicates that the followers of Jesus or the Matthean Christians became nomads, I dismiss this line of reasoning. In fact, Kingsbury believes that when one compares Matthew to Mark and Luke, it becomes clear that Matthew actually downplays any notion of Jesus as an itinerant.[9]

Other scholars also disagree with Schweizer's views. As noted above, Kingsbury believes that the Matthean community must have been an urban group. He provides textual evidence to support this belief. Much of his study focuses on Matthew's usage of the verb ἀκολούθειν ("to follow"). He observes that roughly half of the usages in the Gospel contain no references to "wandering."[10] Other instances of the verb fail to convince him that the Gospel's

---

5. Eduard Schweizer, *The Good News according to Matthew* (trans. David E. Green; Atlanta: John Knox, 1975), 219. There are other instances as well. To be precise, in this case, while explaining 8:20 Schweizer states, "Thus to follow Jesus in fact is to step forth into insecurity, because the one in whom God comes to men has no home among men; they fail to recognize him."

6. Kingsbury, "The Verb *Akolouthein*," 63.

7. Eduard Schweizer, *Matthäus und seine Gemeinde* (Stuttgarter Bibelstudien 71; Stuttgart: KBW Verlag, 1974), 19–20, 61, 67, 147–48.

8. Kingsbury, "The Verb *Akolouthein*," 65. Jesus may have always wished to be "with" his community. See Matt 1:23; 18:20; and 28:20, in which Jesus remains close to his followers.

9. Kingsbury, "The Verb *Akolouthein*," 65.

10. Ibid., 64.

intent is to show that Jesus and his disciples were nomads. G. D. Kilpatrick notes that the Gospel indicates an urban preference. He points out that in Matt 10:23 and 23:34 the disciples flee from city to city, not to the hills, as one would think.[11] The hills, after all, would have provided a better hiding place. Jesus recites in the former passage, "When they persecute you in one town, flee to the next." In the latter passage Jesus cautions that the prophets, wise men, and scribes will be persecuted from "town to town." In both instances the Gospel uses πόλις.

Overman also agrees that the Matthean Gospel must have been written in or near a major city.[12] To begin, the community appears to have lived near a significant center of Jewish life, where officials would reside. The tone of Matthew bears this out. For example, Jesus in the Gospel spends much time debating legal issues.[13] Religiously, this is found in 12:1–8, in which Jesus deliberates with the Pharisees about Sabbath laws. Regarding civil laws, 22:15–22 illustrates Jesus' view of imperial taxation. It seems likely, then, that the community was established in a city near a court.[14]

There are additional cogent reasons for arguing that the Matthean community was an urban group. First, scholars have pointed out that the very language of the Gospel indicates a metropolitan setting. The Koine Greek used by the New Testament writers was spoken primarily in the cities.[15] Harris observes, for example, that in Syria, Judea, and Arabia, Greek was one of the languages of city governments.[16] The rural areas spoke a different Greek dialect. The form of Koine Greek found in Matthew's

11. G. D. Kilpatrick, *The Origins of the Gospel according to St. Matthew* (Oxford: Clarendon, 1946), 125.

12. J. Andrew Overman, *Church and Community in Crisis: The Gospel according to Matthew* (Valley Forge, Pa.: Trinity Press International, 1996), 18.

13. Ibid.

14. J. Andrew Overman, *Matthew's Gospel and Formative Judaism: The Social World of the Matthean Community* (Minneapolis: Fortress, 1990), 159.

15. Gerd Theissen, *Social Reality and the Early Christians* (trans. Margaret Kohl; Minneapolis: Fortress, 1992), 54–55.

16. William V. Harris, *Ancient Literacy* (Cambridge: Harvard University Press, 1989), 187.

Gospel suggests that the text, as well as early Christianity itself, was an urban movement.[17]

Furthermore, the Matthean community must have been located near a Jewish community that also spoke a good deal of Greek.[18] According to Saldarini, many of the cities in Galilee fit this description. They had sizable Jewish populations, as well as many Greek-speaking residents. So both populations must have existed in the same civic region. Likewise, Saldarini writes, "Good-sized cities such as Sepphoris, Tiberias, Capernaum, and Bethsaida would have had the resources to educate and support a leader and writer such as the author of Matthew."[19] As such, I conclude that the Matthean community was located in a major city such as Sepphoris.

Hence, at least two Jewish communities must have been in existence where the Matthean community had settled.[20] The tone of the Gospel implies an awareness of a struggle for power between two Jewish groups. Chapter 23, for instance, finds Jesus addressing "the scribes and Pharisees." The Pharisees, of course, were one of the groups struggling to keep Judaism from disappearing following the disastrous revolt against Rome. Again, this suggests that the Gospel was written from within a large, urban setting.[21]

It is plausible that this oppidan location was established within ancient Israel. Consider Matthew's handling of Mark 1:35–39. Portions of Mark 1:35–39 read, "And in the morning . . . he got up and went out to a deserted place. . . . He answered, 'Let us go on to the neighboring towns.' . . . And he went throughout Galilee, proclaiming the messages in their synagogues and casting out demons." In contrast, the Matthean Gospel omits much of Mark's

---

17. See Meeks, *First Urban Christians*, 9.

18. Anthony J. Saldarini, "The Gospel of Matthew and Jewish-Christian Conflict in the Galilee," in *The Galilee in Late Antiquity* (ed. Lee I. Levine; Cambridge: Harvard University Press, 1992), 26–27. In this paragraph I am following Saldarini's line of thought.

19. Ibid., 27.

20. Saldarini believes that the Gospel was authored in a setting "with an established Jewish community." See Anthony J. Saldarini, *Matthew's Christian-Jewish Community* (Chicago: University of Chicago Press, 1994), 26.

21. Overman, *Matthew's Gospel and Formative Judaism*, 159.

text. Matthew 4:25 states, "And great crowds followed him from Galilee, the Decapolis, Jerusalem, Judea, and from beyond the Jordan." There is no mention here of the "lonely places" or "the next towns." The cities in Israel were of main importance to Jesus.

The Matthean Gospel therefore emphasizes Jesus' mission only to Israel.[22] He does not wander about, as other scholars suggest. Moreover, his actions are largely restricted to Galilee, as 4:23, 9:35, and 11:1 show. Jesus only leaves Galilee for brief periods of time (see 3:13–14; 8:23–9:1; 16:13–20; etc.). On the basis of such evidence Kingsbury concludes, "In reality, a careful consideration of Matthew's treatment of the region of Galilee reveals that it is the wider, not the narrower, setting for Jesus' activity."[23] In other words, Galilee is the main point of reference found in the Matthean Gospel.

The Matthean Community's Location: Antioch vs. Sepphoris

The Traditional Location of the Matthean Community: "The Myth of Antioch"

I argue that the Matthean community was located in Lower Galilee in the city of Sepphoris. Textual and modern archaeological evidence support this position. Yet, traditionally, scholars have placed the Matthean community in Syria, often in the prominent city of Antioch.[24] This trend continues into the twenty-first century, as we shall see.[25] Scholars have provided four primary arguments for this

---

22. Kingsbury, "The Verb *Akolouthein*," 65.
23. Ibid., 66.
24. One of the first scholars to adopt this view was Burntett Hillman Streeter. See *The Four Gospels: A Study of Origins. Treating the Manuscript Tradition, Sources, Authorship, and Dates* (London: Macmillan, 1964), 16, 500–527. Other scholars followed suit. See, for instance, Eduard Schweizer, "Matthew's Church," in *The Interpretation of Matthew* (ed. Graham Stanton; Issues in Religion and Theology 3; Philadelphia: Fortress, 1983), 129–30, or Kingsbury, *Matthew as Story*, 121. There are numerous other scholars that also adhere to this theory.
25. See Donald Senior, "Directions in Matthean Studies," in *The Gospel of*

position. First, the large city of Antioch had become a center of Christianity by the late first century. With the death of James and the destruction of the holy Temple in Jerusalem, the conservative Jewish Christian party's hold on Christianity was weakened, and liberal Christian elements that had existed for some time in Antioch began to gain power.[26] Christianity, according to some scholars, had first spread near Antioch. In fact, the first Gentiles were probably converted there.[27] Acts 11:19–26 indicates that Antioch was an early center of Christianity. Accordingly, many scholars argue this to be the location of the Matthean community.

Second, the tone of the Gospel suggests that friction existed between the church community and a nearby group of formative Jews. This is evident by Jesus' admonishment of the scribes and Pharisees in chapter 23. For this reason some scholars posit a Syrian location for the Gospel. In support of this view, they point to rabbinic literature, which seems to indicate that Syria was involved in Jewish affairs.[28] In fact, the region had a large Jewish population, as Josephus points out.[29] Syria, then, provided an opportunity for Jews and Christians to interact with one another.

Even in the smaller Syrian cities such as Edessa, Hans Drijvers observes that "Gentiles, Jews, and Christians walked along the same streets, did their shopping at the common market-place, suffered from the same diseases, epidemics, and wars, and therefore shared a lot of ideas and concepts about which they talked with

---

Matthew in Current Study (ed. David E. Aune; Grand Rapids: Eerdmans, 2001), 8. See also Warren Carter, *Matthew and Empire: Initial Explorations* (Harrisburg, Pa.: Trinity Press International, 2001), 36–37.

26. John P. Meier, "The Antiochene Church of the Second Christian Generation," in *Antioch and Rome: New Testament Cradles of Christianity* (ed. Raymond E. Brown and John P. Meier; New York: Paulist, 1983), 46–47.

27. Hans Drijvers, "Syrian Christianity and Judaism," in *The Jews among Pagans and Christians in the Roman Empire* (ed. Judith Lieu, John North, and Tessa Rajak; London: Routledge, 1992), 124.

28. Some scholars also posit a Syrian location, but do not necessarily specify a city. See W. D. Davies, *The Setting of the Sermon on the Mount* (Cambridge: Cambridge University Press, 1964), 295–96. See also *m. Hallah* 4:7–8 or *m. Shevi'it* 6:2 for examples of the rabbinic references.

29. See *Jewish War* 7:3:3.

each other."[30] This mixture of Jews and Christians, though, undoubtedly would have created the atmosphere of tension mentioned above. Matthew 23 conveys this growing hostility, according to some scholars. This region may have provided the setting required for the development of such a prominent Gospel.[31]

Third, textual evidence seems to support the Antioch hypothesis. Matthew 4:15 utilizes the phrase "Galilee of the Gentiles." If Galilee were prominently Gentile, then my theory that Matthew must have been written from a Jewish city does not work. In addition, there is the direct mention of Syria in 4:24.[32] Scholars such as Warren Carter have pointed out that the Markan account in 1:28, 39 fails to mention Syria.[33] Furthermore, some scholars have discussed the possibility that Ignatius of Antioch was using Matthew in some of his early-second-century letters, possibly indicating a "hometown bias" toward the text.[34] Peter's place in the Gospel is also quite prominent. After all, in Matt 16:13–20 Jesus gives Peter "the keys of the kingdom of heaven," and the apostle spent much time in Antioch.[35]

Lastly, the Syrian area surrounding Antioch was multilingual. Greek was widely spoken, and, since the Matthean Gospel was composed in the language, some scholars cite this as another reason why the Gospel was written from this location.[36] All these fac-

---

30. Drijvers, "Syrian Christianity," 128.

31. John P. Meier, "Locating Matthew's Church in Space and Time," in *Antioch and Rome: New Testament Cradles of Christianity* (ed. Raymond E. Brown and John P. Meier; New York: Paulist, 1983), 22. The community probably was well-versed in the Septuagint as well as the Jewish Christian Gospel of Mark. So the Jewish Christian viewpoint of Matthew is appropriate.

32. Seán Freyne, *Galilee from Alexander the Great to Hadrian, 323 BCE to 135 CE: A Study of Second Temple Judaism* (Edinburgh: T&T Clark, 1980), 364.

33. Carter, *Matthew and Empire*, 36.

34. For a good discussion of this topic, consult the article by William R. Schroedel, "Ignatius and the Reception of the Gospel of Matthew in Antioch," in *Social History of the Matthean Community: Cross-Disciplinary Approaches* (ed. David L. Balch; Minneapolis: Fortress, 1991), 154–77. In particular, see *Ignatius' Letter to the Trallians 9, Letter to the Philadelphians 8:2*, and *Letter to Polycarp 2:1–2*.

35. See Gal 2:11.

36. David E. Garland, *Reading Matthew: A Literary and Theological Commentary on the First Gospel* (New York: Crossroad, 1995), 3. See also John P.

tors together have led many scholars to argue that Matthew's Gospel most likely was written in Antioch.

Refutation of "The Myth of Antioch"

I first discuss the issue of language. Many scholars posit an urban Syrian location because Greek was spoken there, in contrast to the Aramaic that was allegedly spoken in Palestine. Since Matthew was written in Greek, these scholars eliminate other regions such as Galilee, where Aramaic may have been the colloquial language. They thereby assign the community to a Syrian city such as Antioch.

Is this the case? It is not true that Aramaic was the only language spoken in Palestine. Greek was also widely spoken throughout Palestine.[37] Textual and archaeological evidence support this assertion, especially concerning Galilee. In Beth Shearim, located near Sepphoris, 196 Jewish Greek inscriptions have been found.[38] Many are connected to burial inscriptions. Some catacombs contain both Hebrew and Greek writings, as the tomb of one Rabbi Gamaliel indicates. One inscription reads: זו של רבי גמליאל ם. A second one reads: ΡΑΒΙ ΓΑΜΑΛΙΗΛ.[39] Also, Greek texts have been found in other cities in Galilee, such as Nazareth.[40] Josephus acknowledges

---

Meier, *The Vision of Matthew: Christ, Church, and Morality in the First Gospel* (New York: Paulist, 1979), 13–15. In particular, Meier strongly believes that the most prevalent language in Palestine was Aramaic, not Greek. Therefore, a Greek document such as Matthew must have been written elsewhere, most likely a city like Antioch, in Syria. His reasons for an urban location are also language-based. He claims that Aramaic was a rural language and that Greek was more urban. On the basis of this he hypothesizes that the Matthean Gospel must have been written in a city.

37. Freyne, *Galilee from Alexander the Great to Hadrian*, 139.

38. G. Mussies, "Greek in Palestine and the Diaspora," in *The Jewish People in the First Century* (ed. S. Safrai et al.; Philadelphia: Fortress, 1976), 2:1042–43.

39. Jack Finegan, *The Archeology of the New Testament: The Life of Jesus and the Beginning of the Early Church* (Princeton: Princeton University Press, 1969), 205.

40. Eric M. Meyers and James F. Strange, *Archaeology, the Rabbis, and Early Christianity* (Nashville: Abingdon, 1981), 83–84. Meyers and Strange also contend that Greek was widely used in Palestine, perhaps second only to Aramaic. See pages 77–88 for their complete discussion.

that although Aramaic was the primary spoken language in Palestine, many Jews also knew Greek.[41] Furthermore, Rabbi Yehudah ha-Nasi states, "Why use the Syrian language [Aramaic] in the land of Israel? Either use the holy tongue [Hebrew] or Greek!"[42] This indicates that Jews were encouraged to speak Greek, not Aramaic, in Palestine. In fact, there seems to have been a bias against speaking Aramaic. But was Greek spoken in cities like Sepphoris?

The answer is yes. First, the above quote from Yehuda ha-Nasi, a Galilean known to frequent the larger cities, provides evidence for this view.[43] Second, a lead market weight from the first century C.E., found at Sepphoris, contains Greek writing.[44] Third, Greek writing appears on many first-century Palestinian coins, further attesting to the region's familiarity with the language.[45] Lastly, archaeological evidence from the city of Beth Shearim supports this theory. One particular Greek inscription found on a white marble slab near a mausoleum (by catacomb 11) is worth noting. It is the epitaph of a Jewish man named "Justus." One phrase reads: καὶ γ᾽ ἐλθὼν εἰς Ἅδην. The opening usage of καί γε is common both in the LXX and the New Testament, but is rarely found elsewhere in Greek literature.[46] Perhaps the author of the inscription was familiar with these Greek biblical texts.

---

41. See *Jewish Antiquities* 20:11:1ff. See also J. N. Sevenster, *Do You Know Greek? How Much Greek Could the First Jewish Christians Have Known?* (Leiden: Brill, 1968), 65. Sevenster points out this fact regarding Josephus.

42. *b. Sotah* 49B. Finegan points out this passage. See Finegan, *Archeology of the New Testament*, 204.

43. In fact, Jewish legend states that the Mishnah was recorded by Yehuda ha-Nasi in Galilee. Also interesting is that another prominent rabbi cited in the Mishnah was himself believed to have been a product of Sepphoris. See David Adan-Bayewitz, *Common Pottery in Roman Galilee: A Study of Local Trade* (Ramat-Gan, Israel: Bar Ilan, 1993), 26. See *b. Sanhedrin* 19a, 32b, 109a, 113a, and *b. Eruvin* 86b for confirmation of the fact.

44. Jonathon L. Reed, *Archaeology and the Galilean Jesus* (Harrisburg, Pa.: Trinity Press International, 2000), 121.

45. Sevenster, *Do You Know Greek?* 122.

46. Moshe Schwabe and Baruch Lifshitz, *Beth She'arim*, vol. 2: *The Greek Inscriptions* (New Brunswick, N.J.: Rutgers University Press, 1974), 103. I am following these authors here. Schwabe and Lifshitz identify this inscription. For a complete discussion, see pages 97–110.

Most compelling, though, is the phrase "and having gone to Hades." The same phrase has also been found in another Jewish inscription (from the first century C.E.) in the Egyptian city of Leontopolis. Furthermore, the Greek word Ἅδης is used in the LXX, not in the Hebrew texts. The Hebrew authors would have utilized שאול. The author here has chosen the Greek term. Two things follow from these assertions. First, the Egyptian find indicates that similar Greek colloquial expressions were in use throughout first-century cities. Second, the author's use of "Hades" suggests a preference for a Greek term, not a Hebrew term. This proves that the Greek language was in use throughout Galilee.

It has also been suggested that Greek became prevalent following the Jewish revolt of 66–70 C.E., when the Jewish population was forced to scatter across Judea and Galilee and into other regions. If Greek were already in use to some degree, then it would have spread throughout the rest of Palestine and into places such as Egypt. The above archaeological evidence supports this assertion. Ultimately, then, the Greek language was prevalent in Palestine. The idea that only Aramaic was spoken and written in Galilee is false. Evidence indicates otherwise. I argue, then, that the Matthean Gospel could have been written in Greek from a Galilean city such as Sepphoris.

Yet some scholars insist that the social situation in Antioch supports the theory that the Matthean Gospel was written in the city. I already have noted that Antioch contained a mixture of Jewish and Christian inhabitants, providing the diverse culture that the Gospel presupposes. The Gospel was likely composed within a city that contained a large Jewish population. Recall, of course, that I am presuming that the Matthean community was rooted in Judaism. On this basis, a number of scholars have concluded that Antioch is the most logical choice.

Again, this is mere conjecture. In support of the Syrian view, scholars often cite the Mishnah and Talmud. Since the rabbis mention Syria, the area must have contained a concentrated Jewish population. Some passages do indeed allude to the rabbis' familiarity with the Syrian region. Yet these citations are few in number when compared to the rabbis' discussion of Jewish Galilean affairs.

Galilee is mentioned numerous times by the rabbis. For instance, the Talmud discusses the purchase of wheat in Tiberias and Sepphoris. One passage states, "Had you bought [the wheat] in Tiberias, I would have twenty-five modii; now that you bought it in Sepphoris I have only twenty modii."[47] Another passage from the Talmud discusses whether slaughtered animals found between Tiberias and Sepphoris may be eaten lawfully by a Jew.[48]

Furthermore, many rabbis such as Yehuda ha-Nasi are mentioned in connection with the region, including the city of Sepphoris. Rabbi Yohanan, for example, discusses whether one can assume that a dead body found between Tiberias and Sepphoris is that of a Jewish person.[49] It is not the case, then, that the Matthean community *must* have been located in Syria, since it is obvious from this evidence that a competing group of formative Jews was also located in Galilee. In addition, according to many sources, the Mishnah itself was written in Galilee by Yehuda ha-Nasi around the beginning of the third century.[50] Therefore, it follows that the formative Jewish group in conflict with the Matthean church was Galilean.

In fact, Antioch itself may have been too big to serve as the Matthean community's base of operation. Antioch, one of the largest cities in the Roman Empire, might not have contained the intimate atmosphere necessary for the tension indicated in the Gospel. Scholars estimate its population to have been anywhere from 75,000 to 250,000.[51] Yet in a city that big would the two competing groups have had occasion to come into contact with one another very often? Conversely, a city such as Sepphoris could have provided the

---

47. *y. Bava Qamma* 9:5, 6d–7a. In this section the following passages have been pointed out by Isaiah Gafni in his article, "Daily Life in Galilee and Sepphoris," in *Sepphoris in Galilee: Crosscurrents of Culture* (ed. Rebecca Martin Nagy et al.; Winona Lake, Ind.: Eisenbrauns, 1996), 51–57.

48. *b. Baba Metzi'a* 24b.

49. *y. Sanhedrin* 5:1, 22c.

50. Geza Vermes, *Jesus the Jew: A Historian's Reading of the Gospels* (Philadelphia: Fortress, 1973), 43, 52.

51. Meeks, *First Urban Christians*, 28.

atmosphere necessary for this degree of interaction. Antioch could not. In Antioch, the two groups could avoid each other; in Sepphoris, this would not be as easily accomplished. The conservative Jewish population of Sepphoris no doubt would have heard of the heretical teachings of the nearby Matthean community.

In other strands of thought, scholars claim that because Ignatius of Antioch possibly cites the Matthean Gospel, the text must have been written nearby.[52] There is no concrete evidence that Ignatius was actually writing about Matthew at all. In fact, Ignatius merely mentions "the gospel," a supposed reference to Matthew.[53] Does this necessarily prove that the Gospel itself had to originate in Antioch? Texts could be distributed over wide areas quite rapidly. The same argument from location is made regarding the early Christian writing called the *Didache*, which some scholars claim also was written in Syria.[54] Yet scholars such as R. T. France dispute these claims, pointing out the weakness of such arguments.[55]

Even if Ignatius does mention Matthew's Gospel in passing, this hardly proves that he was using the text as a main reference point based upon a common Antiochan heritage. David Sim has observed that the thought of Ignatius much more closely resembles Pauline theology than Matthew's. Sim states, "Whatever influence the Matthean, Johannine or Lukan traditions exercised over Ignatius, the evidence is overwhelming that of all the forms of the

---

52. Streeter was one of the first scholars to support this view. See *The Four Gospels*, 505–7.

53. See his *Letter to the Philadelphians* 8:2. Other supposed inferences are found in the *Letter to the Trallians* 9:1 and the *Letter to Polycarp* 2:1–2. Yet none of the references is conclusive.

54. Streeter, *The Four Gospels*, 508–11. Again, Streeter brought up this point, and other scholars seemingly followed suit. He alludes to passages such as 8:1–2; 11:3–4, 7; etc. These passages do not prove anything other than the fact that the authors of the *Didache* were familiar with some of the basic principles and sayings circulating throughout the ancient Roman world. The fact, for example, that the *Didache* teaches that men should reconcile with each other before coming to the assembly (see 14:2) does not prove that the Matthean community was located in Antioch.

55. R. T. France, *Matthew: Evangelist and Teacher* (Grand Rapids: Academic Books, 1989), 92–93.

Christian gospel available to him the bishop of Antioch was most influenced by Pauline Christianity."[56] Sim observes Ignatius's continued usage of 1 Corinthians as well as his repeated mention of Paul's mission to the Romans. In fact, in addition to 1 Corinthians, Ignatius may have borrowed directly from Paul's Letter to the Romans. For instance, notice the similarity of the phrase "newness of life" in Rom 6:4 to Ignatius's *Letter to the Ephesians* 19:3.[57] Hence, it is clear that Ignatius was not dependent upon Matthew for his inspiration or theology. Thus I dismiss the Ignatius/ Matthew link to Antioch.

Analysis of Textual Evidence

I now return to the textual evidence that seems to support the Antioch hypothesis and to refute a Galilean location. First, there is the phrase "Galilee of the Gentiles" in Matt 4:15 (taken from Isa 9:1), which seems to prove that the authors of the Gospel viewed Galilee as a region inhabited by a non-Jewish population.[58] Modern scholarship has dispelled this archaic interpretation. Mark Chancey provides a fine analysis of the phrase. He observes that the phrase was used sparingly by both ancient Jewish and Gentile authors. In fact, Isaiah's usage of "Galilee of the Gentiles" in the Old Testament is unique (out of six total references to Galilee).[59] The best contemporary Jewish source of the time, Josephus, never uses "Galilee of the Gentiles," and in all of the rabbinic texts the word "Gentile" is used only three times in relation to Galilee. In the entire New Testament, Matthew's usage in 4:15 is unique; no other text uses the phrase.[60]

---

56. David C. Sim, *The Gospel of Matthew and Christian Judaism* (Edinburgh: T&T Clark, 1998), 259.

57. Ibid., 260.

58. This phrase is still viewed as evidence of Matthew's affinity for Gentiles. See Theodore W. Jennings Jr. and Tat-Siong Benny Liew, "Mistaken Identities but Model Faith: Rereading the Centurion, the Chap, and the Christ in Matthew 8:5–13," *Journal of Biblical Literature* 123 (2004): 480–81.

59. Mark A. Chancey, *The Myth of a Gentile Galilee* (Cambridge: Cambridge University Press, 2002), 171–72.

60. Ibid., 172.

This illustrates two things. First, the phrase itself was not indicative of a typical description of Galilee; most folks simply knew the region as Galilee. Second, Matthew's usage of "Galilee of the Gentiles" must indicate something more than a simple geographical and/or religious designation. The answer lies in the contemporary understanding of the Christian mission in the late first century C.E. Craig Keener observes that Matthew sees the passage in Isaiah as a foreshadowing of the continuing mission to the Gentiles that was to take place in the region in the near future.[61] Remember, Jesus himself spent little time with Gentiles, but the general scope of Christianity was widening by Matthew's time. Therefore, Matthew is not referring to the current population of Galilee; the author is looking toward the future when all nations will be missionized.

Sim takes the issue one step further. He contends that "Galilee of the Gentiles" has little to do with any universal mission. The phrase, rather, is an admonition against the largely *Jewish* population of the region.[62] After all, Jesus' mission is to the Jews, as seen in 10:5–6 and 15:24, so he likely is speaking to them. According to Sim, Jesus tells the Jews that they were living in darkness alongside their Gentile neighbors (who probably bordered them) until he came along.[63] This passage, then, is meant not to flatter Gentiles or describe Galilee; it is meant as a wake-up call to the Jews of the region. Regardless of which viewpoint one follows, what seems clear is that the phrase "Galilee of the Gentiles" is not intended to be an accurate measure of the region's religious preferences.

There is also Matthew's mention of Syria in 4:24. Is this evidence that the Gospel was written from the region? As Carter noted, the reference to Syria is omitted in the Markan version, suggesting that Matthew wished to insert his home community into the text. Evidence for this position, however, is weak. Based on this logic, does it follow that because Mark *does* mention Galilee (by itself, in 1:28) this proves the Markan Gospel was recorded there? Obvi-

---

61. Craig S. Keener, *A Commentary on the Gospel of Matthew* (Grand Rapids: Eerdmans, 1999), 146–47.
62. Sim, *Gospel of Matthew*, 252–53.
63. Ibid.

ously, it does not. Perhaps Matthew chose to "widen the net" and to mention Syria to indicate the pervasiveness of Jesus' fame throughout the Roman Empire as well as to emphasize the importance of the Christian world mission. A similar view is suggested by Keener. He observes that it was common for ancient authors to spread the fame of noted teachers by emphasizing their popularity.[64] In addition, Keener points out that Matthew may have mentioned Syria to convince readers of the Gospel that the mission to the Gentiles (in Syria) was effective.[65] Yet Matthew remained committed to a Galilean Jesus.

In addition, the fact that Peter is prominently mentioned in the Matthean Gospel does not prove that it was written in Antioch. Even if Peter were active in Antioch, it does not mean that the authors of Matthew's Gospel favored Peter in any particular way. It could simply be that the authors wished to emphasize their interest in both the church (remember, Jesus gives Peter the "keys" in 16:13–20) and in the observance of the Torah.[66] In other words, the authors of the Gospel were more concerned with theology than with geography. Peter's location was unimportant. The crux of the matter was the message that Peter could convey to the Matthean community.

Consider also how Matthew portrays Jesus. As Overman points out, the authors of Matthew are hesitant to have Jesus leave Galilee at all. He states, "We have noted Matthew's unusual concentration in Galilee. Matthew seems to know Galilee quite well and essentially limits the activity of the Jesus movement to Galilee"[67] Passages such as 4:13; 8:5; 9:1; and 17:22 confirm this assertion. In the first passage, the reader learns that Jesus "dwelt" in Capernaum, while in 9:1 the city is referred to as Jesus' "own city." Jesus

---

64. Keener, *Commentary on the Gospel of Matthew*, 158.

65. Ibid., 158–59.

66. Henry Thatcher Fowler, *The History and Literature of the New Testament* (New York: Macmillan, 1925), 317. Even at this early date, Fowler alluded to this possibility. The author of the Gospel surely incorporated his or her own beliefs and traditions into the text. Hence, Peter may have been only a prominent character that served the author's needs.

67. Overman, *Matthew's Gospel and Formative Judaism*, 159.

also enters Capernaum (8:5), and "gathers" the disciples in Galilee (17:22). In fact, Jesus himself may have visited cities such as Sepphoris and Tiberias, considering that Lower Galilee seemed to be his home region.[68]

Further evidence for Galilee is found in Matthew's portrayal of the Pharisees. The Pharisees, Jesus' main adversaries, were a Galilean group, as 9:11 and 15:1 indicate. The former passage, for example, discusses Jesus' debates with the Pharisees (in Galilee) concerning the laws of table fellowship. The lone exception to this is found in 27:62–66, but Overman explains that this passage was probably a unique insertion by the Matthean scribes in order to implicate the Pharisees in the death of Jesus.[69] After all, the authors of the Gospel surely wanted to place the blame on their primary adversaries. In this case, the opponents are a Galilean Jewish group. It is logical, therefore, to locate the Matthean community in that region rather than in Antioch. Hence, I dismiss "The Myth of Antioch."

Sepphoris: The Home to the Matthean Community

Admittedly, one cannot be sure of the Matthean community's exact location. Yet there are compelling reasons to locate the community in or near the city of Sepphoris. I begin with a brief overview of the city. Sepphoris was a major Lower Galilean city that thrived until the Byzantine era as a major center of trade and commerce.[70] Scholars have estimated its population to have been between 25,000 and 30,000, making it the largest city in Galilee.[71] Many

---

68. Eric M. Meyers, "Jesus and His Galilean Context," in *Archaeology and the Galilee: Texts and Contexts in the Graeco-Roman and Byzantine Periods* (ed. Douglas R. Edwards and C. Thomas McCollough; Atlanta: Scholars Press, 1997), 60–61.

69. Overman, *Matthew's Gospel and Formative Judaism*, 156.

70. Eric M. Meyers, "Roman Sepphoris in Light of New Archaeological Evidence and Recent Research," in *The Galilee in Late Antiquity* (ed. Lee I. Levine; Cambridge: Harvard University Press, 1992), 321.

71. Richard A. Batey, *Jesus and the Forgotten City* (Grand Rapids: Baker, 1991), 136. Josephus also calls it the largest city. See *Jewish War* 3:2:4. Recently,

factors contributed to this large number. First, the city stood near two major roads: a major east-west highway and a main north-south junction.[72] Dennis Duling's recent map of Roman road networks in Galilee indicates that Sepphoris was centrally located, providing easy access from a number of locations.[73] Hence, a great deal of business was conducted in Sepphoris. This cosmopolitan nature has been cited by scholars as one of the main reasons for the city's reluctance to rebel against Rome during the first-century Jewish revolt.[74] The city was prosperous, and its residents had no real reason to fight the Romans.

Second, according to rabbinic texts, Sepphoris was a prominent Galilean fortress.[75] This would place it among the major Jewish cities of the first century. Third, the area surrounding Sepphoris was quite fertile.[76] As one scholar has observed, "The Hebrew phrase, 'a land flowing with milk and honey,' might best express the exceeding fertility and richness of Galilee at the time of Christ."[77] The city itself was located near a high hill which overlooked the Bet Netofa Valley. This particular valley was noted for its lush green landscape and fertile fields, which served as a breadbasket for the city.[78] These factors indicate that Sepphoris was a vital center of Jewish life in the first century.

A final factor may have contributed to the status of Sepphoris as the most important city in Galilee. Its high status may have been

---

however, the high population count has been challenged. See Reed, *Archaeology and the Galilean Jesus*, 79–80. He believes that the population may have been closer to 10,000.

72. Meyers, "Roman Sepphoris," 321.

73. Dennis C. Duling, "The Jesus Movement and Network Analysis," in *The Social Setting of Jesus and the Gospels* (ed. Wolfgang Stegemann et al.; Minneapolis: Augsburg, 2002), 309.

74. See Stuart S. Miller, *Studies in the History and Traditions of Sepphoris* (Leiden: Brill, 1984), 57.

75. Freyne, *Galilee from Alexander the Great to Hadrian*, 122. Freyne is referring to *m. Arakhin* 9:6, in which "the old castle of Sepphoris" is mentioned.

76. Freyne, *Galilee from Alexander the Great to Hadrian*, 122.

77. Selah Merrill, *Galilee in the Time of Christ* (Oxford: Oxford University Press, 1898), 25.

78. Batey, *Jesus and the Forgotten City*, 136.

due to bureaucratic reasons. It was named as a major governmental seat by Gabinius, the proconsul of Syria, in 55 B.C.E., providing the city with additional status.[79] Therefore, many key institutions were located there, including a royal bank and an archive.[80] This would have made the city vital to Jew and Gentile alike, thereby increasing the amount of traffic passing through the city.

The status of Sepphoris as a well-to-do city is confirmed through recent archaeological evidence. Luxurious houses have been unearthed, some complete with exquisite mosaic floorings.[81] In fact, some of the first-century houses contained luxury items such as molded glass cups and cosmetic products.[82] Paved and colonnaded streets have been found, and a public water works exists near the acropolis.[83] Regarding the wealth of Sepphoris, Arlene Fradkin states, "Archaeological excavations . . . have revealed a sophisticated urban metropolis complete with colonnaded streets, a theater, an aqueduct system, villas, synagogues, and a large public building."[84]

Following the first revolt, many Jewish leaders settled in Sepphoris.[85] Also, the Jewish population in Sepphoris was traditional in nature. Rabbi Yose ben Halafta, who lived in and after the last half of the first century C.E., reported that priests resided in the city even after the war against Rome.[86] If the Matthean community had been in conflict with a surrounding Jewish community, these Jews

---

79. Freyne, *Galilee from Alexander the Great to Hadrian*, 122.

80. Ibid.

81. Carolyn Osiek and David L. Balch, *Families in the New Testament World: Households and House Churches* (Louisville: Westminster John Knox, 1997), 13.

82. Reed, *Archaeology and the Galilean Jesus*, 126.

83. Mark Chancey and Eric M. Meyers, "How Jewish Was Sepphoris in Jesus' Time?" *Biblical Archaeology Review* 26 (2000): 24.

84. Arlene Fradkin, "Long-Distance Trade in the Lower Galilee: New Evidence from Sepphoris," in *Archaeology and the Galilee: Texts and Contexts in the Graeco-Roman and Byzantine Periods* (ed. Douglas R. Edwards and C. Thomas McCollough; Atlanta: Scholars Press, 1997), 107.

85. Ya'akov Meshorer, *City-Coins of Eretz-Israel and the Decapolis in the Roman Period* (Jerusalem: The Israel Museum, 1985), 36.

86. Miller, *Studies in the History and Traditions of Sepphoris*, 103. See *m. Ta'anit* 2:5 for the complete report.

would also have been quite conservative, much like an aristocratic or priestly group that wished to continue practicing a traditional Jewish faith.

In fact, the city's general population was overwhelmingly Jewish.[87] This is important, because Matthew's own Jewish Christian community was in conflict with a nearby formative Jewish group. Therefore, if I am to locate the Matthean church in Sepphoris, there needs to be evidence that a sizable Jewish population existed there as well. Josephus supports this view. He points out that the city's Jewish inhabitants acted as traitors in the war against Rome by refusing to side with the rest of the rebels.[88] Yet as Chancey points out, nowhere does Josephus indicate that the inhabitants of the city were pagans. Chancey further remarks on Josephus' indication that the city's refusal to send reinforcements to Jerusalem was a failure "common to us all," proving that Josephus and his brethren (in Sepphoris) were Jewish.[89] The city was an active center of Jewish learning during the rabbinic age.[90] In fact, the Sanhedrin at times was located in Sepphoris during the first century C.E.[91]

Archaeological evidence also supports the theory that Sepphoris was a Jewish city.[92] First, although thousands of animal bones have been found in the city, almost none are pig bones. Pigs, of course, would not have been consumed by a Jewish population; pigs are

---

87. Meyers, "Roman Sepphoris," 324.

88. *Jewish War* 3:4:1.

89. Mark A. Chancey, "The Cultural Milieu of Ancient Sepphoris," *New Testament Studies* 47 (2001): 133. See Josephus, *The Life* 65.

90. Meyers, "Roman Sepphoris," 330. See the Tosefta, in which Sepphoris is mentioned in conjunction with the rabbis. In particular, see *t. Bava Batra* 2:10 and *t. Ma'aser Scheni* 1:13.

91. Overman, *Matthew's Gospel and Formative Judaism*, 159. Josephus alludes to this as well. See also *b. Rosh HaShanah* 31ab, in which the Great Court moved "from Beth Shaearim to Sepphoris and from Sepphoris to Tiberias." For a brief discussion of the Sanhedrin, see Alexander Guttmann, *Rabbinic Judaism in the Making: A Chapter in the History of Halakhah from Ezra to Judah I* (Detroit: Wayne State University Press, 1970), 27–28.

92. Chancey and Meyers, "How Jewish Was Sepphoris?" 25–27. The archaeological evidence cited in the next two paragraphs is taken from this article.

not kosher. Second, 114 fragments of stone vessels have been recovered by archaeologists. This is relevant since Jews preferred stone vessels to metal or glass ones because they believed that stone could never become impure. Hence, stone vessels were favored by Jews for storing pure water for washing their hands. John's Gospel mentions such stone vessels, which were used for "Jewish rites of purification" (2:6).

Third, many Jewish ritual baths, or *mikva'ot*, have been unearthed in the residential areas of Sepphoris, suggesting a strong Jewish presence in the city. Lastly, coins found in the city dating from the Jewish revolt contain no images of emperors or pagan deities. This indicates that the residents of Sepphoris were concerned with maintaining Jewish law, which prohibited any artificial images or idols. Coins minted in the first century C.E. also contain a double cornucopia intersected by a staff. These two symbols exemplify first-century Jewish coinage.[93] Finally, no remains of any pagan temples or cultic objects dating from the first century C.E. have been found. All of this evidence leads to one conclusion: Sepphoris was a Jewish city.

Accordingly, Sepphoris in Galilee is the most plausible location for the Matthean community. Modern archaeological evidence disproves much of the dated literature concerning the city and its inhabitants. The city fits virtually all of the criteria needed for a Jewish Christian population such as Matthew's. Sepphoris was a wealthy Jewish city with an active economy that allowed Matthew's community the means to produce and distribute a gospel. A city with a wealthy, conservative, aristocratic Jewish population would have provided the perfect setting for the Gospel, since Matthew's own upstart Jewish Christian church appears to have been arguing with just such a Jewish group over the correct interpretation of the Torah and its laws.

Textual evidence supports the assertion that Jews and Christians continued to live as distinct competing groups within Sepphoris for quite some time after the birth of Christianity. A passage from the

---

93. Ibid., 24.

Talmud discusses an incident in Sepphoris in which the famous
Rabbi Eliezer agreed with a follower of Jesus on a point of Jewish
religious law.[94] This follower of Jesus, Jacob of Siknin, is referred
to as "a healer in Yeshua's name."[95] Matthew's own Jewish Christian orientation was evident in that the Gospel clearly exhibited an
intense fervor for the Torah. This zeal was important. A large portion of the Matthean Gospel deals with the group's attempts to
convince other Jews in the city that they alone were the correct
interpreters of the Jewish law.

There is one more interesting feature regarding coinage that
directly involves the city of Sepphoris. Sepphoris was granted per-
mission to mint its own coins toward the end of the Jewish War,
around 67 C.E.[96] This was probably a reward for the city's loyalty
to Rome during the war.[97] Coins minted from this time bear the
Greek inscription ΕΙΡΗΝΟΠΟΛΙΣ ("city of peace").[98]

The Matthean Gospel mentions coinage a number of times, particularly when the higher denominations are concerned. Since silver coins were the normative currency in the markets of the ancient
world, I am not surprised by Matthew's preference for those
coins.[99] This is important for two reasons. First, Matthew's concern for coinage portrays the community as wealthy and engaged
in commercial activity. Second, the Matthean Gospel depicts the
type of coinage which may have easily been struck in the city of
Sepphoris. These factors support the possibility that the Gospel

---

94. *b. Avodah Zarah* 16b–17a. For an analysis of this exchange, see Seán
Freyne, "Christianity in Sepphoris and Galilee," in *Galilee and Gospel: Collected
Essays* (Wissenschaftliche Untersuchungen zum Neuen Testament 125; Tübingen:
Mohr, 1997), 299–307.

95. *t. Hullin* 2:22–23.

96. Meyers, "Roman Sepphoris," 324.

97. Shaye J. D. Cohen, *Josephus in Galilee and Rome: His Vita and Development as a Historian* (Leiden: Brill, 1979), 246–47. Cohen notes that Josephus supports the conclusion that Sepphoris was loyal to Rome. See *The Life* 8, 9, 25, 45,
65, etc. See also Seán Freyne, *Galilee, Jesus, and the Gospels: Literary Approaches
and Historical Investigations* (Philadelphia: Fortress, 1988), 138.

98. Meyers, "Roman Sepphoris," 324.

99. Meshorer, *City-Coins of Eretz-Israel*, 6.

was written from the city. I explore the issue of money and wealth in more detail in the next chapter.

I acknowledge that my attempts to link the Matthean community to the city of Sepphoris are speculative. Yet there is evidence to support this view. The authors of the Gospel were writing from a wealthy urban setting that contained a large, conservative, Jewish population. Sepphoris certainly fits the criteria. Even if one is hesitant to accept this theory, the argument for Antioch is significantly weaker. Antioch is a good guess at best, but Sepphoris is a logical choice supported by archaeological and textual evidence.

3

The Wealth of the Matthean Community

Galilean Economics: A First-Century View

Rome's Relationship to Jewish Politics and Economics

FIRST-CENTURY PALESTINIANS INTERACTED WITH OTHER regions. This resulted in an active Palestinian economy tied to Roman economics and industry. For example, in the Talmud one finds three prominent rabbis discussing the construction of the Roman baths, streets, and bridges in Judea and Galilee.[1] Coinage from the first century B.C.E. also indicates close economic ties between Rome and the Jews. Both Herod's coins and those minted by the Jews had the phrase "King of the Jews" imprinted, suggesting their compatibility. This indicated a desire on the part of Palestine to remain consistent with the Roman system of coinage, thereby allowing for the economic interactions among the two groups. Subsequently, it is relevant to mention the basic economic

---

1. Overman has called my attention to the rabbinic passages in this section. See J. Andrew Overman, "Matthew's Parables and Roman Politics: The Imperial Setting of Matthew's Narrative with Special Reference to His Parables," in *SBL Seminar Papers, 1995* (ed. Eugene H. Lovering Jr.; Atlanta: Scholars Press, 1995), 428–29. The passage cited here is from *b. Shabbat* 33b.

staples of Galilee. Galileans surely would have traded with merchants from many regions.

Galilean Agriculture

Galilee itself was fertile and productive. Josephus, in his description of Galilee, described the soil there as "universally rich and fruitful."[2] In general, throughout Israel (as was the case throughout the Roman Empire) agriculture provided the foundation for the economy.[3] A recent survey conducted on Roman roads in Lower Galilee implies that farming was a pervasive activity.[4] On both sides of the Ptolemais-Diocaesarea Road cultivated terraces and small agricultural tracts have been unearthed. West of the route, the remains of a farmstead have been found. Curbstones of a path that branched from the main road to the farmstead lead one to believe that goods produced there were being transported to and from markets. The Talmud also supports the assertion that large farms existed in Galilee. It states that some of the best wheat in the region was grown near Galilean cities such as Chorazin and Capernaum.[5]

Other rabbinic texts support the pervasiveness of Galilean agricultural pursuits. Much work in this field has been done by Richard Horsley, who believes that the case laws contained in the Mishnah support the point.[6] For example, there is a reference in

---

2. *Jewish War* 3:3:2.

3. Oded Borowski, *Agriculture in Iron Age Israel* (Winona Lake, Ind.: Eisenbrauns, 1987), 162.

4. Israel Roll, "Survey of Roman Roads in Lower Galilee," in *Excavations and Surveys in Israel* (ed. Inna Pommerantz and Ann Roshwalb; Jerusalem: Israel Antiquities Authority, 1994), 14:38–40. The information in this paragraph is taken from this article.

5. Harold W. Hoehner, *Herod Antipas* (Cambridge: Cambridge University Press, 1972), 65. Hoehner points out the passage from the Talmud. See *b. Menahoth* 85a.

6. Richard A. Horsley, *Galilee: History, Politics, People* (Valley Forge, Pa.: Trinity Press International, 1995), 202–7.

the Mishnah to the interest applicable when loaning another person wheat.[7] In addition, the Mishnah carefully discusses the stringent laws governing threshing floors.[8] Finally, there is also mention of field cultivation.[9] Although Horsley believes that such passages allude to agricultural commerce involving small groups of people, one can nonetheless ascertain that trading and commerce also took place on a larger scale. Why would the Mishnah so carefully present the laws, if they did not apply to the majority of the people?

Galilean Trade and Commerce

The Jewish population also seemed to have been quite active in Mediterranean trade and commerce, as Josephus indicates.[10] Trade and commerce were important parts of the Galilean economy. For instance, clay lamp molds found throughout the region (as well as in Palestine and trans-Jordan) suggest the pervasiveness of trade activity taking place in Galilee.[11] Many sources cite Galilee's active participation in the ancient business world.[12] This was due at least in part to the urbanization of Galilee and to the building of many Roman roads in the region by the early first century.[13] In addition to some of the more basic grain crops, other items exported from Galilee included wine, dried figs, cheese, salted fish, meat, honey,

---

7. *m. Bava Qamma* 6:3.

8. Horsley, *Galilee*, 203–4. Horsley points out the law found in the Mishnah. See *Bava Batra* 2:8.

9. *m. Pe'ah* 3:41. For a discussion concerning Galilee, see B. Golomb and Y. Kedar, "Ancient Agriculture in the Galilee Mountains," *Israel Exploration Journal* 21 (1971): 136–40. These authors believe that up to 97 percent of all Galilean mountain ranges had been cultivated at some point, suggesting a large amount of agricultural activity.

10. See *Jewish Antiquities* 12:4:6–8. Already by the third century B.C.E., it appears that some Jewish families conducted business dealings in places as far away as Alexandria.

11. Mark A. Chancey, *The Myth of a Gentile Galilee* (Cambridge: Cambridge University Press, 2002), 163.

12. Ibid., 161. Chancey cites Josephus's note concerning the purchase of Galilean oil by Syrian Jews during the war of 66–70. See *Jewish War* 2:12:2.

13. Marianne Sawicki, *Crossing Galilee* (Harrisburg, Pa.: Trinity Press International, 2000), 119.

dates, pomegranates, mushrooms, and other assorted vegetables.[14] Furthermore, it was likely that other goods were imported and exported from Galilee, such as silk and leather shoes.[15]

Regarding other forms of trade and commerce, marble, luxury items, and ointment bottles have been found throughout Palestine.[16] In ancient times Galilee imported such products as Babylonian beer, Egyptian barley beer, smoked fish and lentils, jewelry, parchment and papyrus, Spanish mackerel, and Tyrian dyes. One type of mollusk was found that came from the Nile River, around five hundred miles from the city.[17] The mollusks must have been imported into the region. This supports the existence of goods imported from places such as Egypt.

---

14. Seán Freyne, *Galilee from Alexander the Great to Hadrian, 323 BCE to 135 CE: A Study of Second Temple Judaism* (Edinburgh: T&T Clark International, 1980), 172. As evidence for the validity of this list, Freyne points out that various ancient papyri contain these items. See Victor Tcherikover, *Palestine under the Ptolemies: A Contribution to the Study of the Zenon Papyri* (Mizraim 4; New York: Hebrew University Press, 1937), 22–24.

15. Shimon Applebaum, "Economic Life in Palestine," in *The Jewish People in the First Century* (ed. Samuel Safrai et al.; Philadelphia: Fortress, 1976), 2:682. Applebaum is citing the evidence of the Mishnah and Talmud here. See *m. Kelim* 26:1 and *y. Ta'anit* 69a.

16. Douglas Edwards, "The Socio-economic and Cultural Ethos in the First Century," in *The Galilee in Late Antiquity* (ed. Lee I. Levine; Cambridge: Harvard University Press, 1992), 60. See also M. Hershkovitz, "Miniature Ointment Vases," *Israel Exploration Journal* 36 (1986): 50–51. Edwards, quoting Hershkovitz, notes that these items have been found as far north as Upper Galilee.

17. Matthew's Gospel seems to contain a special affinity for the fishing trade. This suggests the community's familiarity with the business. Although many pericopes dealing with fishing are similar to passages from Mark or Luke (see Matt 4:18, in which Peter and Andrew are "casting a net"; 13:47, "like a net that was thrown into the sea"), there are others that are unique. Consider, for example, Matt 17:27: "However, so that we do not give offense to them, go to the sea and *cast a hook*; take the first fish that comes up; and when you open its mouth, you will find a coin [*stater*]; take that and give it to them for you and me." The mention of hook-fishing is unique to Matthew's Gospel; no other New Testament writing contains it. It is possible that the Matthean community alone had the expertise necessary to perfect this craft. An interesting study dealing with maritime incidents in the New Testament was written many years ago. See Peter F. Anson, *Christ and the Sailor: A Study of the Maritime Incidents in the New Testament* (Fresno, Calif.: Academy Library Guild, 1954).

Textual evidence also meshes with the existence of Galilean export activity. Tacitus, in the *Historiae*, notes the region's fertility and its ability to produce and export products such as balsam and various rope-making materials.[18] Galilean olive oil, for example, was in high demand throughout the ancient world.[19] Josephus mentions the exploits of a first-century Jew, John of Gischala, who supplied Caesarea Philippi and Syria with olive oil produced in Galilee.[20] Also, the Babylonian Talmud notes an incident in which the people of Laodicea wanted to purchase olive oil, but they could not find it in Jerusalem or Tyre; only Gischala, in Galilee, had enough to satisfy their order.[21]

Furthermore, research has unveiled other export products such as vegetables, grain, and salted fish from the Sea of Galilee. In particular, recent archaeological excavations have yielded startling finds confirming the extensive presence of the fish business in Sepphoris.[22] Dozens of varieties of fish including grouper, catfish, mussels, and mollusks have been uncovered from the Sea of Galilee, the Mediterranean Sea, and the Jordan River. Export of these products seems plausible, judging by the fact that the exchange of local goods and crafts in the urban marketplace was widespread.[23] Recall the example above regarding John of Gischala. Galilee itself was located on a major route to the East, so many traders and merchants were forced to pass through the region on their way to various cities.[24] This resulted in great opportunity for commerce and trade.

---

18. *Historiae* 5:6.
19. Arlene Fradkin, "Long-Distance Trade in the Lower Galilee: New Evidence from Sepphoris," in *Archaeology and the Galilee: Texts and Contexts in the Graeco-Roman and Byzantine Periods* (ed. Douglas R. Edwards and C. Thomas McCullough; Atlanta: Scholars Press, 1997), 112.
20. *Jewish War* 2:21:2.
21. *b. Menahot* 85b. Again, Hoehner points this out.
22. Fradkin, "Long-Distance Trade," 107–16. The following data regarding these archaeological finds comes from this article as well.
23. See also Edwards, "Socio-economic and Cultural Ethos," 58. I agree with Edwards's assertion.
24. Seán Freyne, *Galilee, Jesus, and the Gospels: Literary Approaches and Historical Investigations* (Philadelphia: Fortress, 1988), 156.

Finally, additional information from other Mishnaic passages and archaeological finds supports this position. For example, the Mishnah discusses imported goods, or those manufactured on the coast.[25] Also worth noticing are the large amounts of non-Galilean coinage found throughout the coastal cities, the Decapolis, and other distant locations.[26] This suggests that a great quantity of Galilean goods may have been purchased from those residing outside the area (specifically, Gentiles).[27] The Mishnah confirms this, judging by passages such as *m. Avodah Zarah* 1:5, which states in part, "These things are forbidden to sell to Gentiles: fir cones, white figs, and their stalks, frankincense, and a white cock."[28] Many of the Mishnah's rulings seem to refer to small villages, where merchantry was carried out mostly on a small scale.

The most compelling evidence from the Mishnah concerns the Galilean production of pottery. The pottery trade was prevalent throughout Galilee and contributed greatly to the regional economy. In particular, excavations have isolated a major production center within one region: Kefar Hananya. Kefar Hananya was believed to have been a leading center from the early Roman period through the early Byzantine period.[29] In particular, the vessels produced were designed for the storage of olive oil.[30] In addition to a virtual repertory of pottery items found there, other items, such as cookware found in Sepphoris, were produced at Kefar Hananya.[31] David Adan-Bayewitz infers:

---

25. Martin Goodman, *State and Society in Roman Galilee, A.D. 132–212* (Totowa, N.J.: Rowman & Allanheld, 1983), 45. Goodman points this out. See *m. Avodah Zarah* 2:4.

26. Chancey, *Myth of a Gentile Galilee*, 162.

27. Goodman, *State and Society in Roman Galilee*, 45. It is possible, of course, that Roman soldiers could have been the cause, but even if that is the case, then they would have contributed at least something to the flow of goods in Galilee.

28. Ibid. Once again Goodman points this out.

29. David Adan-Bayewitz, *Common Pottery in Roman Galilee: A Study of Local Trade* (Ramat-Gan, Israel: Bar-Ilan University Press, 1993), 224.

30. See *m. Kelim* 2:2.

31. Adan-Bayewitz, *Common Pottery in Roman Galilee*, 214.

It should be noted that the predominance of Kefar Hananya cooking ware at Sepphoris and, presumably, Tiberias represents the first archaeological evidence of the dependence of these Galilean cities on the manufactured products of a rural settlement. It also represents the first well-defined archaeological evidence for the continual urban-rural commercial interaction within Roman Galilee.[32]

This supports my conclusion that Galilee actively engaged in trade and commerce.

Other rabbinic literature confirms this assertion. For example, the Tosefta refers to "those who make black clay, such as Kefar Hananya and its neighbors."[33] The Mishnah, in turn, discusses market prices for pottery.[34] This early Jewish literature confirms the argument that this region was a center of production and trade. Douglas Edwards sums it up best: "The Lower Galilee [where Sepphoris was located] profited from the *pax Romana,* as its participation in international trade indicated. According to Josephus, 'Acco-Ptolemais served as the maritime city of the Galilee; it dominated the Mediterranean coast west of the Galilee in the early part of the first century.'"[35] Therefore, the region was likely engaged in extensive economic activity in the first century.

Matthew as a Wealthy Galilean Community

There are cogent reasons to believe that the Matthean community was prosperous. Jennifer Glancy points out that Matthew's parables often focus on the topic of slaves.[36] This suggests that the community must have had sufficient wealth to own a number of slaves. Glancy cites a number of passages in which slaves are mentioned and utilized by the authors of the Gospel (see 13:24–30; 18:23–35;

---

32. Ibid., 219.

33. *t. Bava Mezi'a* 6:3.

34. *m. Bava Mezi'a* 5:7.

35. Edwards, "Socio-economic and Cultural Ethos," 60. See Josephus, *Jewish War* 2:10:2.

36. Jennifer A. Glancy, "Slaves and Slavery in the Matthean Parables," *Journal of Biblical Literature* 119 (2000): 67–90.

21:33–41; 22:1–10; 24:45–51; 25:41–30).[37] Notice that many references to slaves deal with those engaged in some kind of managerial function. For example, 24:45 reads, "Who then is the faithful and wise servant, whom his master has put in charge of his household, to give the other slaves their allowance of food at the proper time?" Similarly, 25:14 states, "For it is as if a man, going on a journey, summoned his slaves and entrusted his property to them." This suggests that these slaves could actually read and write. They had to manage properties and keep the finances in order. This is relevant since educated slaves served as teachers to household members or other slaves.[38]

Matthew and Money

Consider the basic nature of references to coinage found in this Gospel. First, unlike Mark, Matthew never makes any reference to the smaller coinage denominations, such as the λεπτόν.[39] Mark's story of the poor widow's two λεπτά (12:41–44) is not found in the Matthean text, although Luke retains it (21:1–4). Luke's Gospel rarely mentions money (see 7:41; 12:6, 59; 19:13; etc.), and when the text does mention denominations they are often far lesser denominations than those in Matthew's Gospel. For example, both Luke and Matthew contain stories about debt. Luke 7:41 discusses a creditor whose two debtors each owed five hundred denarii. Matthew's king, in 18:23, is owed ten thousand talents, a far greater amount. There is no parallel story in either Mark or Luke's Gospel. Only the Matthean Gospel contains a story involving such vast amounts of money. Both Mark and Luke also contain other stories involving denarii, but Matthew once again omits the reference or changes it to read "a large sum."[40]

---

37. Ibid., 73.

38. Stanley F. Bonner, *Education in Ancient Rome from the Elder Cato to the Younger Pliny* (Berkeley: University of California Press, 1977), 37. Cato refers to the practice of using slaves as teachers. See Plutarch's *Cato the Elder* 21:7.

39. Jack Dean Kingsbury, *Matthew as Story* (Philadelphia: Fortress, 1986), 125.

40. Mark's story of the feeding of the five thousand (6:37) and the anointing

In general, Matthew alone mentions the more valuable denominations, such as ἀργύριον, ἄργυρος (silver), χρυσός (gold), and the
τάλαντον (the talent). In fact, the authors use the three terms a total
of twenty-eight times, while Mark mentions silver only once.[41]
Consider the talent. Matthew's Gospel mentions it fourteen times,
while the other Gospels do not mention this sum of money at all.
The lowest denomination of coin mentioned by Matthew is the
κοδράντης (5:26), and it is used only to show how important it is
to reconcile with one's brother down to the last penny.

Some scholars, however, debate the issue of Matthew's references to money. Werner Marx has suggested that Matthew's
Gospel does not favor money. He cites the fact that 10:9 finds Jesus
commissioning the disciples and specifically instructing them not
to take any money with them.[42] The passage reads, "Take no gold,
or silver, or copper in your belts." The parallel Gospel stories show
little similarity. Mark 6:8 mentions only "copper," while Luke 9:3
lists only "silver." Yet Matthew apparently wishes to discard all
denominations.

There is a reasonable solution to this dilemma. The Matthean
church was wealthier than other Jewish Christian communities,
and the authors wished to emphasize nonusage of their many coins
in the practice of missionary work. Although the community had
considerable funds, it was not relevant to the evangelical work of
Jesus' followers. Therefore, Jesus instructs his disciples to preach,
and not to worry about money. Money was certainly important to
the Matthean community, but there were also spiritual concerns
that superseded financial issues.

Other verses are relevant to fiscal matters. First, the authors of
Matthew mention two forms of currency that are found nowhere

(14:5) are good examples. See also Luke's story of the feeding (9:13). Matthew's
story of the feeding of the five thousand (14:15–21) omits Mark's mention of the
two hundred denarii. Matthew 26:9 also changes Mark's anointing story (which
mentions three hundred denarii) to read "a large sum." See also Werner G. Marx,
"Money Matters in Matthew," *Bibliotheca sacra* 136 (1979): 152–57. Marx cites
these passages; I am following his argument here.

41. Kingsbury, *Matthew as Story*, 126.

42. "Money Matters," 155. I am following Marx's argument here.

else in the New Testament. In the story discussing payment of the half-shekel Temple tax, Matt 17:24 includes both the δίδραχμον and the στατήρ.[43] In Matthew, Jesus does not object to the tax. This suggests that the payment of the tax was not problematic for members of this community. Second, the Gospel contains unique usages of the term "gold." Matthew 23:16–17 reads, "Woe to you, blind guides, who say, 'Whoever swears by the sanctuary is bound by nothing, but whoever swears by the gold of the sanctuary, he is bound by the oath.' You blind fools! For which is greater, the gold or the sanctuary that has made the gold sacred?" In these verses Jesus mentions gold three times. He also discusses gold in conjunction with oaths and the Temple, two concepts connected to holiness and purity. This suggests that the community members felt their wealth was so important that they were allowed to proclaim themselves pure. Matthew links their wealth to these important symbols. So the authors of Matthew here caution their community against this practice. The members should never place too high a value on the material wealth that they had accumulated.

A fine analysis of money usage in the New Testament has been offered by Douglas Oakman. Oakman provides a visual analytical model for studying money functions in the New Testament. He organizes the usages of money by their corresponding function (F1 = storage; F2 = measurement; F3 = payment; F4 = exchange-value orientation; F5 = use-value orientation, or money barter).[44] Ten of the fourteen mentions of money as it is related to taxation, debt payments, and purchasing are offered by Matthew's Gospel. This further illustrates the dominance of money-related issues in the Gospel, suggesting that the Matthean community was well-off financially.

Wealth in the Matthean Text

Textual evidence also suggests that the audience of the Gospel was wealthy. Consider, for instance, whom Jesus blesses in the

---

43. Ibid., 155.

44. Douglas E. Oakman, "Money in the Moral Universe of the New Testament," in *The Social Setting of Jesus and the Gospels* (ed. Wolfgang Stegemann et al.; Minneapolis: Augsburg Fortress, 2002), 339–40.

Gospels.[45] In Mark, Jesus blesses the poor (6:20), but in Matthew Jesus instead blesses "the poor *in spirit*" (5:3). This indicates that the authors of Matthew were altering the text in order to suit their audience. The audience was not poor materially; they were only poor spiritually. Mark Allan Powell connotes that Matthew here is referring to those people in the world who have been abandoned and who have lost their "spirit."[46] They have money, but their souls are empty.

Matthew's other modifications of Mark's text denote a wealthy community. For instance, 19:23 modifies the Markan saying of 10:23 ("those who have riches to enter the kingdom of God") to read more directly "a rich man to enter the kingdom of heaven (RSV)."[47] This expresses Matthew's familiarity with affluent members and "rich men." Other scholars have followed this line of thinking. For instance, some scholars feel that Matthew's urban population included many wealthy landowners and businessmen, as passages such as 5:25–26; 6:19; 13:45–46; 20:1–6; and 21:33–46 indicate.[48] These passages provide sound business advice; pearl dealers are mentioned, and landowners are discussed. For example, Matthew in the story of the householder (see 21:33) changes the *man* found in Mark's and Luke's version of the story (12:1 and 20:9, respectively) to *householder*. This conveys a prominent position on the part of the main character.

Consider also Matt 20:29–34, the story of the two blind men who ask Jesus to restore their sight. Unique here is Matthew's

---

45. Kingsbury, *Matthew as Story*, 125. I am following Kingsbury here.

46. Mark Allan Powell, "Matthew's Beatitudes: Reversals and Rewards of the Kingdom," *Catholic Biblical Quarterly* 58 (1996): 464. An excellent article by Robert H. Smith ("Blessed Are the Poor in [Holy] Spirit'? [Matthew 5:3]," *Word and World* 18 [1998]: 389–96) also discusses 5:3. Smith feels that Matthew here is referring to those who are deficient or "poor" in "charismatic endowment." In particular, see pages 390–91 for a summary of his position. Either way, it seems clear that Matthew is not directly addressing an economic crisis in his community.

47. Kingsbury, *Matthew as Story*, 126.

48. Robert H. Smith, "Were the Early Christians Middle-Class? A Sociological Analysis of the New Testament," *Currents in Theology and Mission* 7 (1980): 266.

description of the blind men. At the beginning of the story, both Mark and Luke describe a single blind man, who is *begging*.[49] Oddly enough, this detail is omitted in Matthew's depiction of the two blind men. Instead, the Gospel says that the two blind men were "sitting by the roadside." No mention of begging is included. Have the authors of Matthew skipped this detail because they realize that it is inapplicable to their community's situation? This is likely the case.

Look at those whom Jesus invites to the wedding in the parable of the marriage feast in Matt 22:1–14. In Luke 14:21, the *"poor and maimed and blind and lame"* are invited, but Matthew alters the parable to read, "[I]nvite to the marriage feast as many as you find" (22:9, RSV). Conspicuously absent from the Matthean account is any mention of "the poor."[50] Matthew here differs widely from the Lukan account. The *poor* are eliminated since this group does not seem to apply to the Matthean community.

Particularly interesting is Matthew's parable of the hidden talents (25:14–30; also Luke 19:11–27). First, notice the mention of "bankers" in 25:27, a profession familiar to Matthew's community. Of more interest, though, are the denominations found in the parallel Lukan and Matthean accounts. According to Luke, the slaves are given *pounds*, but in Matthew they are given *talents*. Talents, of course, were by far the more valuable denomination. Why the differences in the story, especially if the brief Markan references (4:24–25; 13:34) contain no mention of money at all? Keener suggests that Matthew inflates the money amounts, and varies the distribution by capability, in order to show that the master (presumably Jesus?) already knew of their differing abilities. Yet that all of the slaves returned *something* illustrates the expectation that everyone must be productive.[51] Hence, if we relate this to Jesus

---

49. Gerd Theissen, *Sociology of Early Palestinian Christianity* (trans. John Bowden; Minneapolis: Fortress, 1978), 36. Theissen notes how both Mark and Luke emphasize begging.

50. Kingsbury, *Matthew as Story*, 125. Again, this example comes from Kingsbury.

51. Craig S. Keener, *A Commentary on the Gospel of Matthew* (Grand Rapids: Eerdmans, 1999), 600–601.

(the master) and the church (the slaves), the meaning becomes clear: all church members may reap big rewards via their active participation regarding their master's interests. And Matthew emphasizes the larger denominations in order to appeal to a wealthy audience that could relate to such large sums of money. In other words, Matthew wanted to convey that a lot was at stake; one should not merely continue to gather wealth and be content. The kingdom of God superseded the community wealth.[52]

Finally, there is the unique Matthean insertion of Judas's suicide in 27:3–10. Here the chief priests take the thirty pieces of silver (returned by Judas) and purchase the potter's field. The story, probably meant to verify the fulfillment of Hebrew prophecy (Zech 11:13; Jer 18–19) as well as to acquit Jesus and implicate the priests, cites "pieces of silver" no less than four times. This is likely another instance in which the Gospel authors find it necessary to convince the audience that their wealth cannot lead them to God. The Matthean community, like the people of Israel, are shown how insignificant and meaningless thirty pieces of silver really are. After all, Jesus had commanded the twelve disciples not to accept any silver (10:9). Their loyalty to Jesus is not predicated upon their financial resources. This would be a lesson that only a wealthy audience could understand. Hence, the other Gospels contain no such story.

The Matthean Community in the Context of the Roman Economy

Taxes and Other Forms of Income

It is important to understand how vital taxes were to the ancient economy. Furthermore, Matthew's Gospel mentions taxes as well as tax collectors. So, the Matthean community must have been linked to Rome. As Finley points out, taxes were the mainstay of income for the Roman Empire. How was this so? The answer is

---

52. Markus Bockmuehl, *Jewish Law in Gentile Churches* (Grand Rapids: Baker, 2000), 125.

simple: through the emperor's taxes on the land.[53] As Garnsey and Saller point out, "The interests and needs of the Roman government were few. Apart from war and diplomacy, its basic concern was to supply and finance the military, bureaucracy and court. . . . It was the tax on agricultural land in all the provinces (but not Italy) which paid for the bulk of this expenditure."[54] In particular, the heaviest burden of the land tax may have fallen on those who worked the hardest: the peasants and tenants.[55] Garnsey elaborates on the subject of taxes, writing that the emperors carried out tax policies different from those in the Republican age.[56] A more systematic method of taxation was enacted through the use of the census. Evidence for this is found in Luke's Gospel, which alludes to a census within Palestine (see 2:1). Scholars have posited that both the Roman and Jewish taxation systems in the first century must have placed a great strain on Palestinian communities (including Matthew's).[57] This is especially true of church members involved in agricultural pursuits. They would be paying money to Rome and Jerusalem.

In addition to the substantial land taxes, there were additional taxes. A poll tax, for example, was levied on both the rich and poor. Other taxes were not as egalitarian in nature, with the property tax serving as an example. The rate seemed to vary depending upon the area, as writers such as Appian seem to testify.[58] In gen-

---

53. Ibid., 89.

54. Peter Garnsey and Richard Saller, *The Roman Empire: Economy, Society, and Culture* (Berkeley: University of California Press, 1987), 56.

55. M. I. Finley, *The Ancient Economy* (updated ed.; Berkeley: University of California Press, 1999), 91.

56. Peter Garnsey, *Famine and Food Supply in the Graeco-Roman World: Responses to Risk and Crisis* (New York: Cambridge University Press, 1988), 245–46. All information contained in this paragraph, with the exception of that provided by the ancient authors, is taken from this source.

57. Douglas E. Oakman, "Jesus and Agrarian Palestine: The Factor of Debt," in *SBL Seminar Papers, 1985* (ed. Kent Harold Richards; Atlanta: Scholars Press, 1985), 63. Oakman is referring especially to the work of F. C. Grant (see F. C. Grant, *The Economic Background of the Gospels* [Oxford: Oxford University Press, 1926], 89).

58. See his *Roman History, Book XL, The Syrian Wars* 50. This account men-

eral, though, Garnsey argues that Rome did not pursue a high level
of direct taxation, due to the uneasiness and discontent that such a
policy could incite. Therefore, with the exception of the emperor
Vespasian, most other rulers kept the rates relatively low and sta-
ble.[59] Regardless of the level of taxes, it seems the Matthean community had no problem paying their debt to the empire.

Matthew and Taxes

I want to examine more closely Matthew's mention of various
taxes. The authors of Matthew do not object to the payment of an
additional Temple tax along with the normal tithing taxes.[60] In
17:24–25 one reads, "[T]he collectors of the half-shekel tax went
up to Peter and said, 'Does your teacher not pay the temple tax?'
He said, 'Yes.'" Later, Jesus endorses the paying of the tax to placate the "kings of the earth" (see 17:25). There is no comparable
passage in Matthew's main source, Mark. Of course, by the time of
Matthew's Gospel the Temple had already been destroyed. So why
does Matthew alone still mention the tax? First, of course, the
authors may be satirizing the Roman two-drachma tax.[61] Second,
the Gospel may have been following Jewish law, which encourages
a peaceful lifestyle. Jesus was paying the tax in order not to disturb
the peace, as the Mishnah advises.[62]

---

tions Vespasian's heavy poll tax on the Jews, which exceeded the poll taxes levied
on their neighbors. This penalty against the Jews was part of their punishment for
their rebellions against Rome. I discussed this in more detail in the first chapter.

59. Information on this found in the writings of Suetonius. See *The Twelve
Caesars* (Vespasian) 10:16, in which he reported that Vespasian levied "new and
heavier ones." See also 10:23. Here Suetonius specifically refers to Vespasian's
love for money.

60. Anthony Saldarini, *Matthew's Christian-Jewish Community* (Chicago:
University of Chicago Press, 1994), 143.

61. David E. Garland, "Matthew's Understanding of the Temple Tax (Matt
17:24–27)," in *SBL Seminar Papers, 1987* (ed. Kent Harold Richards; Atlanta:
Scholars Press, 1987), 193. Garland notes that the Babylonian Talmud also
alludes to the fact that "Kings" are exempt from paying taxes. See *b. Sukkah* 30a.

62. Garland, "Matthew's Understanding," 194. Garland here is referring to
the possibility that Jesus did not wish to withhold the payment of the tax "for the

Matthew may have also been pointing out the group's loyalty (as Jewish Christians) to the authoritative Jewish community then residing in Yavneh. The Jews in Yavneh were instituting another tax (the *fiscus iudaicus*) to help fund new programs designed to preserve the endangered Jewish religion.[63] Maybe the authors included the passage in order to urge the community members to live in harmony with one another as well as with other Jews in the region.[64] Although the Jewish Christian Matthean community disagreed with the formative Jewish population residing in Galilee, they still thought of themselves as Jews. Paying the tax, as opposed to fighting over it, would support the Jewish way of life, which maintained that conflict was not the proper way to handle disputes.

Regardless of which theory is correct, the important thing is that Matthew did not seem concerned about the payment of the tax. These issues never enter into the story. Matthew does not care about the payment of money; that is secondary to the theological or political point. This suggests that the Matthean community was affluent, since the church members had no objection to the payment of taxes. Presumably, they had enough money. As Saldarini concludes, "Jesus thus remains [in Matthew's Gospel] firmly within the Jewish community as a loyal, tax-paying Jew."[65]

Texts and Economics: The Existence of the Book Trade

By the first century there was an active book trade operating throughout the Roman Empire.[66] Cicero, writing in the first cen-

---

sake of the peace." This phrase, סְפְנֵי דְרְכֵי שָׁלוֹם (for the sake of the peace), was coined by the rabbis as a way of allowing the priests not to pay the tax. Priests were not required to pay "for the sake of peace."

63. William G. Thompson, *Matthew's Advice to a Divided Community: Mt 17,22–18,35* (Rome: Biblical Institute Press, 1970), 67–68.

64. Garland, "Matthew's Understanding," 204.

65. Saldarini, *Matthew's Christian-Jewish Community*, 143.

66. Harry Y. Gamble, *Books and Readers in the Early Church: A History of Early Christian Texts* (New Haven: Yale University Press, 1995), 91.

tury B.C.E., reports that he often borrowed books from friends so
that he could have them copied.[67] He writes, "I have sent back the
works of Alexander . . ."[68] Written materials were needed in order
to teach others to read. For the authors of Matthew to have produced a gospel of such great stature, money would have also been
needed to pay the scribes and to transport the texts. The book trade
is also pertinent because this study discusses a community that is
known largely through the written word.

Much work has been done in this field by Harry Gamble, who
believes that early Christian texts were being disseminated throughout the ancient world soon after their completion.[69] Archaeological
evidence supporting this position has been found in Egypt, where
fragments of Irenaeus's *Against Heresies* have been unearthed,
despite the fact that the text could not have been completed anywhere close to the country (Irenaeus was the Bishop of Gaul).[70] The
key to this discovery was that the fragment was dated only about
twenty years after the text itself was written. This suggests that the
text traveled a great distance soon after its completion. Furthermore, a fragment of John's Gospel dating from the early second century has been found in Egypt, suggesting that the Christian Gospels
were in circulation quite soon after their completion.

Other scholars support Gamble's conclusions. D. Moody Smith
argues that the Gospels are misinterpreted if viewed only as
regional worship documents.[71] Often, scholars claim that the
Gospels acted as spiritual guides for an individual church community such as Matthew's. This certainly is true to some extent. Each
community was dealing with local issues, and these issues would
vary depending upon geographical location.

But even if the texts were originally designed to be read only dur-

---

67. Ibid., 280. Gamble points this out. The passage from Cicero that contains
this information is taken from *Epistulae ad Atticum* 2:20, 22.

68. See Cicero, *Epistulae ad Atticum* 2:22.

69. Gamble, *Books and Readers*, 82. See also Colin H. Roberts, "Early Christianity in Egypt: Three Notes," *Journal of Egyptian Archaeology* 40 (1954): 94.

70. Roberts, "Early Christianity," 94.

71. D. Moody Smith, "When Did the Gospels Become Scripture?" *Journal of
Biblical Literature* 119 (2000): 4–6.

ing a local church service, it is likely that they also addressed a broad number of issues that were relevant at the end of the first century C.E.[72] As they became holy texts, the Gospels became spiritually important beyond their original authors' intentions. The Gospels eventually became lasting universal "scriptures."[73] After all, Justin Martyr already was indicating that the Gospels were read during Sunday worship services.[74]

Richard Bauckham also makes the case that the Gospels were disseminated quickly as important Church documents. In fact, he goes one step further. He argues that the Gospels themselves were *intended* for a mass audience, not a single isolated Christian community, as many scholars before him have argued.[75] In fact, he believes that there was a sophisticated "network" of Christian communities that were in constant contact with one another.[76] I am not prepared to accept Bauckham's latter hypothesis. Why would the authors of Matthew need to edit Mark's text so precisely and vigorously if the communities were sharing so much common information? Matthew's Gospel clearly seems intended for a different audience, as this study indicates. Yet Bauckham's hypothesis concerning the quick circulation of information is right on the mark. It is clear that early Christian texts such as Paul's letters and the Gospels circulated rapidly, as the Papias fragment and the letters of Ignatius indicate.

This denotes that by the second century the texts were considered sacred and were used in church services. Therefore, it is likely that the Gospels would already have been well known if they were to be used as worship documents for early Christian churches. Also, the early Christian movement was largely a missionary movement, so the followers of Jesus would have needed texts that

---

72. Ibid., 6.
73. Ibid., 19.
74. Ibid., 6. See Justin Martyr's *First Apology* 67.
75. Richard Bauckham, "For Whom Were Gospels Written?" in *The Gospels for All Christians: Rethinking the Gospel Audiences* (ed. Richard Bauckham; Grand Rapids: Eerdmans, 1998), 30–31. Bauckham discusses his argument as it relates to Matthew's Gospel here.
76. Ibid.

could be distributed and used for religious purposes. Finally, there is evidence that the codex was already being used (albeit in small numbers) by the late first century, as Loveday Alexander observes in a recent study.[77]

This position is not without its skeptics. Some scholars have assumed that little can be learned about the circulation of books because evidence is sparse regarding book trading in the ancient Roman world.[78] Yet that is not necessarily the case. Raymond J. Starr states, "In fact, we know a great deal about book circulation, even though we know little about the book trade."[79] Early authors bring up the topic of books and their distribution. For instance, Cicero mentions books a number of times in his various works.[80] Cicero discusses how he sends a rough copy (copied perhaps by a slave) of a text to Atticus for copying and criticism.[81] As Starr points out, once the text had been recorded by the author, the next step was to send (or recite) the manuscript to a small group of friends for further revision.[82] This small audience would discuss the work, then the original author might send some corrected copies to other friends as gifts.[83]

Once the book had been sent to friends it was ready to be purchased by the larger public.[84] Sometimes this involved no copying

---

77. Loveday Alexander, "Ancient Book Production and the Gospels," in Bauckham, *Gospels for All Christians*, 75. She refers to *The Epigrams of Martial* 14:86 and to other places where Martial discusses the form.

78. Raymond J. Starr, "The Circulation of Literary Texts in the Roman World," *Classical Quarterly* 37 (1987): 213. In particular, he is referring to studies produced by scholars such as E. J. Kenney (see E. J. Kenney, "Books and Readers in the Roman World," in *The Cambridge History of Classical Literature* [ed. E.J. Kenney; Cambridge: Cambridge University Press, 1982], 3–32).

79. Starr, "Circulation of Literary Texts," 213.

80. See the *Epistulae ad Atticum* 13:21a; 15:27.

81. *Epistulae ad Atticum* 15:27. Here Cicero relays to Atticus that he is sending him a copy of his book *On Glory* for his perusal.

82. Starr, "Circulation of Literary Texts," 214. See Pliny the Younger, *The Letters* 5:12.

83. Pliny the Younger, *The Letters* 5:12. See Cicero's *Epistulae ad Atticum* 13:21a. Here Cicero exclaims, "I am in such a hurry to send what I have written to Varro, as you suggested, that I have sent it already to Rome to be copied."

84. Starr, "Circulation of Literary Texts," 215.

on the author's part. Each text to be purchased could be copied by a bookseller, who in turn would charge the patron for the book.[85] I do caution, however, that Jewish scribes—the focus of this study—were not to be equated with literary authors such as Cicero or Martial.

Some points can be made generally regarding book trading. First, there was an active book-dealing business by the first century. For example, it is known that Trypho dealt with the books of Martial.[86] Starr states, "The book trade appears to become more important during the first century A.D., so that by Pliny's time it seems to have become an accepted method for the circulation of literature, although by no means the only method."[87] It does appear that small urban shops sold books along with other "luxury" items.[88]

This is important, since I am arguing that literacy and books were reserved for the upper class. Some scholars believe that literacy and education went hand in hand with social mobility.[89] Starr observes that literature was linked to social status.[90] In other words, the wealthy wrote and purchased books. They were bought and sold in stores that contained items such as perfume or expensive fabric. In fact, Martial notes that a bookseller's profit margin could reach as high as 50 percent.[91] It also follows, then, that the wealthy would have had a particular interest in the written word.

---

85. Ibid. Starr looks to Martial for evidence. Martial relates sending a willing purchaser to a bookstore because he did not feel like taking the time to make another copy. See *The Epigrams of Martial* 4:72. Often, this practice resulted in little or no profit for the author.

86. Starr, "Circulation of Literary Texts," 220. See *The Epigrams of Martial* 13:3. Martial was a contemporary of Pliny the Younger.

87. Ibid., 222.

88. Ibid., 220. Starr feels that books were probably considered a luxury item; thus, they were sold in shops.

89. Richard P. Saller, *Personal Patronage under the Early Empire* (Cambridge: Cambridge University Press, 1982), 137.

90. Starr, "Circulation of Literary Texts," 223.

91. *The Epigrams of Martial* 13:3. See also Richard Duncan-Jones, *The Economy of the Roman Empire: Quantitative Studies* (Cambridge: Cambridge University Press, 1964), 48.

For instance, consider the earlier citation from Cicero, who had a great interest in books. The statement reveals that books could easily have been obtained by a wealthy citizen upon entering a retail shop.[92] Gamble agrees:

> One of the social consequences of the transition from the republican to the imperial order was a shift in the composition of the literary public. The weakening of the senatorial aristocracy and the rise of imperial power were attended by the greater social differentiation and increased opportunity for upward social mobility. In this social change the book trade found its opportunity. Since literary interest was traditionally a mark of high social standing, the development of commerce in books indicated a "weakening of the hold of the traditional aristocracy on the control of access to social status." Thus, under the empire, books were often status symbols.[93]

It appears, then, that the buying and selling of books was essentially predicated upon wealth and social rank.

Interest in Christian religious texts may have exceeded interest in other traditional forms of literature. The church, after all, would have needed both scribes and merchants to carry on the production and trade of its writings. The Matthean Gospel may have been in widespread use by the middle of the second century. The writings of Justin Martyr support this assertion. By the middle of the second century, Justin already was referring to the Gospels (including Matthew).[94] For example, in his *First Apology* 1:67 Justin speaks of the "memoirs of the apostles."

---

92. Ibid.

93. Gamble, *Books and Readers*, 91. See also Starr, "Circulation of Literary Texts," 223.

94. See Harry Y. Gamble, *The New Testament Canon: Its Making and Meaning* (Philadelphia: Fortress, 1985), 28-29. Gamble points out some of Justin's usages. See Justin's *First Apology* 1:66.3; 1:67.3; *Dialogue with Trypho* 100:4; 101:3; 102:5; etc.

It is even possible that Matthew's Gospel was in use as early as the *beginning* of the second century. This would be remarkable for a text completed only twenty years earlier. Gamble mentions that Eusebius, quoting the words of Papias, an early-second-century bishop of Hieropolis, discusses Mark's arrangement of sayings.[95] Yet at the end of the section, Eusebius adds, "Matthew collected the oracles in the Hebrew language, and each interpreted [translated?] them as best he could."[96] Although it is generally accepted that Matthew was written in Greek, the quote from Eusebius is curious. Could Matthew's Gospel have been in use only years after its completion? This is probable.

The significance of these discoveries is that they allow a conclusion that the Matthean Gospel was in circulation soon after its completion. Why is this so? I believe it was because religious texts had generated much interest by the late first century. Specifically, Gamble argues that written accounts about Jesus were in great demand.[97] This includes the Gospels, and it seems unlikely that they were known only by their respective congregations. For instance, Justin Martyr refers to early-second-century non-Christians who were taking an interest in the Gospels.[98] Based on the meticulous construction and carefully designed style of each Gospel (especially Matthew), one may argue that the texts were designed for circulation among the general public.[99] After all, were not these congregations evangelical in nature? Would not they have wanted to spread their message?

I agree, therefore, with scholars such as Abraham J. Malherbe,

---

95. Gamble, *New Testament Canon*, 27.

96. *The Ecclesiastical History* 3:39:15–16.

97. Gamble, *Books and Readers*, 102.

98. Ibid., 286. See Justin Martyr's *First Apology* 1:28. Gamble points out this reference. See also Tertullian's *Apology* 31.

99. Gamble, *Books and Readers*, 102. See also C. W. Votaw, *The Gospels and Contemporary Biographies in the Graeco-Roman World* (Philadelphia: Fortress, 1970), as well as Elisabeth Schüssler Fiorenza, "Miracles, Mission, and Apologetics: An Introduction," in *Aspects of Religious Propaganda in Judaism and Early Christianity* (ed. Elisabeth Schüssler Fiorenza; Notre Dame, Ind.: University of Notre Dame Press, 1976), 1–25.

who writes, "Suffice it here to say that, with some exceptions, the New Testament writings are . . . designed for mass consumption. They represent the literary forms congenial to the masses and speak of the people's concerns."[100] The most obvious evidence may be that the authors of Matthew used Mark's Gospel. And most scholars agree that Mark was only written about twenty years before Matthew. This implies that the first Gospel must have already been in circulation within twenty years of its origin.[101] Of course Luke's community also used Mark, and if Luke were written from a different location, this would further support this position. How could two church communities located in different cities have utilized the same Gospel if it was not readily available to them? In light of the economic evidence presented in this chapter, the Matthean community would have had the monetary means to access and possess circulated texts. Similarly, Sepphoris was located in the midst of significant trade routes, increasing the possibility of the acquisition of such items. Therefore, it is feasible that the Gospels were circulating and in use soon after their completion.

100. Abraham J. Malherbe, *Social Aspects of Early Christianity* (2nd ed.; Philadelphia: Fortress, 1983), 18-19.

101. Gamble, *Books and Readers*, 102.

4

Scribes and Conflicts

Leadership in the
Matthean Community

The Role of the Scribe in the First Century

I BEGIN BY EXAMINING THE ROLE AND FUNCTION OF
a first-century Jewish scribe.[1] The term "scribe" is mentioned as
early as the apocryphal text of the Wisdom of Ben Sira, which
accounts for the origin of the Septuagint.[2] A Greek Jewish pseudonymous letter from the second century B.C.E. describes how an
Egyptian king supposedly hired seventy-two translators to formulate a Greek version of the Hebrew Bible.[3] This story would

---

1. The role of the first-century scribe is relevant, since some scholars have
argued that the parables (13:1–52), which mention scribes, are intended to allow
the reader (in addition to the scribal author) to enter into the action as a scribe.
See Gary A. Phillips, "Training Scribes for a World Divided: Discourse and Division in the Religious System of Matthew's Gospel," in *Religious Writings and
Religious Systems: Systemic Analysis of Holy Books in Christianity, Islam, Buddhism, Greco-Roman Religions, Ancient Israel, and Judaism*, vol. 2: *Christianity*
(ed. Jacob Neusner et al.; Atlanta: Scholars Press, 1989), 69. Phillips feels that the
rhetoric of the parables allows for this conclusion.
2. See Wisdom of Ben Sira, or, as it is sometimes called, Sirach, or Ecclesiasti-
cus 38:24–39:11. The "divine wisdom" of the scribe is noted here.
3. Anthony J. Saldarini, *Pharisees, Scribes, and Sadducees in Palestinian Society: A Sociological Approach* (Wilmington, Del.: Michael Glazier, 1988), 259–60.
The rest of the information regarding this letter is taken from Saldarini as well.

account for the existence of the Septuagint. Evidence indicates that
the scribal profession was already recognized and respected by the
community. George Foot Moore believes that by this time the
scribe was an "institution."[4] Even at this early date, the profession
was highly regarded and accepted as a necessary vocation within
ancient Jewish communities.

The translators of these texts were educated, scholarly, and cognizant of the laws. As Saldarini notes, "The description of this
group [the translators] also fits the wisdom ideal of the scribe
attached to the highest levels of the ruler's court and has much in
common with the scribe as depicted in Ben Sira."[5] This evidence
surmises that the scribe existed as early as the time of the Maccabees. Yet what exactly did work in this profession entail?

Originally, the scribe, or סֹפֵר, had administrative responsibilities.
The office is mentioned numerous times in the Hebrew Bible,
mostly in connection with positions involving finance and admin-
istration.[6] In the Greek secular world, one finds similar views of the
scribe. Consider, for example, Thucydides' "secretary of the coun-
cil," which uses the scribal term γραμματεύς.[7] Similarly, in the New
Testament, Acts 19:35 speaks of the scribe as more of a "town
clerk" than anything else. Yet, as Overman points out, by the Second Temple period scribes had gained status and became prominent in society. This was probably due in part to the fact that they
could read and write, which was a rare achievement.[8]

According to Birger Gerhardsson, two main aspects of the scribe
came to the forefront.[9] First, the scribe was learned in the written

---

For further information see also George Nickelsburg, *Jewish Literature between
the Bible and the Mishnah* (Philadelphia: Fortress, 1981), 165–69.

4. George Foot Moore, *Judaism in the First Centuries of the Christian Era:
The Age of the Tannaim* (Cambridge: Harvard University Press, 1962), 1:41.

5. Saldarini, *Pharisees, Scribes, and Sadducees*, 260.

6. J. Andrew Overman, *Church and Community in Crisis: The Gospel according to Matthew* (Valley Forge, Pa.: Trinity Press International, 1996), 205. See, for
instance, 1 Kgs 22 and Jer 36:10.

7. Overman, *Church and Community in Crisis*, 205. Overman provides this
example from the ancient Greek world, and it is a good one.

8. Ibid.

9. Birger Gerhardsson, *Memory and Manuscript: Oral Tradition and Written
Transmission in Rabbinic Judaism and Early Christianity* (trans. Eric J. Sharpe;

word as a skilled writer and copyist. In addition, the scribe would write everyday documents such as bills of divorce and legal records.[10] Throughout the centuries their importance gained momentum, and they became associated with Scripture interpretation as well as legal decisions. In fact, Old Testament and intertestamental texts indicate that the scribes became as important as the law itself.[11] By the first century the scribe had become one specifically "trained." The Gospel of Matthew supports this assertion. Matthew 13:52 states, "And he [Jesus] said to them, "Therefore every scribe who has been trained for the kingdom of heaven is like the master of a household who brings out of his treasure what is new and what is old."

Simply put, the role of the first-century scribe could be designated by the labels student, scholar, and teacher.[12] Strictly speaking, though, the scribe was a "Scripture specialist."[13] He made his living by teaching and copying sacred texts.[14] Yet the scribe was more than a writer. In fact, the early scribe eventually would evolve into the modern-day rabbi.[15]

According to N. T. Wright, before the Jewish War of 66–70 C.E., Judaism contained two prominent symbols: Temple and Torah.[16] In particular, the Temple was thought of as the "spiritual center of Judaism."[17] Even the bickering rival Jewish sects such as the Pharisees and Sadducees were to some degree content to leave the

---

Copenhagen: C. W. K. Gleerup, 1964), 44. The following two aspects come from Gerhardsson as well.

10. William Richard Stegner, "Leadership and Governance in the Matthean Community," in *Common Life in the Early Church: Essays Honoring Graydon F. Snyder* (ed. Julian V. Hills; Harrisburg, Pa.: Trinity Press International, 1998), 148.

11. Ibid. See, for example, Ezra 7:6; *1 Enoch* 72–82; etc.

12. Moore, *Judaism in the First Centuries*, 41.

13. Gerhardsson, *Memory and Manuscript*, 44.

14. M. D. Goulder, *Midrash and Lection in Matthew* (London: SPCK, 1974), 11.

15. Jacob Neusner, *Judaism: The Evidence of the Mishnah* (Atlanta: Scholars Press, 1988), 233.

16. N.T. Wright, "The Divinity of Jesus," in *The Meaning of Jesus: Two Visions* (ed. Marcus J. Borg and N. T. Wright; San Francisco: Harper, 1999), 166.

17. David Flusser, "The Jewish Religion in the Second Temple Period," in *Society and Religion in the Second Temple Period* (ed. Michael Avi-Yonah and Zvi Baras; The World History of the Jewish People 8; Jerusalem: Massada, 1977), 17.

administrative practices of the Temple in the hands of the priests, out of reverence for it.[18] The Temple was holy, and virtually every Jew recognized this. Some scholars observe that by the time of the New Testament, the role of the scribe had already expanded to cover this spiritual element. In other words, the scribe had evolved into a spiritual leader, in addition to being a person learned in the written texts.[19] Howard Clark Kee, agreeing with the other scholars, points out that many of the issues mentioned in rabbinic texts such as the Mishnah are believed to have existed in some form before 70 C.E.[20] Hence, many debates regarding the laws of the Torah surely began to surface by the end of the first century.

As stated earlier, following the Jewish War of 66–70 C.E. and the destruction of the Temple in Jerusalem, a central concern of the survivors was the preservation of the Torah. Neusner states, "First, the destruction of the temple constitutes a noteworthy fact in the history of the law. Why? Because various laws about rite and cult had to undergo revision on account of the destruction."[21] Thus the scribe began to play an even more prominent role for the remaining Jewish population. Judaism became a religion based on the book, not on the Torah and the Temple, as had been the case for centuries. The Temple was gone.

Therefore, the scribes helped to sort out these issues. They became adept at interpreting the Torah and began implementing numerous hermeneutical principles, which aided in this endeavor.[22] The role of the scribe began to be more clearly defined, especially by the late first century. They were skillful writers as well as respected teachers, interpreters, and spiritual leaders.

---

18. Ibid.

19. Emil Schürer, *The History of the Jewish People in the Age of Jesus Christ* (vol. 1; ed. and trans. Geza Vermes and Fergus Millar; Edinburgh: T&T Clark International, 1973), 324.

20. Howard Clark Kee, "The Transformation of the Synagogue after 70 C.E.: Its Importance for Early Christianity," *New Testament Styudies* 36 (1990): 12.

21. Jacob Neusner, "Beyond Myth, after Apocalypse: The Mishnaic Conception of History," in *The Social World of Formative Christianity and Judaism: Essays in Tribute to Howard Clark Kee* (ed. Jacob Neusner et al.; Philadelphia: Fortress, 1988), 97.

22. Stegner, "Leadership and Governance," 148.

After the destruction of the Temple in 70 C.E., the scribe was regarded as a specialist in the Torah, both as a writer and a teacher.[23] Written copies of the Torah remained at a premium. The scribe, therefore, was first and foremost an adept writer. In fact, the Hebrew word for scribe, ספר, comes from a Semitic root word referring to a written message.[24] Similarly, the Greek term, γραμματεύς, is derived from a reference to something "written," such as letters.[25] So it is evident that the scribe largely dealt with the written word. Specifically, though, how did the scribe copy the text?

As a general rule, the Torah could not be copied from memory. A written text had to be used, as the Hebrew phrase כתב מן הכתב states. Evidence for this rule is clearly outlined in the Talmud.[26] Yet the scribe was far more than a writer with a gifted pair of eyes. He had to engage the text actively, to the point of reading it aloud and carefully constructing each letter.[27] Even today the practice of vocal prayer is still quite prominent, especially within Orthodox Judaism. As the scribe was copying the text, there was also a chance that issues would arise, such as where the division of a paragraph should be allowed. Often it was up to the scribe to determine what should be done. It was likely that the decision rendered was based upon his particular school of training, for different copyists were trained by different teachers.[28]

Outside the Gospels, the resourceful work of the scribe is nowhere more evident than in the Mishnah. Although not found within the text itself, the work of the scribes is quite obvious.[29] As Neusner puts it, "They write the script, arrange the stage, raise the curtain—and play no role at all."[30] For instance, a typical passage of Mishnah might read something like, "*He who does so and so is*

---

23. Gerhardsson, *Memory and Manuscript*, 45.
24. Saldarini, *Pharisees, Scribes, and Sadducees*, 241.
25. Ibid.
26. See *b. Megillah* 18b. Gerhardsson points this out within his analysis of the scribe. See Gerhardsson, *Memory and Manuscript*, 46.
27. Gerhardsson, *Memory and Manuscript*, 47.
28. Ibid., 49.
29. Neusner, *Judaism*, 234.
30. Ibid. The following analysis and examples come from Neusner as well.

such and such . . ."[31] At first, the clause appears relatively mundane. But upon closer examination, one notices the tight, compact format and the neat placement of the subject, verb, and object. These techniques are not included by accident; they form a distinct pattern throughout the text.

The formulation of the Mishnah is also worth noticing. The layout often consisted of equations such as, "*the X which has lost its Y is unclean because of its Z. The Z which has lost its Y is unclean because of its X.*"[32] In short, one can say that the scribes who composed the Mishnah were cognizant of rhetoric, grammar, and syntax. This further illustrates that the Jewish scribe was a learned writer and copyist of texts.

Jewish Education, the Scribe, and the Roman Empire

Recent Scholarship Concerning Jewish Education

In recent years, some scholars have begun to doubt the pervasiveness of education in the Jewish Roman world. Of interest here, of course, are studies of first-century communities in Palestine, since I argue that Matthew's community was located there. A fine, thorough study is Catherine Hezser's *Jewish Literacy in Roman Palestine*. Although she devotes much of the text to issues beyond the scope of the first century, Hezser draws some relevant conclusions. In sum, Hezser argues that a lack of written documentation such as letters, creative texts, and graffiti suggests a much lower Jewish literacy rate than scholars such as Samuel Safrai have put forth.[33]

In addition, she offers many other interesting summations. First,

---

31. For examples, see *m. Pe'ah* 5:8e; *m. Kil'ayim* 8:3a; *m. Nedarim* 10:7g; etc.

32. Again I am following Neusner, *Judaism*, 243, here. Such structured reasoning is reminiscent of the precise Jewish exegetical techniques found in Matthew's Gospel, which I discuss later.

33. Catherine Hezser, *Jewish Literacy in Roman Palestine* (Tübingen: Mohr-Siebeck, 2001), 500.

she claims that Jewish schools probably only taught reading skills rather than a complete curriculum of writing, arithmetic, and other nonbiblical subjects. She bases this claim on what she deems an "idealized rabbinic view" that alluded to a more thorough education.[34] Second, she argues that in the Roman world little emphasis was placed on formal education.[35] Below I contrast this view with the state of Jewish education. Third, Hezser argues that when placed side by side, the state of Jewish and Roman education is "strikingly similar" in that both groups lacked any formal system of education at the elementary level.[36]

I critique the findings of Hezser within my own analysis of Palestinian Jewish education in the first century C.E. In sum, I argue that the Jewish population may have been more literate than the general Roman population.[37] For ancient Romans, education was more than mere academic training; it relied upon family conditions.[38] Yet by the first century C.E., the character of Roman children was in question. Many ancient writers harshly criticize the laziness and extravagance of the younger generation. Writers such as the elder Seneca and Quintilian believed that the young men of the time were lazy and bizarre, almost "feminine" in nature, concerned more with fashioning their hair than with receiving an education. They were content to sit at the baths and consume themselves in pleasure. Seneca states, "Look at our young men: they are lazy, their intellects asleep. . . . Braiding the hair, refining the voice till it is as caressing as a woman's, competing in bodily softness with women, beautifying themselves with filthy fineries—this is the pattern our youths set

---

34. Ibid., 39.

35. Ibid., 60–61.

36. Ibid., 64–65.

37. John Meier discusses this in some detail, ultimately recognizing the possibility that the Jewish population could have been more literate than the Roman population in general. As indicated earlier, we may assume that the literacy rate of the Roman Empire hovered around 10 percent, but again this is only speculation. See John P. Meier, *A Marginal Jew: Rethinking the Historical Jesus* (New York: Doubleday, 1987), 1:271–78.

38. Stanley F. Bonner, *Education in Ancient Rome from the Elder Cato to the Younger Pliny* (Berkeley: University of California Press, 1977), 98.

themselves."[39] Quintilian observes that the people of his time (the first century C.E.) spend too little time in general studying.[40] This behavior suggests a declining state of education. So in this regard I agree with Hezser's assertion regarding the lack of emphasis placed on formal education in the Roman world.

I also concur with Hezser regarding educational opportunities in the Roman Empire. Education itself was largely a privilege of the wealthy.[41] Harris points out that writing materials could be quite expensive. Papyrus, for example, was used only by the elite due to its high price.[42] There were some Roman schools available, but many of these had poor reputations. Harris refers to the conditions of schooling in the Roman Empire as "wretched."[43] Many schools were merely makeshift places where little or no privacy could be had.[44] The students were troublemakers, and, as Seneca the Younger pointed out, often the teachers were corrupt. He states, "You surely do not believe that there is good in any of the subjects whose teachers are, as you see, men of the most ignoble and base stamp?"[45] Also, Quintilian notes, "It is held that schools corrupt the morals. It is true that this is sometimes the case."[46]

Therefore, many families were forced to seek alternative educational methods. This often involved the hiring of a tutor. The practice of private education was common by the third and second centuries B.C.E.[47] In the first century C.E., it appears this method

---

39. Ibid., 98–99. Bonner points out these quotations from Seneca and Quintilian. See Seneca's *Controversiae* Preface 1:8 as well as Quintilian's *Institutio oratoria* 12.11.18. Other passages from Quintilian include 1.6.44; 2.2, 9–12.

40. *Institutio oratoria* 12.11.18.

41. William V. Harris, *Ancient Literacy* (Cambridge: Harvard University Press, 1989), 194–96.

42. Ibid., 194. Most likely prolific writers such as Julius Caesar wrote their long books on papyrus. See Suetonius's *The Twelve Caesars* 56 (Julius Caesar). Also, Pliny the Younger refers to having to erase and use "the paper" again. No doubt he is referring to papyrus here. See *The Epistulae* 8.15.

43. Harris, *Ancient Literacy*, 236.

44. Ibid.

45. Seneca the Younger's *Epistles* 88:2.

46. *Institutio oratoria* 1.2.4

47. H. I. Marrou, *A History of Education in Antiquity* (trans. George Lamb; New York: Mentor Books, 1956), 359.

was still preferred.[48] Quintilian, for instance, discusses the debate concerning which method of education is better, the schools or a private tutor.[49] The preferred method seemed to have been a private tutor. Pliny the Younger mentions the practice in his letters. In his discussion of one of Cornelia Fistula's sons, he writes:

> Now his studies must be carried farther afield, and we must look for a tutor in Latin rhetoric whose school shall combine a strict training along with good manners and, above all, moral standards; for, as our boy happens to be endowed with striking physical beauty amongst his natural gifts, at this dangerous time of life he needs more than a teacher. A guardian and mentor must be found.[50]

Hezser also makes this point in her book.

However, only wealthy families could afford to hire pedagogues to educate their children.[51] In general, most families were poor agricultural peasants, who were forced to work long hours just to survive the harsh life of the ancient Roman world. Therefore, it is likely that most of the population would not have had the opportunity to learn to read or write. Hezser seems to be correct in her conclusions thus far.

Jewish Education and the Scribes in the First Century

It is here where I disagree with Hezser's findings. Despite Rome's problems in the first century, the Jewish population may have fared much better regarding education. Specifically, the Matthean community, being wealthy, would have had a great advantage from the start. Furthermore, the Mishnah supports the argument favoring literacy. Regarding a young man's schooling, Judah ben Tema states, "At five to Scripture, ten to Mishnah . . ."[52] The Jewish

---

48. Ibid.
49. *Institutio oratoria* 1.2.
50. *The Epistulae* 3.3.
51. Bonner, *Education in Ancient Rome*, 105.
52. See *m. Avot* 5:21. In fact, the Mishnah even states that it is a "curse" if one cannot read certain prayers.

scribes would serve as the primary teachers according to this system of education.

Hezser, though, at times seems to dismiss such claims from the rabbis while at other times upholding their writings as truthful. For instance, she refers to an "idealized rabbinic view."[53] She also calls the rabbinic writings "wishful thinking."[54] Yet in her discussion of written and oral transactions, for example, she bases her conclusions almost solely on those very writings.[55] In addition, my other major critique of Hezser's study deals with the omission of texts. When discussing the state of Jewish affairs in the first century she almost never mentions any of the New Testament writings, despite the fact that the texts reflect, at the very least, the remnants of Jewish thought prevalent at the time. For instance, she mentions just three passages from Matthew, arguably the most Jewish Gospel, and the passages are only utilized in the context of other authors' work.[56] Nevertheless, Hezser's study remains a high-quality, contemporary analysis of education and literacy in the first century and beyond.

Returning to the current study, I focus my thoughts on the scribes' role in Jewish education. In the first century, each synagogue contained a "house of learning" called the בית ספר (literally, "house of book"), where the written Torah was studied.[57] The Torah was the textbook, and the scribe was the teacher. Young children were taught the Hebrew alphabet as well as the laws of the Torah.[58] As a young student progressed, more in-depth forms of study were introduced. If a student was truly gifted, he would progress up to a secondary school called the בית מדרש ("house of study"). Here the student would be introduced to more intense

---

53. Hezser, *Jewish Literacy in Roman Palestine*, 39.
54. Ibid., 75.
55. Ibid., 111–17.
56. Ibid., 172, 341.
57. Goulder, *Midrash and Lection*, 11. The early Jewish sources supporting this information include the *y. Megillah* III, 73d; *y. Ketubbot* XIII, 35c.
58. Numerous rabbinic sources confirm this. In particular, *m. Avot* 5:21 spells out the specific ages for learning. Scripture at 5, Mishnah at 10, religious duties at 13, Talmud at 15, and so on.

scholarly study and debate with sages and teachers.[59] The scribe would play a large role in this form of study as well.

In addition to the above duties, the scribe was also active in the synagogue. In ancient times, two major components were included in synagogue services: a reading from the Torah scroll and a reading from the books of the prophets. Regarding these aspects of worship, much of the responsibility fell on the scribe, since he was often the most educated man in the city or village.[60] In smaller towns that lacked formal leadership, it is even likely that the scribe was called upon to interpret passages of Scripture, or to preach on them.[61]

The role of the first-century Jewish scribe, then, was a prominent one. He was a teacher, scholar, interpreter, lecturer, copyist, and, in the smaller villages, the most educated authority on the Torah. He must have possessed a great command of the language, since he was in charge of writing and interpreting a large number of documents. Yet there were likely additional scribal functions.

For instance, a good deal of trade and commerce took place in Galilee. Since that was the case, then other tasks such as recording transactions and bookkeeping would have been necessary for the economy to function properly. And who would have done such tasks? The responsibility would have fallen to the scribes. As Martin Goodman states, "As places for exchange the markets needed moneychangers and scribes."[62] Thus the scribe would have had a direct role in the Galilean economy.

How does this discussion relate to the Matthean community? Were the authors of the Gospels learned scribes, capable of deploying numerous rhetorical and literary techniques? Would the audience have been learned enough to comprehend these techniques if scribes used them? Finally, what does the Gospel itself

---

59. Samuel Safrai, "Education and the Study of the Torah," in *The Jewish People of the First Century* (vol. 2; ed. Samuel Safrai and M. Stern; Philadelphia: Fortress, 1976), 953.

60. Goulder, *Midrash and Lection*, 11.

61. Ibid., 11–12.

62. Martin Goodman, *State and Society in Roman Galilee, A.D. 132–212* (Totowa, N.J.: Rowman & Allanheld, 1983), 57.

say regarding the role of the scribe? The rest of the chapter will begin to answer these questions. Therefore, I now examine what the Matthean Gospel says about the Greek term for scribe, γραμματεύς.

Matthew's View and Usage
of the Term "Scribe"

In the past, scholars such as Sjef van Tilborg have dismissed the relevance of the "scribes" to the Matthean Gospel.[63] In recent years this negative trend has continued in some scholarly circles. Christine Schams has argued that Matthew cared little for the title "scribe" and, in fact, often mixed up the names of Jesus' opponents due to this lack of interest.[64] She points out that some passages in Matthew illustrate this (9:9–13; 12:22–32; 22:41–46). In essence, she makes the case that Matthew's redaction of Mark clarifies this point. Sometimes the term "scribe" is left unchanged; other times it is altered or omitted. Matthew's disorganization is taken as proof of the authors' disinterest in the specific titles of Jesus' opponents.[65] The scribes have a generally negative connotation and are basically unimportant.

I disagree with this assertion. Overman has pointed out the scribe's central role in the Matthean Gospel.[66] This is in contrast to other Gospels, particularly Mark. To illustrate, then, I examine Mark's usage of the term "scribe," since Matthew copied much material from Mark. Mark's Gospel mentions the Greek term for scribe, γραμματεύς, twenty-one times.[67] Yet these notations are not usually flattering. In Mark, the scribes are often the villains of the

---

63. Sjef van Tilborg, *The Jewish Leaders in Matthew* (Leiden: Brill, 1972), 3.

64. Christine Schams, *Jewish Scribes in the Second Temple Period* (Journal for the Study of the Old Testament Supplement Series 291; Sheffield: Sheffield Academic, 1998), 182.

65. Ibid., 183.

66. J. Andrew Overman, *Matthew's Gospel and Formative Judaism: The Social World of the Matthean Community* (Minneapolis: Fortress, 1990), 115.

67. Goulder, *Midrash and Lection*, 13.

story.[68] The scribes in Mark should not be trusted (see 12:38), and they constantly question, harass, and doubt Jesus. Ultimately, they share much of the blame regarding Jesus' passion (see Mark 14:1–2). So, one finds only two complimentary usages of the term in Mark's Gospel.

Matthew, although following Mark much of the time, reverses the trend. The noun γραμματεύς is mentioned a total of twenty-two times, but much is changed concerning context. In particular, of the nineteen hostile references in Mark, Matthew retains only six, and those may have been kept only because they are necessary for the story.[69] The rest are either dropped entirely, or are changed in some manner. For instance, Mark 12:38 recounts Jesus' teaching that one should "beware of the scribes." Also, in 12:40 the scribes "devour widows' houses and for the sake of appearance say long prayers." Matthew, however, changes these passages considerably. Matthew 23:2–3 reads, "The scribes and the Pharisees sit on Moses' seat; therefore, do whatever they teach you and follow it; but do not do as they do, for they do not practice what they teach." Here Matthew acknowledges the authoritative and scholarly nature of the scribes, while omitting Mark's statement concerning the devouring of widows. Matthew has thus altered the text to "soften" the image of the scribal profession. Schams is incorrect regarding her claim that Matthew indiscriminately utilized the term. The authors of the Gospel, indeed, were careful and deliberate regarding the usage of the word "scribe."

Passages from Matthew Alluding to Scribes: A Brief Discussion of 16:19

I now examine some of the usages of "scribe" in Matthew's Gospel. This will clarify Matthew's attitude toward the profession.

---

68. Ibid. For specific references, see Mark 1:22; 2:6–12, 16–17; 7:1–12; 8:31; 9:14; 14:1; etc.

69. Goulder, *Midrash and Lection*, 13. The rest of the information in this paragraph also comes from this source.

Beyond the obvious favorable reference to scribes in Matt 13:52, one finds many indirect references to the scribe. For instance, consider Matt 16:19, in which Jesus gives Peter the "keys" of the kingdom of heaven and the authority to "bind and loose." Since this passage is unique to Matthew, the Evangelist composed it himself. But what does this phrase mean? Why does Matthew use it here?

The answers are connected to the role of the scribes as teachers and interpreters of the halakah (Jewish legal codes).[70] In rabbinic sources the phrase "bind and loose" was linked to legal decisions. Celia Deutsch interprets Matthew's "binding and loosing" (in Greek, δέω and λύω) to be synonymous with the rabbinic references using the verbs "permit" and "forbid."[71] She cites several passages from the Mishnah as evidence, including *m. Pesahim* 4:5h, which states, "And the House of Hillel permit," as well as *m. Terumot* 5:4, which states, "But the House of Hillel permit." In addition, the latter passage discusses what is "forbidden." Finally, Josephus briefly uses the phrase. He states that when the Pharisees of the Maccabean era gained power "they bound and loosed [men] at their pleasure."[72] This textual evidence implies that the phrase referred to one's ability to administer important decisions regarding laws. Scribes similarly rendered decisions concerning laws. They had the power to "bind" and to "loose," which actually meant to "permit" and "forbid."

The term "keys" (from the Greek, κλείς) is also important. First, this is the only place in the Gospel where κλείς appears.[73] Second, the term "keys" also had a connection to the profession of teach-

---

70. Stegner, "Leadership and Governance," 148–49. I am following Stegner's line of thinking here. Other scholars such as Overman also agree with Stegner's thinking. See Overman, *Church and Community in Crisis*, 243.

71. Celia Deutsch, *Lady Wisdom, Jesus, and the Sages: Metaphor and Social Context in Matthew's Gospel* (Valley Forge, Pa.: Trinity Press International, 1996), 211 n. 128. The following examples are taken from here as well.

72. Josephus, *Jewish War* 1:5:1.

73. W. D. Davies and Dale C. Allison Jr., *The Gospel according to Saint Matthew* (vol. 2; ed. J. A. Merton et al.; International Critical Commentary; Edinburgh: T&T Clark International, 1991), 605. They also note Matthew's unique usage of a number of other words in 16:17–19, which illustrate Matthew's ability to edit the text radically.

ing in Judaism, as rabbinic texts indicate.[74] In the New Testament, Luke's Gospel (see 11:52) makes an interesting reference to the "key of knowledge," which suggests that the term was linked to the process of education and teaching.

Likewise, the keys might have been a symbol for authority and leadership, to which Isa 22:22 alludes.[75] The passage refers to a future time when God will call Eliakim, and God will place upon his shoulders "the key of the house of David." This notation, linking the keys to the Temple in Jerusalem, is similar to other biblical references that also link the term "keys" to either authority and/or Temple. Recall also how Rev 3:7 has Jesus holding "the key of David." This powerful imagery conjures up the picture of the scribe as a learned leader of the community. Matthew does nothing to discourage this view in his Gospel. In 16:19 Peter is given the "keys" to the kingdom of heaven, thereby granting him the authority to teach and interpret the Jewish halakah, just as a Jewish scribe would. The keys, along with the corresponding allusion to the scribal profession of teaching, are pictured in a positive light.

One other point regarding Matt 16:19 is relevant. Note that Matt 23:13 gives a more negative assessment of the term "scribe." In this pericope, Matthew states that the scribes, along with the Pharisees, have "shut the kingdom of heaven against men" (RSV). One can assume that the scribes used their own "keys" to "shut" the door. Gundry claims that this passage is intentionally used as a contrast to 16:19 to illustrate how Peter, as the scribe, will undo what others who do not follow Jesus or believe in him as the Messiah and Son of God have done.[76] They have locked the kingdom of heaven. Peter, as the representation of the good disciple, can unlock the door. According to Gundry, discipleship in Christ entails that one become a scribe as well, so that he or she may

---

74. Ibid., 635. For the Jewish sources, consult the *b. Shabbat* 31a–b.

75. Overman, *Church and Community in Crisis*, 241–43. Overman lists several other ancient biblical texts that similarly place the term within the context of either Temple or authority. Specifically, see *2 Baruch* 10:18; *3 Baruch* 11:2; as well as *4 Baruch* 4:4.

76. Robert H. Gundry, *Matthew: A Commentary on His Literary and Theological Art* (Grand Rapids: Eerdmans, 1982), 334–35.

instruct or teach others regarding the kingdom of heaven (see 13:52).[77]

Finally, in chapter 16, Peter acts in the present, not the past. The other false scribes have locked the door; Peter will now open it. The Temple has been destroyed. According to Matthew, Peter, representing the Matthean scribal leadership, will take the keys and lead the people into the kingdom of heaven.[78] In sum, Matt 16:19 may serve as an analogy regarding the identification of the true interpreters of the Torah. They are Matthew's scribal community.

Matthew 23:13 acts as a contrast to 16:19. Peter, as the typical pious scribe, is given the *keys*, an allusion designed to remind the reader of his role (probably representing the Matthean scribes) as an instructor. Simply put, Gundry believes that Jesus, as the new and improved Moses, produces through his teachings new and improved scribes. While Gundry emphasizes the Moses/Jesus analogy too much, I do think he is correct regarding the scribal connection to keys. The evidence clearly indicates that the term was understood by the Matthean community as a symbol of instruction and authority.

Matthew 23 in More Detail

Chapter 23 is important since it reflects the conflicting situation of the Matthean community more than any other chapter in the Gospel.[79] It has often been cited for its negative tone.[80] The scribes and Pharisees are charged with hypocrisy and blindness, apparently confirming a bleak image of the Matthean scribes. In particular, this

---

77. Ibid., 281. The ensuing point is from this source as well.

78. Overman, *Church and Community in Crisis*, 242–43. See Celia Deutsch, "Christians and Jews in the First Century: The Gospel of Matthew," *Thought* 67 (1992): 399–409. Deutsch believes the scribes were vital to the Matthean community. See also David E. Horton, *The Understanding Scribe: Matthew and Apocalyptic Ideal* (Journal for the Study of the New Testament Supplement Series 25; Sheffield: Sheffield Academic, 1989), 50–52.

79. Overman, *Matthew's Gospel and Formative Judaism*, 142.

80. Anthony J. Saldarini, "Delegitimation of Leaders in Matthew 23," *Catholic Biblical Quarterly* 54 (1992): 659.

chapter has served as evidence of Matthew's hatred for the Jewish scribe.[81] Yet there are alternative solutions to such theories.

To begin, Jesus aimed seven woes at the scribes and Pharisees. One question may be asked immediately: *whose* scribes is Matthew talking about? Saldarini concludes that in chapter 23 Matthew is indeed chastising the "scribes," *but not his own.* In other words, the scribes and Pharisees to which Matthew refers are his opponents, the protorabbinic leaders of the Jews.[82] Meier has also observed that in much of the Gospel the scribes and Pharisees are only mentioned together as a unit. In other words, Matthew coined a unique formula to indicate when he is discussing the leaders of the opposing formative Jewish community.[83] Matthew is not denigrating the general profession of the scribe; the authors are instead defending their own scribal group against Jewish leaders in Galilee who threaten the beliefs (such as the Messiahship of Jesus) of the community.

What evidence supports this assertion? Saldarini notes that in late-first-century Judaism, many diverse Jewish groups and sects existed.[84] Matthew's community itself represented one of these groups. In fact, many of the sins that Jesus points out in chapter 23 are the same sins to which the early rabbis alluded.[85] Matthew was just pointing out some of the inconsistencies in Jewish practice that offended his community. Within any religion there are good and

---

81. Benedict T. Viviano, "Social World and Community Leadership: The Case of Matthew 23:1–12, 34," *Journal for the Study of the New Testament* 39 (1990): 15. Scholars such as Viviano claim that Matthew has a "dread" of scribal arrogance. David E. Garland has noted the chapter's abusive language, which mentions "hypocrites," "double sons of hell," "blind fools," "blind guides," "sons of murderers," and "brood of vipers." See David E. Garland, *Reading Matthew: A Literary and Theological Commentary on the First Gospel* (New York: Crossroad, 1993), 227.

82. Saldarini, "Delegitimation of Leaders," 678–79.

83. John P. Meier, *Law and History in Matthew's Gospel: A Redactional Study of Mt. 5:17–48* (Analecta biblica 71; Rome: Biblical Institute Press, 1976), 111.

84. Saldarini, "Delegitimation of Leaders," 664.

85. C. G. Montefiore, *Rabbinic Literature and Gospel Teachings* (New York: Ktav, 1970), 332.

bad leaders, and Judaism was no exception. Therefore, Jesus was referring to the corrupt Jewish leaders (scribes?) of his time (see Matt 10:6). This theory concerning differences of opinion is supported by the Jerusalem Talmud, which pointed out instances of rabbis contradicting each other.[86] So not all scribes are being criticized in chapter 23, only the scribes that Matthew feels are wrong.

Mark Allen Powell offers a similar solution regarding the dilemma of the scribes and Pharisees in chapter 23. He maintains that the scribes and Pharisees mentioned by Jesus in chapter 23 represent the traditional Jewish purveyors of the Torah. These Jews are knowledgeable regarding the specific laws of the Torah, but they are incorrect in the interpretation of the developing legal code.[87] The laws of the Torah are important to Jesus. Therefore, Jesus warns his disciples to respect those who know and follow the law. The Torah is not abrogated in any manner. "Do not think that I have come to abolish the law or the prophets; I have come not to abolish but to fulfill. . . . Therefore, whoever breaks one of the least of these commandments, and teaches others to do the same, will be called least in the kingdom of heaven . . ." (Matt 5:17, 19). Yet Jesus also warns his disciples not to follow incorrect interpretations of the law. Only Jesus and the church can fulfill the Torah in the proper manner. Powell observes that several passages from the Gospel mention the church's ability to do this (16:19; 18:18), but nowhere does Jesus or his disciples ever boast of superior general knowledge of the Torah.[88]

According to Powell, two things are necessary for teachers to fulfill the laws of the Torah: "First, they must know the word of Moses, which may be designated the 'word of God' (15:4–6) and which will remain authoritative until heaven and earth pass away (5:18). Second, they must be able to interpret the words of Moses for the present day."[89] On the basis of these presumptions, then,

---

86. Ibid., 323. Montefiore is here referring to *y. Berachoth* I, 3a.

87. Mark Allan Powell, "Do and Keep What Moses Says," *Journal of Biblical Literature* 114 (1995): 434–35.

88. Ibid., 434.

89. Ibid., 433–34.

Jesus is stating that the scribes of the competing Jews indeed fulfill the first prerequisite, but fail regarding the second. They know the laws, but they interpret them incorrectly. Furthermore, Powell concludes that Matthew at this point appears to compliment them for their knowledge of Scripture, although he disagrees with their interpretation of the Torah (see Matt 12:1–8, for example). For as Powell himself admits, "The religious leaders of Israel are denied authority to interpret the law even though they repeatedly give evidence that they know what the law says."[90]

Although Powell strengthens the case concerning the scribes to whom Matthew is referring, I remain skeptical regarding his conclusions. Powell seems unable to deal with the inconsistencies and contradictions that he finds in Matthew's text.[91] The Gospel is not as contradictory as Powell wants the reader to believe. If one accepts that Matthew's own scholarly Jewish Christian group is in serious competition with other Galilean protorabbinic scribes, the text is quite cohesive. Negative portrayals of the scribe may be dismissed if one accepts that Matthew is referring to the scribes of the formative Jews. Also, nowhere does Powell mention the positive role of the scribe in Matthew's own community. Therefore, I reaffirm that Matthew does nothing to denigrate the role of the scribes, especially those in his community.

Matthew the Scribe:
The Transfiguration as Evidence

Matthew viewed the scribe as a positive figure. In particular, scholars like William Richard Stegner have noted that scribes were the primary leaders of the Matthean community.[92] Much evidence supports this claim. First, Matthew did not denigrate the office of the scribe; he was only upset with the scribes and leaders of the competing formative Jewish movement.

---

90. Ibid., 435.
91. For examples, see ibid., 425 and 429.
92. Stegner, "Leadership and Governance," 156.

Consider the scene of the transfiguration (Matt 17:1–9), in which the heavenly voice speaks to Peter, James, and John. Scholars have argued that this passage confirms the vital role of the scribe, although the term is not mentioned by name. How is this so? Stegner notes that upon receiving the vision as well as upon hearing the heavenly voice, Peter, James, and John now possess knowledge which surpasses that of other humans.[93] They have witnessed something beyond ordinary human experience. This is relevant because Matthew apparently wished to elevate their status and to place them in roles as community leaders. Paul confirms this in Gal 2:9 when he refers to them as "pillars." Who were the community leaders in Matthew's church? The answer is the Jewish scribes.

Support for Stegner's conclusion has come from scholars such as Overman and Deutsch. Overman, for instance, points out that the phrase spoken by the heavenly voice in 17:5 ("listen to him") confirms Jesus' role as an authority figure.[94] Specifically, his authority carries weight regarding interpretation of the Torah. Therefore the phrase "listen to him" may have been Matthew's way of further distinguishing the scribes. Deutsch also points out the connection of the transfiguration to scribal authority. In particular, she views 17:1–9 as a legitimization of Jesus' as well as the scribes' authority within the Matthean community.[95] The vision received by the three disciples is central to Matthew's view of the group's leadership; it confirms the role of the scribe as student, scholar, teacher, and community leader.

Also interesting is that immediately following the story of the transfiguration Matthew uses the word "scribe" in 17:10. Here Matthew is directly copying from the Markan version of the story. The passage reads, "And the disciples asked him, 'Why, then, do the

---

93. Ibid., 154–55. Unless otherwise noted, I am following Stegner's reasoning here.

94. Overman, *Church and Community in Crisis*, 254.

95. Celia Deutsch, "The Transfiguration: Vision and Social Setting in Matthew's Gospel (Matthew 17:1–9)," in *Putting Body and Soul Together: Essays in Honor of Robin Scroggs* (ed. Virginia Wiles et al.; Valley Forge, Pa.: Trinity Press International, 1997). 125.

scribes say that Elijah must come first?'" One could argue that this proves Matthew had no direct feelings concerning the role of the scribe; he was merely copying another account. Luke, in fact, has deleted the line altogether. Why does Matthew retain it? A brief analysis reveals a possible answer. Orton argues that the formula "why do the scribes say" resembles the Mishnaic introductory phase "the sages say."[96] This was a traditional form of authoritative ruling according to Jewish tradition. Matthew has no need to alter it. In fact, as Orton notes, Jesus accepts this teaching; he does not dispute the basic principle regarding the coming of Elijah.[97]

Similarly, Orton makes the claim that Mark has misinterpreted the phrase by linking it to the Pharisees in 9:14. Matthew realizes that the scribes mentioned here have nothing to do with the Pharisees, so there is no reason to include them (unlike in chapter 23).[98] Hence, Matthew upholds the Jewish scribal tradition rather than denigrating it, as is suggested by critics. The scribes that Matthew chastises would only be those with whom he is in disagreement. In the case of chapter 23, that group would be the scribes of the Pharisees.

Additional passages support the validity of Jewish scribes. For instance, consider Matt 11:25–30, in which Jesus' light φορτίον, or "burden," is mentioned. Verse 28 is noteworthy, since Matthew uses the term πεφορτισμένοι. This usage is similar to the word φορτίον in 23:4. Recall that chapter 23 deals primarily with interpretation of Jewish halakah. Deutsch writes that this similarity is no coincidence.[99] Matthew intentionally links the two passages. Jewish interpretation of the Torah relied upon one's being able to link passages of text together. Matthew, as a Jewish scribe, is using this rabbinic technique of interpretation.

---

96. David E. Orton, *The Understanding Scribe: Matthew and the Apocalyptic Ideal* (Journal for the Study of the New Testament Supplement Series 25; Sheffield: Sheffield Academic, 1989), 32–33. He notes passages such as *m. Berakhot* 6:4 and 7:5.

97. Orton, *Understanding Scribe*, 32–33.

98. Ibid.

99. Deutsch, *Lady Wisdom*, 118.

Furthermore, the general invitation by Jesus to "all that are weary and are carrying heavy burdens" suggests a competition between "the teachers of Matthew's community and those of the opposition."[100] In addition, the language of the passage suggests that Mathew was referring to the scribes in his community.[101] Consider, for example, a word such as νήπιοι ("infants"), which suggests humility and lowliness. Even Jesus refers to himself as being "gentle and humble in heart." This is relevant because such language is common in Jewish circles when referring to the status of Torah sages (see *Mekilta Amalek* 4:63–70; *Sifre Deuteronomy* 43; etc.).[102] Jesus is again placed within the realm of the Jewish sage through his humility and lowliness. The Matthean community members (Jesus' disciples) are also "infants." They are able to receive revelation, in contrast to those "wise" ones who lack such a humble status (see 10:5–25; 12:2, 14, 24, 38; 23:4). Matthew's scribes are truly the humble, learned ones. This textual evidence suggests that Matthew envisions his disciples and community members as the authentic teachers and interpreters of the Torah.[103] The scribal profession thrives within the Matthean community.

Therefore, 11:25–30 seems to deal strictly with Jewish matters of Torah. Yet the passage has been compared to Hellenistic documents, thereby suggesting some sort of dependence upon Greek origins. I reject this assertion. Matthew 11:27 in Greek reads: Πάντα μοι παρεδόθη ὑπὸ τοῦ πατρός μου, καὶ οὐδεὶς ἐπιγνώσκει τὸν υἱὸν εἰ μὴ ὁ πατήρ, οὐδὲ τὸν πατέρα τις ἐπιγνώσκει εἰ μὴ ὁ υἱὸς καὶ ᾧ ἐὰν βούληται ὁ υἱὸς ἀποκαλύψαι. Similarly, a line written about Hermes reads: οἰδε σε, Ἑρμῆ, καί σύ ἐμέ.[104] At first, the two passages appear to be somewhat similar, but upon careful review one sees otherwise. According to Dale Allison, there is one key differ-

---

100. Ibid.
101. Ibid., 117.
102. Ibid., 37–38.
103. Ibid., 118.
104. Dale C. Allison Jr., "Two Notes on a Key Text: Matthew 11:25–30," *Journal of Theological Studies*, n.s., 39 (1988): 478. For further formulations, see *Corpus Hermeticum* 1.31; 10.15a. Unless otherwise noted, I am following Allison here.

ence: Jesus and the Father have an exclusive relationship, while the line about Hermes contains no such emphasis. It is more vague.

A more appropriate parallel to Matt 11:27 is found in the MT, in Exod 33:12–13.[105] It reads in part: "Yet you have said, 'I know you by name [בשם ידעתיך; LXX has οἶδά σε παρὰ πάντας], and you have also found grace in My sight.' Now therefore, if I have found grace in your sight, show me your ways, so that I may know you [ואדעך; LXX has γνωστῶς ἵνα ἴδω σε] and find favor in your sight." Here, as in Matt 11:25–30, the notion of reciprocal knowledge is reinforced. God knows Moses and Moses knows God. Furthermore, Allison believes that the ancient Jews surely would have recognized such a mutually exclusive knowledge, just as Matthew does.[106] This is also evident in Deut 34:10, where it is written, "Never since has there arisen a prophet in Israel like Moses, whom God knew [ידעו; LXX has ἔγνω] face to face." The term "face to face" shows the intimate relationship Moses had with God. Ordinarily, no mortal could view God on this level (see also Num 12:8, which utilizes the phrase "mouth to mouth").[107]

Paul recognizes this concept in 1 Cor 13:12. The passage contains an allusion to Moses as well as a reference to seeing one's self in a mirror (presumably "face to face"). This evidence leads me (I am agreeing with Deutsch) to conclude that Matthew remains concerned with interpretation of the Torah. So I reject the notion of a Hellenistic influence here; there is simply not enough evidence to support that notion. The authors of Matthew are illustrating their scribal nature through the skillful usage of the Old Testament. They recognize the Semitic nuances of the MT and incorporate them into the Gospel.

I can therefore say with confidence that the scribal profession was highly regarded by the Matthean community. As Dennis Duling has stated, "In the Matthean brotherhood good scribes are

---

105. Allison, "Two Notes," 479.
106. Ibid.
107. Ibid. Allison notes the work of P. J. Budd here as well. See P. J. Budd, *Numbers* (ed. David A. Hubbard and Glenn W. Barker; Word Biblical Commentary 5; Waco, Tex.: Word Books, 1984).

honoured, and indeed the author of the Gospel is most likely a scribe (13:52). He is educated, literate and sees the secrets of scripture in a sophisticated fashion."[108] This suggests a great deal of scribal activity and thought within the Matthean community. Finally, due to the prevailing evidence, I also assert that the leaders of the Matthean community were most likely scribes themselves. In the next chapter I provide illustrations of the authors' scribal prowess through a number of examples.

---

108. Dennis C. Duling, "The Matthean Brotherhood and Marginal Scribal Leadership," in *Modeling Early Christianity: Social-Scientific Studies of the New Testament in Its Context* (ed. Philip F. Esler; London: Routledge, 1995), 179.

5

Evidence of a
Learned Community

Matthew's Use of the Old Testament
and Targums

KRISTER STENDAHL'S *THE SCHOOL OF ST. MATTHEW* WAS A
cornerstone work regarding Matthew's use of the Old Testament.
Stendahl refers to the use of the Old Testament by the writers of
Matthew as "ingenious interpretation."[1] Stendahl believes that
Matthew uses a form of rabbinic interpretation called the *midrash
pesher*.[2] He believes that the *midrash pesher* method explains
Matthew's liberal interpretation of the text. Some principles incorporated in this method include the examination of textual pecu-
liarities, the presumption of allegorical meanings, and the use of
analogous passages.

For example, these principles help to interpret Matt 12:18–21
(which refers to Isa 42:1–4).[3] Often, the interpreter can reveal a
hidden eschatological meaning. In fact, Stendahl shows that this

---

1. Krister Stendahl, *The School of St. Matthew and Its Use of the Old Testament* (Uppsala, Sweden: C. W. K. Gleerup, 1954), 34.

2. Ibid., 35.

3. Phillip Sigal, *The Halakah of Jesus of Nazareth according to the Gospel of
Matthew* (New York: University Press of America, 1986), 191–92.

111

liberal, intricate *midrash pesher* method was utilized by the Qumran community in its commentary on Habakkuk. The style closely
resembles Matthew's method. This claim is controversial, yet the
authors of Matthew seem to follow a concise, complex methodology.

William Brownlee points out that one of the main purposes of
the *midrash pesher,* from a teacher's standpoint, is to instruct the
community as well as to prepare them for the future.[4] The scribal
authors of Matthew would have possessed a thorough knowledge
of the MT and the LXX. This is also true concerning many members
of the community. They would have had to know the Old Testament in order to comprehend the underlying meanings in the text.

Matthew 12:18–21 helps to clarify Stendahl's position regarding
the *midrash pesher.* Notice the formula quotation in Matt 12:17,
in which the author cites the prophet Isaiah (42:1–4). This long
New Testament pericope, which contains both MT and LXX material, is the longest Old Testament quotation in Matthew.[5] The
Greek text of Matt 12:18–21 reads:

ἰδοὺ ὁ παῖς μου ὃν ᾑρέτισα,
    ὁ ἀγαπητός μου εἰς ὃν εὐδόκησεν ἡ ψυχή μου·
θήσω τὸ πνεῦμά μου ἐπ᾽ αὐτόν,
    καὶ κρίσιν τοῖς ἔθνεσιν ἀπαγγελεῖ.
οὐκ ἐρίσει οὐδὲ κραυγάσει,
    οὐδὲ ἀκούσει τις ἐν ταῖς πλατείαις τὴν φωνὴν αὐτοῦ.
κάλαμον συντετριμμένον οὐ κατεάξει
    καὶ λίνον τυφόμενον οὐ σβέσει,
ἕως ἂν ἐκβάλῃ εἰς νῖκος τὴν κρίσιν.
    καὶ τῷ ὀνόματι αὐτοῦ ἔθνη ἐλπιοῦσιν.

This passage contains many curious features. For example, verse
18 includes some notable changes from both the MT and LXX mate-

---

4. William H. Brownlee, *The Midrash Pesher of Habakkuk* (Missoula, Mont.:
Scholars Press, 1979), 36.
5. Both Stendahl and Gundry agree on this point. See Stendahl, *School of St.
Matthew,* 109, and Robert H. Gundry, *The Use of the Old Testament in St.
Matthew's Gospel* (Leiden: Brill, 1967), 149.

rial concerning the terms παῖς μου and ἀγαπητός.[6] The former phrase is found in the LXX, yet the latter term is not, leading Stendahl to believe that Matthew was following another Greek translation, such as the one by Theodotion. This implies that Matthew possessed knowledge of numerous texts. Further, Matthew selects the verb θήσω instead of using ἔδωκα from the LXX or the Hebrew form of the verb, נתתי.

Consequently, Stendahl, Gundry, Davies, and Allison all agree that the authors of the Gospel were relying upon an alternative source.[7] They believe this source could be the *Targums*, the Aramaic versions of the Hebrew Bible. (Aramaic biblical texts were necessary as the language became widely spoken in the Near East.)[8] Although they were only recorded formally in later centuries, it is possible that an oral form of these texts existed as early as the first century C.E. In fact, some scholars trace their origins as far back as the time of Ezra. Even if that date is unrealistic, firm evidence is found in the Dead Sea Scrolls, which date to the second century B.C.E.[9]

If an Aramaic form was in existence by the late first century C.E., the verb אתין found in the Targum seems to be a natural match for Matthew's selection, based upon both word choice and tense.[10] Moreover, Matthew's ἀπαγγελεῖ is looser (in keeping with the *pesher* method of interpretation) than the LXX's ἐξοίσει, again indicating a possible reliance upon the Targums.[11] Other examples

---

6. I am following Stendahl here. See Stendahl, *School of St. Matthew*, 108–10.

7. Ibid., 111; Gundry, *Use of the Old Testament*, 113; and W. D. Davies and Dale C. Allison Jr., *A Critical and Exegetical Commentary on the Gospel according to Saint Matthew* (ed. J. A. Merton et al.; International Critical Commentary 2; Edinburgh: T&T Clark International, 1991), 2:325. See also *Targum Pseudo-Jonathan*'s rendering of Isa 42:1–4.

8. John Bowker, *The Targums and Rabbinic Literature* (Cambridge: Cambridge University Press, 1969), 3. Bowker provides a fine section on the background of the Targums.

9. Daniel Patte, *Early Jewish Hermeneutic in Palestine* (Society of Biblical Literature Dissertation Series 22; Missoula, Mont.: Scholars Press, 1975), 49–50. A fragment of a Targum on Job has been found at Qumran.

10. Gundry, *Use of the Old Testament*, 113.

11. Ibid.

engaging the Targums can be found, but here I wish merely to illustrate that the authors of Matthew were integrating a number of diverse sources.

Matthew 12:19a shows the author's adept interpretation of the Old Testament. Davies and Allison note that the opening phrase of the verse, οὐκ ἐρίσει οὐδὲ κραυγάσει, clearly differs from the LXX's rendering, οὐ κεκεράξεται οὐδὲ ἀνήσει. So, they conclude that Matthew is following a different source here.[12] This suggests an independent interpretation taken from the Hebrew לא יצעק ולא ישא, from the Targums, or from some other version such as an additional Aramaic version of Matthew.[13] Matthew reworks the Greek ἐν ταῖς πλατείαις from the Hebrew term בחוץ in 12:19b, yet Stendahl points out that the LXX would have been the more logical choice here based upon the natural translation ("in the streets").[14]

Conclusions Regarding Matt 12:18–21: The Nature of Jesus' Ministry

This pattern of a loose, "pick and choose" redaction of Matt 12:18–21 continues in the ensuing verses. However, one question arises. Why do the authors of Matthew's Gospel stray from the MT or LXX norm here and continually rework the text instead of following the accepted formula quotation from Isaiah? Assuming the audience knew something about the Old Testament prophets, they would probably have been more comfortable accepting the more familiar quotation. According to Stendahl, this shows the genius of the *midrash pesher*. Matthew has carefully changed the existing Old

---

12. Davies and Allison, *Critical and Exegetical Commentary on Matthew*, 2:325.

13. Ibid. Davies and Allison accept the similarities in the Hebrew. Gundry believes that Matthew follows the Targums again at this point judging by the similarities between "cry aloud" in Matthew's Greek (κραυγάσει) and the Targums (יכלי). See Gundry, *Use of the Old Testament*, 114. Stendahl suggests the possible reliance upon a Syriac version of the text. See Stendahl, *School of St. Matthew*, 111.

14. Stendahl, *School of St. Matthew*, 113.

Testament prophecy of Isaiah into a compelling story about the fulfillment of Jesus. The Matthean scribes chose their words very carefully, so much so that they are not afraid to incorporate a few different languages into the Gospel. Stendahl states, "Thus there are reasons to presume that the form of the text in Matthew is an interpretation of the prophecy in the light of what happened to Jesus. This interpretation was not made without textual support."[15]

In other words, the authors of Matthew were doing more than translating; they were interpreting through their own *midrash pesher* formula. Matthew employs an exegetical method in order to convey precisely how Jesus represents the epitome of the divine servant. Davies and Allison believe that this emphasis on Jesus as the servant is relevant to the meaning of the Gospel itself.[16] After all, Matthew states that one's primary duty is to love one's neighbor (22:39), which is the unselfish service of others (5:43–48). Therefore, there can be no love without some form of service to others. So Matthew has skillfully woven together a variety of texts to demonstrate for the readers how this is accomplished through Jesus. As Davies and Allison state, "As the perfect embodiment of God's moral demand, Jesus the servant lives the commandment of love."[17]

Overman provides another motive for the inclusion of Matthew's fulfillment citations. Matthew depicted Jesus as the fulfillment of prophecy. Overman believes that the citations go a step further; they help to explain the life of Jesus to an audience, made up of many Jews, that would have had some difficulty believing in him as the Messiah.[18] The authors of the Gospel include these important prophetic passages to lend credence to the Jesus story. This makes it easier for the audience to accept Jesus as the Messiah.[19] According to Overman, Matthew's exegetical prowess

---

15. Ibid., 112.
16. Davies and Allison, *Critical and Exegetical Commentary on Matthew*, 2:329. The following conclusion is taken from them.
17. Ibid.
18. J. Andrew Overman, *Matthew's Gospel and Formative Judaism: The Social World of the Matthean Community* (Minneapolis: Fortress, 1990), 75.
19. Ibid.

serves more than a biographical purpose. The Matthean scribes perform a foundational task; they proclaim Jesus as the Messiah.

Of course, some changes in the text may be explained in straightforward terms. Matthew simply chose words that he liked the best. For example, the scribes may have deleted certain words from the LXX's version of Isaiah that they felt did not fit into the Gospel.[20] But there are other reasons for the editing. The primary reason for these changes is to explain the fulfillment of the prophecy through Jesus, specifically as it relates to his ministry in ancient Israel.[21] In sum, the authors of Matthew wanted to make sure that their Palestinian audience understood the vital role Jesus was to play in their past, present, and future.

Recall Matthew's addition of the word ἀγαπητός in 12:18. The LXX contains no such term; in Isaiah it utilizes ἐκλεκτός, a weaker term often meaning "chosen" or "elected." Similarly, both the MT and the Targums contain בחירי, which means the same thing. The term "beloved," which Matthew uses, signifies a more intense, personal relationship. In fact, no Greek version of Isa 42 uses the more intimate term, ἀγαπητός.[22] Why does Matthew alone select it? Matthew linked this prophetic quotation to the baptism that had already occurred (in 3:17) and the transfiguration of Jesus that was yet to come (in 17:5). The authors did this to retain and emphasize the consistent theme of servitude and love.[23] Also, this form of inclusion was selected by ancient scribes to emphasize important aspects of recorded texts.

Consider the crucial placement of the Greek noun παῖς in 12:18. Matthew follows the LXX here. Yet in the baptism story the voice

---

20. Gundry, *Use of the Old Testament*, 112. For example, the LXX adds the words Ἰακώβ and Ἰσραήλ to 12:18, while Matthew omits them. Gundry suggests that Matthew may have realized that the LXX simply added them, and elected to drop them since they are not found in MT version of Isaiah. Matthew chose to remain true to the more original form of the text in this case.

21. Davies and Allison, *Critical and Exegetical Commentary on Matthew*, 2:324. Recall I am arguing that the Gospel was recorded in Israel, so the need to explain Jesus' doings in Israel is self-evident.

22. Stendahl, *School of St. Matthew*, 112.

23. Gundry, *Use of the Old Testament*, 112. I agree with Gundry here.

from heaven uses the phrase ὁ υἱός μου ὁ ἀγαπητός ("my beloved son"). Strictly speaking, the term παῖς can be translated as "servant." So why did Matthew follow the LXX instead of changing the noun? First, Matthew probably wished to reinforce the servant-love motif. So, it was necessary to use the more precise term. Second, Matthew followed the LXX because it allowed him to link this passage (12:18–21) more effectively to the voice in the story of the baptism (3:17). The term παῖς can also mean "son," of course.[24] It seems that the authors of the Gospel cleverly addressed two issues with one noun. They remained true to the servant-love motif while at the same time reminding the reader that the baptism story is linked to the present. Jesus remains connected to the Old Testament. As O. Lamar Cope observes, "In this shaping of the text, he [Matthew] again testifies to his belief that the OT, and especially the prophets, point forward to Jesus and the coming of his kingdom."[25]

This type of midrash interpretation is seen elsewhere. For example, in 12:18 the phrase ὃν ἡρέτισα, immediately following, is inconspicuously reconstructed in the aorist indicative instead of the imperfect Hebrew אתמך־בו (which Matthew usually prefers). This tense adaptation was probably done to illustrate the changeover from the promise of Isaiah to the fulfillment that is now Jesus.[26] Also, Matthew deviates from the LXX by using the ἀπαγγελεῖ ("proclaim") instead of ἐξοίσει. Matthew, following the Targums, selects the former verb because it conveys the sense of accomplishment lacking in both the LXX as well as the MT (the Hebrew יוציא).[27] Finally, near the end of the passage Matthew chooses the most striking verb, ἐκβάλῃ, a more powerful term than either the θῇ of the LXX or the ישים of the MT. The scribes do this intentionally to

---

24. O. Lamar Cope, *Matthew: A Scribe Trained for the Kingdom of Heaven* (Washington, D.C.: Catholic Biblical Association of America, 1976), 45. See also W. C. Allen, *The Gospel according to St. Matthew* (Edinburgh: T&T Clark, 1912), 130–31.

25. Cope, *Matthew*, 49.

26. Davies and Allison, *Critical and Exegetical Commentary on Matthew*, 2:324.

27. Gundry, *Use of the Old Testament*, 113.

continue the theme of ἐκβάλλειν τὰ δαιμόνια, which is vital to the chapter (see 12:24, 26, 27).[28] Matthew once again deviates from the norm in order to produce a flowing, forceful Gospel.

The authors of Matthew do more than merely translate various versions of Isa 42:1–4. They convey the larger message of Jesus' fulfillment to their audience. Stendahl sums it up best:

> The unique interweaving of traditions of interpretation supported on different sides, and the completely original readings, render it difficult to understand the quotation in Matthew 12:18–21 as a "free citation" or to be satisfied that it shows a dependence upon the M.T. It can only have a satisfactory explanation as a targumized text which is the fruit of reflection and acquaintance with the interpretation [midrash] of the Scriptures.[29]

I conclude that only the Matthean scribes would have been educated enough to use this *pesher* form of exegetical interpretation. I also concur with Stendahl when he states that the method "presupposes an advanced study of the Scriptures and familiarity with the Hebrew text and with the traditions of interpretation known to us from the Versions."[30] The Jewish Matthean scribes were not merely literate; they were educated scholars.

Opponents of Stendahl: A Threat to the Conclusion?

Stendahl's groundbreaking work, however, is not without its critics. Numerous scholars disagree with many of Stendahl's presuppositions and conclusions. Gundry claims that Stendahl is incorrect. He questions Stendahl's statements regarding the link between the Matthean scribal community and the Qumran community.[31] In particular, Gundry disagrees with Stendahl's belief that

---

28. Stendahl, *School of St. Matthew*, 114. I agree with Stendahl's conclusion.
29. Ibid., 115.
30. Ibid., 203.
31. Gundry, *Use of the Old Testament*, 156–57.

the Matthean *midrash pesher* form of exegesis was markedly similar to the one used by the Qumran community in the Habakkuk commentary.

First, Gundry points to the numerous differences between the two communities. For example, the Qumran community's isolated, monastic nature differs greatly from the Matthean group's more social tendencies (he cites Matt 9:37–38; 10:5–11; 24:14; and others).[32] Tracy Howard agrees with Gundry, citing the many textual and social differences between the two groups. For example, Howard observes that the fulfillment citations in Matthew (see 2:15) contain the introductory ἵνα πληρωθῇ, while the Qumran texts lack the phrase.[33] So, there is little agreement between the two documents. R. T. France is also skeptical of such a comparison.[34]

Most relevant of all the charges leveled against Stendahl is the one claiming Matthew did not use a *pesher* methodology at all. This is the view of some scholars, including Raymond Brown and Daniel Patte.[35] They claim that Matthew's pick-and-choose analysis differs from the authentic *pesher*, which emphasizes a more strict, line-by-line approach.[36] Patte argues that this format was not intended for use in the Scriptures. As far as rabbinic literature goes, it was more inclined to be used for the interpretation of prophetic texts (in relation to dreams and visions).[37]

In response, I point out that often a prophetic dream or vision deals directly with what is to happen in the future. Therefore, if Matthew intended to convey a message to the audience regarding the past, present, and future role of Jesus, why not use a method of

---

32. Ibid. The rest of Gundry's arguments in this paragraph are also taken from here.

33. Tracy L. Howard, "The Use of Hosea 11:1 in Matthew 2:15: An Alternative Solution," *Bibliotheca sacra* 143 (1986): 318–19.

34. R. T. France, *Matthew: Evangelist and Teacher* (Grand Rapids: Zondervan, 1989), 175. France feels that Matthew is much more radical in his interpretation than the Qumran scribes were.

35. Raymond R. Brown, *The Birth of the Messiah* (New York: Doubleday, 1993), 102. See also Patte, *Early Jewish Hermeneutic in Palestine*, 308.

36. Patte, *Early Jewish Hermeneutic in Palestine*, 308.

37. Ibid.

study that discusses future events? Richard Longenecker has stated, "But at least a pesher treatment is involved [by Matthew] in the variations within the text and the stress on fulfillment, whether Isa. 42:1–4 was taken as having individual messianic significance or understood more along the lines of corporate solidarity."[38] Therefore, some scholars also defend Matthew's usage of the *pesher* method.

Matthew does deviate from the methodology in some instances. James Kugel and Rowan Greer observe, "Most of our examples of this form [the *pesher*] consist of verse-by-verse explanations of passages from various prophets and the psalms."[39] That Matthew deviates from the line-by-line method is not important. What is important is that the Matthean scribes knew *how* to use the method. Otherwise, how would they have possessed the ability to provide such a loose form of analysis in the Gospel? Whether the scribes perfectly incorporated the method is not crucial. The argument rests upon the fact that the authors of Matthew were able to manipulate the text in order to serve their own purposes. The Jewish scribes do that quite skillfully in Matt 12:18–21.

Gundry offers a final criticism of Stendahl by noting that *The School of St. Matthew* examines only those formula quotations found in the LXX. It ignores many others. This results in a biased analysis of the text, which allows Stendahl to manipulate the data and formulate his own conclusions. I disagree with Gundry's assertion. Stendahl provides a respectable number of examples. He cannot provide an in-depth analysis of every formula citation. Furthermore, a scholar should not dismiss Stendahl's conclusions merely on the basis that he does not cover as much material as one would like. Even Gundry himself admires the efforts of Stendahl, despite dismissing many of his specific theories as noncredible.

However, I concede that some of Gundry's arguments are valid. For example, I acknowledge that the Qumran community was

---

38. Richard N. Longenecker, *Biblical Exegesis in the Apostolic Period* (Grand Rapids: Eerdmans, 1975), 148.

39. James L. Kugel and Rowan A. Greer, *Early Biblical Interpretation* (Philadelphia: Westminster, 1986), 77.

probably not linked to the Matthean church. Stendahl's conclusions do seem to be based upon limited analysis and speculation at times. Also, Matthew may not use the *pesher* method flawlessly. Yet for the purposes of this discussion, Stendahl's work remains credible and useful. Regardless of how they did or did not relate to the Qumran community, Stendahl proves that the Matthean scribes were *learned*.

In conclusion, the authors skillfully redacted the numerous texts of the Hebrew, Greek, and Aramaic versions of the Old Testament for their Gospel. Brown points out that it was Stendahl who reminded scholars of the vast number of scriptural traditions that existed by Matthew's time.[40] The authors of Matthew included their *midrash pesher* method of interpretation in order to unify these numerous textual traditions. As Gundry states, "Such a detailed application of Scripture [in this case the OT prophetic texts], designed to create a unity between the life and ministry of Jesus and the Old Testament, reflects a sophisticated understanding of Scripture."[41]

Matthew's Jewish Exegetical Techniques

Jewish exegetical techniques help prove that the validity of the existing oral laws was confirmed in the Torah.[42] In order to interpret the written Torah, one was required to follow customary methods of argumentation and logic. The early rabbis formulated many rules to facilitate the process. These rules came to be known as the *Middoth* of Hillel, or the rules of R. Ishmael. Each rule represents a unique and precise method of argumentation that must be followed carefully. Sometimes the rules were engaged specifically

---

40. Brown, *Birth of the Messiah*, 103. In fact, Brown states that Stendahl's great contribution to later scholars was his realization that numerous textual traditions in Scripture already existed by the first century.

41. Gundry, *Use of the Old Testament*, 75.

42. H. L. Strack and G. Stremberger, *Introduction to the Talmud and Midrash* (trans. Markus Bockmuehl; Minneapolis: Fortress, 1992), 18.

for the purpose of settling interpretive disputes involving two or
more passages from the Old Testament.

The examination of some of these techniques is both helpful and
necessary to my discussion of Matthew's literacy. Charles Kimball
points out, "Since Jesus was a Jew like all the NT writers, since he
claimed to fulfill OT prophecy and Judaism as a whole . . . it is necessary to investigate the exegetical practices of first-century
Judaism for a proper understanding of his exposition of Scripture."[43] Hence, my examination of the Jewish exegetical techniques will also clarify who the Matthean Jesus was and how he
implemented Jewish teachings.

In particular, I look at some of the rules of Hillel and R. Ishmael,
including the בנין אב מכתוב אחד־משני כתובים (for our purposes I refer
to this rule as the *binyan av*), and the קל וחמר (*kal vehomer*).
Although I discussed Matthew's usage of the Old Testament earlier,
the examples below reinforce the Gospel authors' reliance upon the
text (as well as the Jewish nature of the community). It was the
practice of first-century Jews to appeal to Old Testament passages
for the basis of their arguments.[44] As David Daube observes, "It
was the essence of the Rabbinic system that any detailed rule, any
halakha, must rest directly, or indirectly, on an actual precept promulgated in Scripture."[45]

Example One: Reasoning, Methodology, and the Binyan Av

I begin by examining the Jewish exegetical technique of the *binyan
av*. The Matthean pericopes I have selected for examination are the
divorce teachings in 5:32 and 19:9. I will be especially thorough in
the first example so the reader can fully comprehend how Matthew

---

43. Charles A. Kimball, *Jesus' Exposition of the Old Testament in Luke's
Gospel* (Sheffield: JSOT Press, 1994), 44.
44. Longenecker, *Biblical Exegesis*, 96.
45. David Daube, *The New Testament and Rabbinic Judaism* (New York:
Arno Press, 1973), 68.

used this Jewish technique. I have selected these passages partially due to the fact that the divorce citations in Matthew are among the most studied by scholars.[46] In particular, Matt 5:32 is well known since it is included among the antitheses of Jesus. Furthermore, the divorce antithesis of 5:31–32 is possibly one of the authentic sayings of Jesus, due to its unique structure.[47] The two verses, comprising the so-called exception clauses, show how Matthew incorporates Jewish forms of reason and logic into the Gospel.

Briefly, the *binyan av* is a Jewish exegetical technique that shows how one or two passages of Scripture serve as the authority for another passage when a legal ruling is disputed. In other words, one or two main passages allow the interpreter to reach the same conclusion for all other texts that contain the common elements.[48] Therefore, the main passage(s) then remains authoritative, allowing for a similar decision in the case of the other disputed passages.[49]

Matthew's version of the Old Testament divorce rule, in 5:32 and 19:9, has often been understood as an example of how Jesus contradicts the Torah.[50] Matthew's ruling on divorce, I maintain, actually *enforces* the halakah of the Torah; it does not contradict it. David E. Garland states, "Some scholars considered Jesus to have abrogated the law [Torah] in these so-called antitheses, but one must heed the warning of 5:17–19. Rather than abrogating the law . . . Jesus restores its original intention."[51]

---

46. Ulrich Luz, *Matthew 1–7: A Commentary* (trans. Wilhelm C. Linss; Minneapolis: Augsburg, 1985), 298–99.

47. Robert Banks, *Jesus and the Law in the Synoptic Tradition* (Cambridge: Cambridge University Press, 1975), 183. Banks provides a fine section outlining the differences between the authentic sayings of Jesus and those that are likely pseudonymous.

48. Strack and Stremberger, *Introduction to the Talmud*, 22.

49. Jacob Zellel Lauterbach, "Talmud Hermeneutics," *The Jewish Encyclopedia* (vol. 12; ed. Cyrus Adler; trans. Isidore Singer; New York: Funk and Wagnalls, 1904), 31–32.

50. Daniel J. Harrington, "Not to Abolish, but to Fulfill," *Bible Today* 27 (1989): 334. I concur with Harrington.

51. David E. Garland, *Reading Matthew: A Literary and Theological Commentary on the First Gospel* (New York: Crossroad, 1993), 63.

Some scholars believe that Matthew intended for Jesus to "reinterpret" radically the Torah, or to supersede Moses as the new lawgiver, but this seems to be overstated and untrue.[52] These passages show how the authors of Matthew incorporated the Jewish law into the Gospel. Also, the scribes recorded the teachings of the Gospel based upon constructs taken from their own native Jewish background. As educated scribes, this would have been their manner of study.

The Old Testament passage from which Matthew quotes, Deut 24:1–4, reads in Hebrew and English as follows:

כי־יקח איש אשה ובעלה והיה אם־לא תמצא־חן בעיניו כי־מצא בה ערות
דבר וכתב לה ספר כריתת ונתן בידה ושלחה מביתו: ויצאה מביתו והלכה
והיתה לאיש־אחר: ושנאה האיש האחרון וכתב לה ספר כריתת ונתן בידה
ושלחה מביתו או כי ימות האיש האחרון אשר־לקחה לו לאשה: לא־יוכל
בעלה הראשון אשר־שלחה לשוב לקחתה להיות לו לאשה אחרי אשר
הטמאה כי־תועבה הוא לפני יהוה ולא תחטיא את־הארץ אשר יהוה
אלהיך נתן לך נחלה:

Suppose a man takes a wife, and marries her, then it comes to pass, if she finds no favor in his eyes, because he has found some unseemly thing for her, that he writes her a bill of divorcement, and gives it in her hand, and sends her out of his house, and she departs out of his house, and goes and becomes another man's wife, and the latter husband hates her, and writes her a bill of divorcement, and gives it in her hand, and sends her out of his house; or if the latter husband dies, who took her to be his wife, after that she is defiled; for that is abomination before the LORD; and you shall not cause the land to sin, which the LORD thy God gives you for an inheritance.[53]

---

52. See, in particular, W. D. Davies, *The Setting of the Sermon on the Mount* (Cambridge: Cambridge University Press, 1966), 102; M. D. Goulder, *Midrash and Lection in Matthew: The Speaker's Lectures in Biblical Studies* (London: SPCK, 1974), 290–91; as well as Banks, *Jesus and the Law*, 146–59, for a discussion of the topic.

53. This translation is taken from the A. Cohen, ed., *The Soncino Chumash* (New York: Soncino Press, 1975), 1108–9.

Matthew's rendering of the text reads in 5:32 and 19:9 respectively:

ἐγὼ δὲ λέγω ὑμῖν ὅτι πᾶς ὁ ἀπολύων τὴν γυναῖκα αὐτοῦ παρεκτὸς λόγου πορνείας ποιεῖ αὐτὴν μοιχευθῆναι, καὶ ὃς ἐὰν ἀπολελυμένην γαμήσῃ μοιχᾶται.

"But I say to you that every one who divorces his wife, except on the ground of unchastity, makes her an adulteress; and whoever marries a divorced woman commits adultery" (RSV).

λέγω δὲ ὑμῖν ὅτι ὃς ἂν ἀπολύσῃ τὴν γυναῖκα αὐτοῦ μὴ ἐπὶ πορνείᾳ καὶ γαμήσῃ ἄλλην μοιχᾶται.

"And I say to you, whoever divorces his wife, except for unchastity, and marries another commits adultery" (RSV).

Some of Matthew's divorce material is taken from Mark 10:11–12 and Q, although the Markan version contains no mention by Jesus of any exception to the rule of divorce. This leads one to believe that Matthew has expanded upon the Markan ruling. Why would this be so? I believe the authors of Matthew were using their knowledge of halakah and Jewish exegetical techniques in order to show how Jesus upholds and fulfills the Torah (see 5:17–19). As Markus Bockmuehl claims, "Jesus, although he may hold to uncommon exegetical distinctions and priorities (see 19:8; cf. 23:23), does not abrogate the Torah (5:17ff). . . . [I]t was essential for Matthew's partly Jewish Christian community to affirm that their otherwise strict divorce halakah did not at this point contravene the Torah."[54] So, how is Matthew using a Jewish exegetical technique?

The Relationship between Deuteronomy 24:1–4 and Matthew 5:32 and 19:9

First, I must establish that some relationship exists between Deut 24:1–4 and Matt 5:32 and 19:9. The easiest way is first to look at

---

54. Markus Bockmuehl, "Matthew 5:32; 19:9 in the Light of Pre-Rabbinic Halakah," *New Testament Studies* 35 (1989): 294.

what the Old Testament says concerning divorce. Deuteronomy 24:1–4 appears to be acknowledging a man's right to divorce under certain circumstances (the meaning of ערות דבר is unclear; some sort of "abomination"), although the law is not stated in a perfectly clear manner.[55] Furthermore, additional textual evidence implies that Deut 24:1–4 may have been intended especially to refer to divorces granted on the basis of the "abomination" of adultery.[56] This legal allowance for divorce is accomplished via the exegetical technique of the *gezerah shavah*, a so-called argument from analogy in which the decision of one case is based upon the similarity of another case. Matthew deploys the technique numerous times in the Gospel.[57]

In this instance, Deut 24:1–4, on the basis of the exegesis of similar biblical and rabbinic texts, has extended divorce to include cases of adultery.[58] Some rabbinic texts even require divorce in the case of adultery. At such times divorce is actually considered a necessary *mitzvah*.[59] I should caution, however, that other scholars feel the true meaning of ערות דבר remains unknown.[60] I am offering one of the more plausible explanations. One may never know for sure what the authors meant. What is certain is that Deut 24:1–4 allows for divorce in certain instances.

What do Matt 5:32 and 19:9 have in common with the above Old Testament passage? First and foremost, both texts seemingly allow for divorce in the case of adultery. The phrases ערות דבר (from the MT) and πορνεία (from Matthew) both refer to adultery.[61] I have indicated above how the former phrase alludes to infidelity, but can the same be said about πορνεία, as found in Matthew? I believe the answer is yes, based upon the following evidence.

55. Sigal, *Halakah of Jesus of Nazareth*, 87.

56. Bockmuehl, "Matthew 5:32," 292–93.

57. Shedinger, "Must the Greek Text Always Be Preferred?" 457. Shedinger points out the example found in Matt 2:6, for instance.

58. See Bockmuehl, "Matthew 5:32," 292–93, for a more complete explanation. The point here is to affirm that adultery by one's partner permits one to be granted a divorce.

59. Ibid., 292.

60. Sigal, *Halakah of Jesus of Nazareth*, 87.

61. Ibid., 88.

Davies and Allison point out that in antiquity the term referred to one of three instances: fornication, incest, or adultery.[62] Of the three choices, the first is the least plausible since Matt 5:32 and 19:9 allude only to sexual matters in marriage. The passages are not referring to the general act of fornication. Some evidence exists for the second meaning on the basis of textual as well as social evidence (see 1 Cor 5:1; Acts 15:20; 21:25; and possibly Lev 17–18, for example). Incest was more prevalent among Gentiles, which probably constituted a small portion of the Matthean community. Matthew 4:15, of course, mentions Gentiles, but I have already refuted that reference in an earlier chapter. Davies and Allison feel that πορνεία probably does not refer to incest. It rather refers to the act of adultery.

They cite numerous reasons for this conclusion.[63] For example, there is no patristic textual evidence to support the incest theory. Early Christian literature does not discuss the subject. Furthermore, the argument suggesting that Acts incorporates the Holiness Code (which bans incest) is not convincing, and Lev 17–18 itself contains no term comparable to πορνεία. Consider also Jer 3:1–10, in which God grants a bill of divorce to Israel on the grounds of adultery. Matthew's discussion of adultery in 5:32 and 19:9 is then consistent with the Old Testament version.[64] Finally, the Mishnah notes that the Jewish School of Shammai interprets the ערות דבר of Deut 24:1 as "unchastity" on the woman's part.[65] In this Jewish

---

62. Davies and Allison, *Critical and Exegetical Commentary on Matthew*, 1:529–31. The following explanation for the meaning of πορνεία is also taken from this section.

63. Ibid. Again, I am following Davies and Allison in this paragraph. See *m. Gittin* 9:10.

64. See Jer 3:8, in which God says, "She saw that for all the adulteries [from the Hebrew, נאוף] of that faithless one, Israel, I had sent her away with a decree of divorce." Davies and Allison agree with Sigal's line of thinking here. See Sigal, *Halakah of Jesus of Nazareth*, 94–102, for the entire discussion.

65. Taken from Jacob Neusner's *The Mishnah: A New Translation* (New Haven: Yale University Press, 1988), 487. Some scholars have noted that Matthew's word order is more similar to the School of Shammai's than to either the Old Testament or the Hillelites. See W. D. Davies and Dale C. Allison Jr., *The Gospel according to Saint Matthew* (ed. J. A. Merton et al.; International Critical Commentary; Edinburgh: T&T Clark International, 1991), 1:530.

tradition, the authors of Matthew formulate their own divorce creed, engaging the phrase in a similar manner (to mean adultery).

The Relationship between ערות דבר and πορνεία: Agreement or Exegesis?

Based upon the evidence stated above, can one claim that Matthew and Deuteronomy are related? If so, what kind of relationship is it? Sigal states, "The question to be more carefully examined is whether these terms represent the same grounds for divorce or whether the latter exegetes the former."[66] First, consider how the LXX replaces the MT's ערות דבר in Deut 24. The preferred term seems to be ἄσχημων πρᾶγμα (see Deut 24:3), which can mean a variety of things.[67] In many contexts where the Hebrew phrase appears, the LXX responds with the above translation (see Deut 23:15 and compare with 23:14 from the LXX).[68] Regardless of the meaning, the two phrases are usually considered together.

It seems there is a measure of consistency on the part of the MT and the LXX. This implies that Matthew was probably following a consistent corpus of textual sources when he inserted πορνεία into the Gospel. The next step is to return to the question of how Matthew's divorce text is related to the version found in Deuteronomy. Sigal concludes that Matthew was interpreting the Old Testament, not merely agreeing with it.[69] I concur; more is happening than a simple confirmation of Old Testament halakah. The authors of the Gospel are not just reciting law; as educated scribes, they are interpreting it for their own needs.

If Deut 24:1–4 extends divorce to include adultery, the authors of Matthew (through Jesus) may have been clarifying their position on the matter, since the topic was open for debate throughout the

---

66. Sigal, *Halakah of Jesus of Nazareth*, 88.

67. Ibid.

68. I concede that the example from Deut 23:15 does not deal with the topic of sex. Yet the phrase always seems to be used when discussing extremely serious matters.

69. Sigal, *Halakah of Jesus of Nazareth*, 89, 91.

early centuries. This applies to the Gentile and Jewish world. For example, a deed of divorce dating from the Hellenistic period around 13 B.C.E. clearly spells out the terms between the couple "Zois" and "Antipater."[70] Within the agreement, one notices specific provisions concerning remarriage. In this case both parties are freely allowed to remarry without any fear of repercussions. Furthermore, personal property is divided in a unique manner: the former wife receives the dowry along with an allotment of clothes and two gold earrings.

In contrast, a divorce certificate from Masada dated 111 C.E. is different in style.[71] Here, both parties are also allowed to remarry freely, yet the division of goods is legally centered. The former wife gets back the dowry plus all goods that have been damaged or destroyed multiplied four times. This suggests that laws pertaining to divorce and remarriage were quite varied throughout the ancient world, let alone in Judaic circles where these laws were debated. Situations were often resolved on an individual basis. The Matthean scribes probably felt the need to include Jewish forms of argumentation to unify the divorce laws within their own diverse community.

The authors of Matthew were dealing with two important dilemmas regarding divorce. First, as noted above, they faced stringent opposition from formative Jews concerning the halakah of the Torah, which included divorce laws. Second, they wanted to resolve the debates surrounding divorce that probably plagued the members of the Matthean community. In other words, the Matthean community faced dissension both from the outside as well as internally. As a result, Matthew felt the need to reinterpret the divorce law clearly in order to placate a volatile situation. Therefore, I argue that Matthew (in 5:32 and 19:9) has Jesus pronounce a strict ruling regarding divorce. In fact, Sigal notes, "Nevertheless, he [Matthew] cannot do more than exegete [Deut] 24:1, and so he exegetes it in the strictest possible way; for πορνεία alone

---

70. M. Eugene Boring, Klaus Berger, and Carsten Colpe, eds., *Hellenistic Commentary to the New Testament* (Nashville: Abingdon, 1995), 117.

71. Ibid., 58.

may a person terminate his marriage."[72] But how did Matthew accomplish this?

The Use of the Binyan Av by the Matthean Jesus

Now I come to the crux of the matter. Recall that the authors of Matthew interpret Deut 24; they do not just copy it verbatim. In addition, if there were dissension in the Jewish community regarding the definition of ערות דבר, Matthew needed to clarify its meaning. The authors chose to define the phrase simply as πορνεία.[73] Therefore, based upon their understanding, the Matthean scribes allowed for divorce only in the case of πορνεία; no other instance made it permissible. As Luz puts it, "Thus, in the Matthean community Jesus' prohibition of divorce was promulgated, unless there was a case of adultery."[74]

One final objection remains. What does one do with the term μοιχᾶται as it relates to πορνεία? Do they not both mean "adultery" in the passages from Matthew? A plausible answer is that Matthew had to use the term "adultery" twice in the passages to avoid confusion. The first term would indicate the only permissible reason for divorce (a woman's infidelity), while the latter term referred to the man's resulting action if he remarries (he is committing adultery).[75] The skillful Matthean redactors would not wish to choose the same word twice in one line. So they use both terms at this point to refer to the gender-divided action of adultery.[76]

How does Matthew resolve the issue of divorce in the community while at the same time being faithful to the halakah of the Torah? The answer is that the scribes use the *binyan av*, the Jewish exegetical technique noted above. As I stated, this technique calls

---

72. Sigal, *Halakah of Jesus of Nazareth*, 89.

73. Ibid., 95.

74. Luz, *Matthew 1–7*, 306.

75. Sigal, *Halakah of Jesus of Nazareth*, 97.

76. Ibid. I am also agreeing with Luz here. He also suggests that the term can only refer to a married woman's act of adultery. See Luz, *Matthew 1–7*, 304.

for one to formulate a major decision based upon one or two exist-ing texts. In this instance, Jesus (through Matthew's scribes) engages the *binyan av*. But how does Jesus accomplish it?

First, Deut 24:1–4 allows for divorce in certain instances. Exactly when, no one is sure. Deuteronomy seems to allow for divorce in the instance of adultery. But if the authors of Matthew's Gospel wish to put forth an even stricter halakah regarding divorce while at the same time not contradicting the Torah, they must be able to incorporate a Jewish exegetical technique competently. Based upon the definition of the *binyan av*, the authors of Matthew's Gospel must find alternative Old Testament texts so that they can establish a principle over and above the unclear Deut 24:1–4. This allows them to follow the precepts of the Torah properly.

Jesus finds his authoritative passages in Gen 1:27 and 2:24. These passages state that God created man, as well as women, in God's own image and that they become of "one flesh." This was important to Jesus. Procreation within marriage was God's pri-mary intention for humankind. Marriage, then, was the most holy of relationships. Divorce was not granted, except in extreme cir-cumstances.

How does this relate to Deut 24:1–4? Jesus includes the Genesis texts to "supersede" Deuteronomy. This allows him to proclaim his own principle regarding divorce.[77] In other words, the *binyan av* principle has been put to the test here. Deuteronomy 24:1–4 itself contains no authoritative halakah; it only provides informa-tion about an *existing* law.[78] On this basis, Jesus invokes the authority of God's plan for humankind contained in Genesis to override the confusing, vague text of Deuteronomy. He is able to state the only permissible reason for divorce: adultery.

Jesus permits only πορνεία (adultery) to void a marriage—a strict interpretation of Jewish law on Matthew's part. But how does Jesus get away with allowing for divorce at all in light of the strict Genesis passages? The answer is found within the Jewish

---

77. Sigal, *Halakah of Jesus of Nazareth*, 98–99.
78. Ibid.

halakah. Bockmuehl states, "We have seen . . . a clear pre-rabbinic attestation for the halakhic idea that any sexual interference with an existing marriage bond produces a state of impurity which precludes a resumption of that marriage."[79] In addition, consider *m. Sotah* 5:1. It states that a woman becomes "unclean" to her husband if she commits an act of adultery.[80] No sexual relations can take place after the woman's violation, which breaks the code put forth by God in Gen 2:24 (to become *one* flesh). Logically, then, Jesus is justified in establishing his own principle of divorce "by πορνεία only" via the Genesis codes. A divorce must be permitted in a case in which sexual relations are no longer possible.

Conclusion

It is clear that the authors of Matthew's Gospel have formulated their own version of the divorce law by invoking the Jewish exegetical technique of the *binyan av*. They have taken two different authoritative texts and used them to supersede Deut 24:1–4. This justifies their conclusion, while at the same time remaining true to the halakah of the Torah. In fact, Matthew's version of the law is still strict—probably stricter than many other schools of Jewish thought in the first century. The Matthean scribes were opposed to divorce and approved of it only in emergency situations, as the authors continued to operate within the confines of Jewish law. Sigal states, "In this interpretation of the pericopae the halakah of Jesus concerning divorce as presented in Matthew neither abrogates nor transcends the Torah's divorce halakah. It brings it into focus."[81]

Certainly, the authors of Matthew needed to clarify the divorce law for the community. But the scribes may also have been carefully constructing a solid defense of the Jewish law in order to deflect the arguments of competing formative Jews. They com-

---

79. Bockmuehl, "Matthew 5:32," 294.
80. Sigal, *Halakah of Jesus of Nazareth*, 97.
81. Ibid., 98.

pleted both tasks by formulating a divorce code for the community and establishing their authority as competent Jewish scribes and scholars. This is evident in the cases of Matt 5:32 and 19:9.

Matthew's Continued Use of Jewish Exegetical Techniques: The *Kal Vehomer*

The Matthean scribes continue using Jewish exegetical techniques throughout the Gospel. The next example, the discussion of the Sabbath in Matt 12:1–8, again illustrates Matthew's adept redaction of the text. Some scholars argue that Jesus negates or modifies the rules and tradition of the Jewish holiday.[82] Graham Stanton has offered two interesting conclusions pertaining to Matthew's view of the Sabbath: the community either observed the Sabbath strictly, or they did not keep its commandments at all.[83] He favors the latter conclusion.

Stanton cites textual evidence to support this position.[84] First, he proposes that outside of Matt 12:1–14 and 28:1, there is no mention of the Sabbath in the Gospel. Furthermore, he claims that Matt 12 focuses not on Sabbath observance, but on the Temple's precedence over the Sabbath. Three passages serve as evidence. He cites 12:6, in which Jesus states, "I tell you, something greater than the Temple is here." Stanton believes that Jesus is referring to himself here. Then, Jesus proclaims in 12:8, "For the Son of Man is lord of the Sabbath." Finally, he feels that 12:12 serves as the climax to the story. Jesus announces, "So it is lawful to do good on the Sabbath." These passages, according to Stanton, illustrate Matthew's disdain for Sabbath observance as a whole. Jesus seems to shift the focus of the story away from the Sabbath by portraying himself and the Temple as greater than the law.

---

82. Graham N. Stanton, "'Pray That Your Flight May Not Be in Winter or on a Sabbath' (Matthew 24:20)," *Journal for the Study of the New Testament* 37 (1989): 17–21. Stanton's article is an informative survey of prevailing views concerning Matthew and the Sabbath.

83. Ibid., 24–25.

84. Ibid., 25. The information in this paragraph comes from this source.

I disagree with Stanton. To begin, no one knows for sure who or what Jesus refers to when he states "something" greater than the Temple is here. Next, Matt 12:8 may only be reaffirming Jesus' status as the authoritative teacher of the Torah. Nothing in the passage dismisses Sabbath observance altogether. Finally, doing "good" is always considered a *mitzvah* in the Jewish religion, even on holidays. According to the rabbis, there is nothing wrong with doing good deeds on the Sabbath. For example, the Mishnah clearly points out that it is permissible to save someone's life on the Sabbath.[85]

The ensuing textual analysis supports the hypothesis that the authors of Matthew were learned Jewish scholars intent on upholding the halakah of the Torah. This, of course, includes the Sabbath, which was important to the community. Even among scholars who believe that Jesus upholds the Sabbath regulations, few actually attempt to prove their case through an analysis of Jewish exegetical principles.[86] I attempt to do so here.

The exegetical principle of the *kal vehomer* relies upon the movement of reasoning from the simple ("light") to the complex ("heavy"), or the complex to the simple.[87] This form of deductive reasoning is narrowed in the sense that one may only base a conclusion upon evidence contained in the premise. Typically, the technique contains three parts: two premises and one conclusion based upon these premises.[88] For example, I may make the equation: if the Sabbath is more important than an ordinary holiday and if working is forbidden on the ordinary holiday, then how much more is work forbidden on the Sabbath.[89] In mathematical terms:

---

85. *m. Yoma* 8:6.

86. Many scholars do support the notion that Jesus, in chapter 12, is teaching his own interpretation of halakah. For example, see Garland, *Reading Matthew*, 136.

87. *The Jewish Encyclopedia*, 12:32.

88. Dan Cohn-Sherbok, *Rabbinic Perspectives on the New Testament* (Studies in the Bible and Early Christianity 28; Lewiston, N.Y.: Edwin Mellen, 1990), 37.

89. Ibid., 28. The idea for this example comes from Cohn-Sherbok. I have reformulated it into mathematical terms.

if $b > a$, and if $c < a$, then how much more the case must $b > c$. This technique often has been used within biblical interpretation. Therefore, I believe I can show that Matthew comes up with a reliable conclusion while incorporating this method. Please note that my solution may not agree perfectly with the above equation. I have only provided it as a sample of the method.

Matthew 12:1–8, the Sabbath, and the Kal Vehomer

Although some of Matt 12:1–8 has been taken from Mark 2:23–28, the authors of Matthew's Gospel have based much of the passage upon their own reasoning and/or interpretation of the Old Testament.[90] For example, it will become clear how Matthew adds certain key words such as ἐπείνασαν to the basic story (the disciples plucked grain because "they were hungry"). Here is the passage in English:

> At that time Jesus went through the grainfields on the sabbath: his disciples were hungry, and they began to pluck heads of grain and to eat. When the Pharisees saw it, they said to him, "Look, your disciples are doing what is not lawful to do on the sabbath." He said to them, "Have you not read what David did, when he and his companions were hungry? He entered the house of God and ate the bread of the Presence, which it was not lawful for him or his companions to eat, but only for the priests. Or have you not read in the law that on the sabbath the priests in the temple break the sabbath and yet are guiltless? I tell you, something greater than the temple is here. But if you had known what this means, 'I desire mercy, and not sacrifice,' you would not have condemned the guiltless. For the Son of man is lord of the sabbath."

In the story Jesus rebukes the Pharisees regarding the disciples' supposed violation of the Sabbath. According to the Pharisees,

---

90. Davies and Allison, *Gospel according to Saint Matthew*, 2:304–16. Davies and Allison provide a fine analysis of the passage. Again, it is not the point of this study to exegete each passage from Matthew's Gospel. I am merely attempting to discern Matthew's line of thought.

"plucking" is considered one of the forms of work, or עבודה, that is not permitted on the holiday. The Pharisees question Jesus on the matter, and he, as usual, provides a clever answer. But how so? Are the disciples actually violating the Sabbath? As alluded to above, some scholars view this passage as an indication that Matthew's community did not observe all the rules of the Sabbath.[91] However, this is not necessarily the case.

I believe the disciples were not violating the Sabbath by "plucking" the grains. The Mishnah appears to contain contradictory views. As Sigal points out, the Mishnah itself does not specifically list "plucking" as one of the forbidden forms of work.[92] Furthermore, Josephus agrees with Deut 23:24–25 and records that the poor should be allowed to gather crops from the fields.[93] The Tosefta seems to confirm this practice as well.[94] But the act could be considered more like "trimming" or other forms of gardening, which represent violations of the Sabbath.[95] Moreover, there seems to be an implied understanding of the Pharisees in 12:2 that this type of labor (plucking) is not allowed on the Sabbath.[96] Finally, Jesus clearly does nothing to stop the disciples. So how does one resolve the issue?

The answer may at first seem disappointing. There is no apparent resolution. Yet, as Davies and Allison state, there are two noteworthy considerations. First, Exod 34:21, which prohibited plowing or harvesting on the Sabbath, must have been well known

---

91. Günther Bornkamm, Gerhard Barth, and Heinz Joachim Held, eds., *Tradition and Interpretation in Matthew* (trans. Percy Scott; Philadelphia: Westminster, 1963), 81. This is one of the possibilities that the authors are alluding to here.

92. Sigal, *Halakah of Jesus of Nazareth*, 129. He is referring to *m. Shabbat* 10:6.

93. *Jewish Antiquities* 4:8:21.

94. See, in particular, *t. Pe'ah* 2:10–19.

95. Sigal, *Halakah of Jesus of Nazareth*, 129. As Sigal points out, passages in defense of this view are also found in the Mishnah. See *m. Shabbat* 7:2 and 10:6. Specifically, the act of "plucking" as meaning "separation" is not among the thirty-nine main forbidden forms of "work."

96. Bornkamm, Barth, and Held, *Tradition and Interpretation*, 81.

and authoritative, considering the Pharisees' line of questioning.[97] They likely had this law in mind when they came across the disciples plucking the heads of grain. Second, there were exceptions to the law when it came to the Torah's halakah. This is clarified in passages such as Lev 18:15, in which prophets are given supreme authority, seemingly over and above the law (as in 1 Kgs 18). Likewise, various Jewish circles may have accepted a rule prohibiting the practice of fasting on the Sabbath (see *Jub.* 50:11; Jdt 8:6).[98] Saldarini points out that even the strictest holiday of all, Yom Kippur, allowed legal exceptions based upon extreme hunger.[99]

I asserted that only Matthew's version of the story contains the word ἐπείνασαν ("were hungry"). If Jesus' disciples had not eaten that day, they may have been required to eat in order to observe the celebration of the Sabbath. One may not fast on the Sabbath. Another Matthean redaction is also curious. Although the Matthean scribes accept much of the Markan material here, they curiously omit one notable phrase. Mark 2:27 states, "The sabbath was made for man, not man for the sabbath" (RSV). Why is this important? This phrase is omitted from Matthew's text because putting the Sabbath in the hands of man (and his desires), instead of God, could make the holiday appear less important. This could have led to members of the community becoming lax in their observance.[100] Having heard arguments from both sides concerning Sabbath observance in Matthew, is there no satisfactory resolution?

Sigal provides the best conclusion.[101] I agree that many Jews of the first century would not have viewed the plucking as a violation. Further, as noted above, the Old Testament and rabbinic texts are not clear concerning whether the act of plucking was a violation of the Sabbath at all. Also, Jesus' disciples, cognizant of the Old Tes-

---

97. Davies and Allison, *Gospel according to Saint Matthew*, 2:307. Both considerations are from this source.

98. Sigal, *Halakah of Jesus of Nazareth*, 130.

99. Anthony J. Saldarini, *Matthew's Christian-Jewish Community* (Chicago: University of Chicago Press, 1994), 128. Saldarini quotes from *m. Yoma* 8:1.

100. Ibid., 131.

101. Sigal, *Halakah of Jesus of Nazareth*, 130–31. The following two summations are from Sigal.

tament, may have chosen to follow Isa 58:13, which commands one to "call the sabbath a delight." It is well known that Jesus quoted numerous times from the prophets. This excused the disciples of any guilt regarding the act of plucking. The main purpose of the Sabbath was to revel in its blessing, not to argue over specific laws. Remember, prophetic passages were authoritative in ancient Judaism. It is likely, therefore, that the prophet Isaiah acted as the authoritative mediator in the dispute.

Finally, Judaism already contained precepts stating that if one had a measure of doubt regarding the halakah, the halakah did not have to be enforced.[102] So even if there was some doubt concerning the legality of the disciples' actions, the Pharisees may have been forced to acquiesce to Jesus' teaching. In the final analysis, then, one can say that there is no evidence proving that Jesus or his disciples were violating any of the rules of the Sabbath. This is central to my discussion, since it places even more doubt upon the arguments of those who say that the Matthean community was "relaxing" many Jewish laws and customs.[103] The Gospel does not violate Jewish law; it reaffirms it.

Matthew 12:1–8 and the Kal Vehomer

Having confirmed Matthew's loyalty to the Jewish laws, I intend to show how the authors use the *kal vehomer* in this passage. After two introductory verses, Jesus responds in verses 3–4 by citing 1 Sam 21:2–6, in which David and his hungry men ate the holy

---

102. Ibid., 130. Sigal also cites *Thesaurus Talmudis* (ed. Chaim J. Kosowski; Jerusalem: Israel Ministry of Education and Culture, 1971), xxvii, 304–18, which discusses the issue at length.

103. For example, see Eric Kun-Chun Wong, "The Matthean Understanding of the Sabbath: A Response to G. N. Stanton," *Journal for the Study of the New Testament* 44 (1991): 3–18. Specifically, Wong feels that Matthew "indirectly affirmed" the Sabbath, but it was not the "central ethic" of the Gospel. What is interesting concerning Wong's analysis is the omission of any authoritative rabbinic textual evidence. How can one compare Matthew to Judaism without the use of any Jewish legal texts?

bread of the Presence (meant for the priests of the Temple only). As in the case of the disciples, this was a supposed violation of the Jewish law. David and his men violate the law by eating what is considered "holy." Similarly, the disciples have violated the holiness of the Sabbath. Jesus binds together the two stories. This usage of two parallel instances illustrates Matthew's knowledge of another Jewish hermeneutical rule, the *hekish*, which is the use of two parallel instances within a case.[104]

Additionally, Jesus states in his conclusion (12:6) that "something greater than the temple is here." This point is debated, and many scholars insist that Jesus is referring to himself.[105] Comparing Jesus to the Temple is like comparing apples and oranges. Jesus and the Temple are not synonymous; a building and a human are not comparable. It makes more sense to compare two obligations. These two obligations, according to Sigal, are the love of humans and the cult.[106] As 12:7 shows, God demands *chesed* (love, or mercy) above all, and one should consider that in light of the disciples' hunger. Mercy takes precedence over the Sabbath or the cult.

Recall Matthew's unique insertion of ἐπείνασαν into the story. I believe this word is central to understanding the passage. The message of the story revolves around hunger. If so, then the usage of the *kal vehomer* becomes clearer. As Sigal states, "Matthew's pericope is quite coherent. Hunger supersedes the halakhic stringencies attached to the holy food and, in turn, requirements of the cult supersede the holiness of the Sabbath. This in itself issues in a kal vehomer. If hunger supersedes an element of the cult, how much more so the Sabbath which is superseded by the cult."[107] In other words, Jesus is arguing from the simple to the complex, or from the lesser to the greater. One can formulate a possibly clearer equation:

---

104. Sigal, *Halakah of Jesus of Nazareth*, 131.

105. For example, see Saldarini, *Matthew's Christian-Jewish Community*, 130; Bornkamm, Barth, and Held, *Tradition and Interpretation*, 82; John P. Meier, *Matthew* (New Testament Message 3; Collegeville, Minn.: Liturgical Press, 1980), 129; Garland, *Reading Matthew*, 137; and others.

106. Sigal, *Halakah of Jesus of Nazareth*, 131.

107. Ibid., 133–34.

if sacrifice > the Sabbath, but God says that *chesed* > sacrifice, then
how much more is *chesed* > the Sabbath.[108]

Objections to Matthew's Usage of the Kal Vehomer

Some scholars disagree with this line of reasoning. For instance,
Cohn-Sherbok believes that Jesus did not use the *kal vehomer* at all
in Matt 12:1–8.[109] He observes that the principle can only be formulated from the premises of two biblical passages, not from the
comparison between two people or things, such as Jesus and the
Temple. In other words, the equation is formulated something like
this: if Jesus > the Temple (and its laws), and if the Temple law
(which allows offerings; see Num 28:9) > the Sabbath, then how
much more must Jesus and his disciples (who similarly neglect the
Sabbath law) > the Sabbath.[110] In this equation, only one Temple
law is taken directly from the Torah, and Jesus himself is compared
to the Temple.

Cohn-Sherbok's methodology is flawed. To begin, Daube states
that rabbinic arguments must rest upon scriptural authority. He
merely asserts that Matthew's usage of the *kal vehomer*, although
largely based upon the tale of a patriarch (David), is still connected, albeit in story form, to the Torah. Although not stated as a
law, it still merits authority in this case.[111] Daube understands the
rule regarding biblical law and hermeneutics; he was following the
thought of the early rabbis. The rabbis of the first century probably were not interpreting the rule quite so stringently.

Sigal supports Daube's defense by observing how 1 Sam 21:2–6,
along with Lev 24:5–9, is useful to the formulation of the *kal
vehomer*.[112] Specifically, 1 Sam 21:2–6 parallels David and the
actions of Jesus' disciples, while Lev 24:5–9 clearly links the Sab-

---

108. Ibid., 134. Bornkamm, Barth, and Held also agree with the primary
authority of God's mercy as seen in verse 7 (*Tradition and Interpretation*, 83).

109. Cohn-Sherbok, *Rabbinic Perspectives*, 38–39.

110. Daube, *New Testament and Rabbinic Judaism*, 67–71.

111. Ibid.

112. Sigal, *Halakah of Jesus of Nazareth*, 128.

bath activities to the current situation. As I suggested above, Jesus does not have to be compared to the Temple at all. Sigal adeptly sees the real comparison between the concept of God's love for humans (*chesed*) and the cult (God's people). The Old Testament supports this, as Hos 6:6 ("I desire steadfast love and not sacrifice") indicates.[113] Thus, Cohn-Sherbok competently argues his case, but falls short in the end. Matthew in 12:1–8 clearly uses the *kal vehomer*. Matthew's comparison is supported by the authoritative words of the Torah. In closing, one must remember that Matthew did this while remaining under the umbrella of the Jewish halakah. Surely, the authors of the Gospel do nothing here to break any Jewish laws; in fact, they uphold them.

Conclusions Regarding the Sabbath

The preceding evidence indicates that the Sabbath has been superseded legally via the Matthean scribes' usage of Jewish exegetical principles. The authors cite Hos 6:6 to reinforce the message that mercy and love for the cult are greater than the laws.[114] The magnitude of this argument should not be minimized. The Sabbath itself was, and is, extremely important to Jews. To this day it remains one of the most sacred celebrations on the Jewish calendar. For one to make the case that *chesed* supersedes the Sabbath was a calculated, daring maneuver on the part of the authors of the Gospel.

In fact, some scholars have suggested that Matthew engaged in a typical form of first-century debate regarding the observation of the holiday.[115] As far back as the second century B.C.E., disputes regarding Sabbath rules and observance are alluded to (see *Jub.* 2:17–28). The Qumran community, as well as the later rabbis, carefully explicated their views on the matter, leading one to believe that Sabbath observance remained a topic open for discus-

---

113. Ibid., 133–34.
114. Meier, *Matthew*, 129–30.
115. Saldarini, *Matthew's Christian-Jewish Community*, 126–28.

sion.[116] For example, *m. Shabbat* 1:6 points to differences in opinion regarding Sabbath observance.[117] The authors of Matthew, as educated scribes, also wished to address the issue. Saldarini surmises, "Matthew argues the case for his interpretation of the Sabbath with great sophistication."[118] As Jewish scholars, they must have had strong opinions concerning Sabbath observance.

I have shown that the authors of the Matthean Gospel incorporated numerous Jewish exegetical techniques into the text. This signifies that the Matthean scribes remained faithful to the Jewish laws. There is no conclusive evidence that the Matthean community relaxes the Sabbath laws in any way. Through the use of masterful rabbinic hermeneutics, the Gospel authors uphold the halakah of the Torah. Redactions such as the insertion of ἐπεί-νασαν and the subtraction of the Markan "the sabbath was made for man, not man for the sabbath" reinforce the Gospel's promotion of Sabbath observance.

The Matthean Gospel and Additional Literary Techniques

Two rhetorical techniques are found frequently in the Matthean Gospel. They are the *inclusio* ("inclusion") and chiastic arrangement. Briefly, an inclusion may be defined as a key idea or phrase that is repeated at the beginning and the end of a scriptural passage.[119] Authors often used this technique to emphasize important concepts. Additional force was added by "bracketing off" crucial references and terms. In a chiasm, or chiastic arrangement,

---

116. See the *Covenant of Damascus* 10:14–11:18 and *m. Shabbat* 7:2, respectively.

117. See E. P. Sanders, *Jewish Law from Jesus to the Mishnah* (Philadelphia: Trinity Press International, 1990), 9. Specifically, the House of Shammai does not allow certain tasks to be done the day before the holiday unless they can be completed the same day. This includes the baking of flax, the dying of wool, and the casting of nets. Yet the House of Hillel permits these tasks to be done.

118. Saldarini, *Matthew's Christian-Jewish Community*, 128.

119. Richard Soulen, *Handbook of Biblical Criticism* (Atlanta: John Knox, 1976), 94.

sequences of parallel words or ideas are inverted.[120] A simplistic example might be: the dog [a] bites the man [b], so the man [b'] bites the dog [a']. There are many examples of greater complexity, but all follow a similar basic pattern.

Inclusion: Two Examples

Consider Matt 6:25-31 (from the Sermon on the Mount), in which Jesus is teaching about care and anxiety.[121] Notice especially the lines marked with the letters [a] and [b]:

Therefore I tell you, do not worry about your life, [a]
What you will eat or what you will drink, [b]
Or about your body, [a] what you will wear. [b]
Is not life more than food,
and the body more than clothing?
Look at the birds of the air:
they neither sow nor reap nor gather into barns,
and yet your heavenly Father feeds them.
Are you not of more value than they?
And can any of you by worrying add a single hour to your span
    of life?
And why do you worry about clothing? [a]
Consider the lilies of the field how they grow;
they neither toil nor spin
yet I tell you, even Solomon in all his glory was not clothed like one
    of these.
But if God so clothes the grass of the field,
which is alive today and tomorrow thrown into the oven,
will he not much more clothe you, you of little faith?
Therefore do not worry, saying, [a]
What will we eat? Or what will we drink? Or what will we wear? [b]

---

120. Ibid., 40–41.

121. Goulder, *Midrash and Lection in Matthew*, 86–87. The following example is taken from Goulder. I concur with his conclusions regarding the use of the inclusion here.

Beyond the noticeable poetic flow and rhythm of the stanza, one notices the positioning of the [a]'s and [b]'s within the discourse. Jesus repeats line [a] ("do not be anxious") of his speech at the beginning, middle, and end of the section. The [b] phrase, "what to wear or eat," is placed at the beginning and the end. Jesus accentuates salient concepts by repeating phrases and words. He brackets them off, allowing the reader to follow where his passages begin and end, while revealing what is important. Therefore, Matt 6:25–31 is a fine example of inclusion. As Goulder states, "Matthew's version ends with his favourite inclusion, the (a) and (b) lines being repeated."[122] The theme of the two-line repetition is prevalent throughout the Gospel (see also 12:41–42, for example).

This technique is also seen twice, after the Sermon on the Mount, in 8:1–3, in which Jesus cures the leper. I offer this example in Greek:

8:1 Καταβάντος δὲ αὐτοῦ ἀπὸ τοῦ ὄρους ἠκολούθησαν αὐτῷ ὄχλοι πολλοί. 2 καὶ ἰδοὺ λεπρὸς προσελθὼν προσεκύνει αὐτῷ λέγων· κύριε, ἐὰν θέλῃς δύνασαί με καθαρίσαι. 3 καὶ ἐκτείνας τὴν χεῖρα ἥψατο αὐτοῦ λέγων· θέλω, καθαρίσθητι· καὶ εὐθέως ἐκαθαρίσθη αὐτοῦ ἡ λέπρα.

Notice the expression ἠκολούθησαν αὐτῷ ὄχλοι πολλοί at the end of verse 1. In 4:25, preceding the sermon, the Greek text reads ἠκολούθησαν αὐτῷ ὄχλοι πολλοί. According to Davies and Allison, this identical phrasing of text, which conveniently borders the Sermon on the Mount, is an inclusion.[123] It appears that the scribes have intentionally bracketed the text in order to highlight the sermon's distinctiveness, while preparing the audience for the shift in themes.

The use of inclusion is unmistakable within the passage as well. In verses 2 and 3, Matthew employs inclusion to bracket off relevant stories from each other. Consider how the term λεπρός ("leper") neatly borders the little story of the leper's healing. Also,

---

122. Ibid., 87.
123. Davies and Allison, *Gospel according to Saint Matthew*, 2:9.

the authors of Matthew cleverly moved the noun λέπρα to the end of the sentence, after the verb, to bracket the key term off. As William Thompson states, "The narrative is beautiful in its simplicity. Matthew frames it in an inclusion. . . . The two sentences [vv. 2–3] are parallel in style and construction, and attention is drawn to the key-word *katharizein* which is repeated in the leper's request, Jesus' response and Matthew's description of the cure."[124]

Therefore, the Matthean scribes express their knowledge of literary techniques in at least four ways in this one verse. They begin the passage with an inclusion that allows the audience to turn its focus away from the sermon. Further, as Thompson points out, Matthew uses a *Stichwort* to attract attention to salient features. Often, keywords were inserted into a text and explained throughout other portions of the document. The *Stichwort* was an exegetical technique common in first-century Jewish literature. (This also shows that the authors may have been Jewish scribes.)[125] Subsequently, the authors formulate an inclusion through the usage of the word λεπρός. The scribes constructed the pericope in a proficient, uniform manner, meticulously arranging each word.

The most compelling instance of inclusion is found in three passages: 1:23; 18:20; and 28:20. Although I have not discussed the topic of Matthew's Christology at length, I wish to mention it briefly. A significant christological title in the Gospel is Jesus as the Divine Presence, or שכינה in Hebrew.[126] This Jewish title appears throughout Matthew's Gospel, especially in the above three passages. Confirmation of the term's Jewish derivation is in the Mishnah, which reads, "If two sit together and the words between them are of Torah, then the *Shekinah* is in their midst."[127] In Matthew's Gospel, the phraseology of the three passages is similar enough

---

124. William G. Thompson, *Matthew's Advice to a Divided Community: Mt 17,22–18,35* (Rome: Biblical Institute Press, 1970), 89. I think Thompson is correct regarding this passage. His analysis is provided here.

125. Cope, *Matthew*, 46.

126. W. Richard Stegner, "Breaking Away: The Conflict with Formative Judaism," *Biblical Research* 40 (1995): 18. For an interesting perspective regarding Matthew's Christology, see Stegner's entire article, 7–36.

127. *m. Avot* 3:6.

that it may serve as the largest example of inclusion in the entire text.[128]

The three passages, conveniently placed at the beginning, middle, and end of the Gospel, contain a single, primary message: Jesus remains with the Matthean community eternally as the new Divine Presence. Consider some excerpts from the three pericopes. The first passage discusses Jesus, and the last two are quotes from Jesus.

> 1:23 . . . and they shall name him Emmanuel, which means "God is with us."
>
> 18:20 . . . "For where two or three are gathered in my name, I am there among them."
>
> 28:20 . . . "And remember, I am with you always, to the end of the age."

First, these phrases and the phrase from the Mishnah are quite similar. Also, the authors of Matthew have marked off virtually the entire Gospel within the confines of one coherent unit of thought: Jesus is always with his community. Meier observes, "In Jesus, we find fulfilled the great promise of God to the patriarchs and prophets: 'I shall be with you.' It is Jesus, 'God-with-us' in person [as stated in Matt 1:23], who concludes Matthew's gospel by promising his church: 'Lo, I am with you always to the close of the age.'"[129]

One may ask whether the presence of Jesus was crucial enough to merit the use of such a large inclusion. The answer is yes. Although the passage numbers are different, the presence is a central theme. Thompson has stated, "Matthew highlights the theme of presence. He announces it at the beginning of his gospel (1,23), and includes it in the final commission to the disciples (28,20)."[130] The Matthean scribes present this information in the form of an inclusion that brackets the entire Gospel, while including Jewish terminology (not to mention a Jewish theme) in the process.

---

128. Stegner, "Breaking Away," 18.
129. Meier, *Matthew*, 8.
130. Thompson, *Matthew's Advice*, 198.

Therefore, Jesus' presence was vital to the Jewish Christian Matthean community. The Gospel would not continually emphasize Jesus as the Divine Presence without a significant purpose. The theme functions as a focus for the whole community gathering. As Rudolph Pesch states, "Der Bedingungssatz in Mt 18.20 bindet die Gegenwart des erhöhten Herrn an die Versammlung von wenigstens zweien oder dreien 'auf seinen Namen hin.'" ("The conditional clause in Mt 18.20 binds the presence of the risen Lord to the congregation where at least two or three 'are gathered in His name.'")[131] Likewise, Matthew has incorporated another Jewish principle into the Gospel. Davies and Allison state, "As in the Mishnah, so in Matthew."[132] The Matthean scribes again return to their Jewish roots. Moreover, they do so within the confines of a scrupulously created, uniform text.

Chiastic Arrangement in the Gospel: Matthew 18

The chiastic arrangement consists of a section of text arranged in an inverted structure. Matthew's Gospel contains many examples of this technique. I put forth a simple example, a portion of Greek text from Matt 18:8. Once again I diagram the section for easier recognition.

εἰσελθεῖν εἰς τὴν ζωὴν [a]
κυλλὸν ἢ χωλὸν [b]
ἢ δύο χεῖρας ἢ δύο πόδας ἔχοντα [b']
βληθῆναι εἰς τὸ πῦρ τὸ αἰώνιον [a']

The chiasm is formed through Matthew's usage of infinitive phrases and modifiers.[133] Note the similar infinitive form of the

---

131. Rudolph Pesch, "'Wo zwei oder drei versammelt sind auf meinen Namen hin . . .' (Mt 18.20): Zur Ekklesiologie eines Wortes Jesu," in *Studien zum Matthäusevangelium: Festschrift für Wilhelm Pesch* (ed. Ludger Schenke; Stuttgart: Verlag Katholisches Bibelwork, 1988), 240.

132. Davies and Allison, *Gospel according to Saint Matthew*, 2:790.

133. Thompson, *Matthew's Advice*, 115. I am following Thompson's reasoning here.

verbs in [a] and [a'] (εἰσελθεῖν and βληθῆναι). The modifiers in [b] and [b'] seem to sway the reader into concentrating on their starkly contrasting meanings.

A more recognizable, yet complex, example appears in 18:1–4.[134] Some of the material is borrowed from Mark 9:33–37, but Matthew has made significant changes. Here is a portion of the text:

μείζων ἐστὶν ἐν τῇ βασιλέα τῶν οὐρανῶν [a]
παιδίον [b]
μὴ . . . ὡς τὰ παιδία [b']
οὐ μὴ . . . εἰς τὴν βασιλείαν τῶν οὐρανῶν [a']
ὡς τὸ παιδίον τοῦτο [b'']
ἐστιν ὁ μείζων ἐν τῇ βασιλείᾳ τῶν οὐρανῶν [a'']

One notices first the striking similarity in word selection among these lines. As Thompson points out, the keywords are repeated in an "elaborate" pattern.[135] Jesus is responding to a question regarding who is the greatest in the kingdom of heaven. He repeats many of the same words in his answer [a''] as he does in the question [a].[136]

Notice also how central the term παιδίον ("child") is to the structure of the passage, arranged in chiastic order. Why is this done? Often, one associates children with innocence. Yet Davies and Allison believe that the term is placed in the foreground to illustrate for the reader the status of the child in the community. Children have no privileged status, and this message of equality is what Matthew wishes to show the audience.[137] In other words, Jesus is teaching a lesson about hubris and humility to his disciples. All people must be treated as equals. Matthew, emphasizing this concept, organizes the text in a neat, chiastic arrangement.

Numerous other examples of chiastic arrangement appear in the Gospel.[138] The particular distribution of keywords within passages

---

134. Ibid., 80. Again, I owe this example to Thompson.
135. Ibid.
136. Ibid., 81.
137. Davies and Allison, *Gospel according to Saint Matthew*, 2:757.
138. Thompson, *Matthew's Advice*, 162. Thompson provides many other examples. See Matthew 18:9, 21, 35; 19:30; 20:16; etc.

illuminates meaningful themes. In the current example, Matt 18:1–4, the authors illustrate for the audience the importance of the kingdom of heaven.[139] Furthermore, much of what I have demonstrated above is unique to this Gospel. Only the Matthean scribes use many of these rhetorical techniques. This is true even in passages borrowed from Mark or Q. Again, considering 18:1–4, Thompson notes, "At first sight the discussion about greatest in the kingdom of heaven seems to resemble the parallel passages in Mark (9,33–37) and Luke (9,46–48). But a more careful comparison reveals that the literary contacts are limited and the differences are far from negligible."[140] Once again the Matthean scribes have proven their prowess.

Unity, Irony, Allusion, Allegory, and Multiple Levels of Meaning

Several literary and rhetorical techniques are pervasive in the Gospel. In a portion of Matt 18:15–20, one can identify some unique characteristics:

18:15a . . . μεταξὺ σοῦ καὶ αὐτοῦ μόνου ("between you and him alone")

18:16a . . . μετὰ σοῦ ἔτι ἕνα ἢ δύο . . . δύο μαρτύρων ἢ τριῶν ("with you one or two others") ("two or three witnesses")

18:19 . . . δύο . . . ἐξ ὑμῶν ἐπὶ τῆς γῆς ("two . . . of you on the earth")

18:20 . . . δύο ἢ τρεῖς ("two or three")

Observe Matthew's intentional repetition of key words and phrases. Within 18:15–20, Thompson found four similar phrases repeated, as shown above.[141] The technique helps to establish a literary unity within the text. As Pesch states, "Durch wichtige Stichworte sind

---

139. Ibid., 81. I agree with Thompson. The kingdom of heaven was certainly at the forefront of Jewish thought in the first century.

140. Ibid., 82.

141. Ibid., 199.

die beiden in Mt 18, 19–20 überlieferten Sprüche Jesu mit den
Worten im voraufgehenden Kontext verbunden" ("By means of
important keywords both sayings of Jesus transmitted in Mt 18,
19–20 are bound to the words in the preceding context").[142]

One finds other examples of repeated words within this passage.
For example, μὴ ἀκούσῃ, παρακούσῃ, and παρακούσῃ are all found
in the pericope in verses 16, 17a, and 17b.[143] Thompson believes
this technique "connects" the various sayings of Jesus.[144] Also, rep-
etitions may be used to magnify key points, such as the ὁ ἀδελφός
σου and τὸν ἀδελφόν σου of 15a and 15b. (The emphasis here is on
brotherhood.) These examples point to Matthew's desire for a
flowing, coherent Gospel, both pleasing and effective.

The Use of Irony in the Gospel

Although the Matthean scribes incorporate irony in many ways, I
concentrate only on the usage of irony as it pertains to the political
leaders of the Gospel. Irony may be thought of as a "two-leveled"
story in which the surface level (the victim's situation) contrasts
with the upper level (the readers' observations).[145] As Dorothy Jean
Weaver discerns, "Between the lower and the upper levels there is,
secondly, an 'opposition' consisting of 'contradiction, incongruity,
or incompatibility,' such that 'what is said may be contradicted by
what is meant' or 'what the victim thinks may be contradicted by
what the observer knows.'"[146] Ironies can deal with many subjects,
including people, beliefs, attitudes, religions, and so on.[147]

---

142. Pesch, "Wo zwei oder drei," 233.

143. Thompson, *Matthew's Advice*, 199.

144. Ibid. See also the next example.

145. Dorothy Jean Weaver, "Power and Powerless: Matthew's Use of Irony in
the Portrayal of Political Leaders," in *Teasures New and Old: Recent Contributions to Matthean Studies* (ed. David R. Bauer and Mark Allan Powell; Atlanta:
Scholars Press, 1996), 180.

146. Ibid. Weaver here is quoting from another source. See D. C. Muecke, *The
Compass of Irony* (London: Methuen, 1969), 19–20.

147. Muecke, *Compass of Irony*, 34.

In Matthew's Gospel, irony appears in the stories of the political leaders. For instance, Herod the king is mentioned first in 2:1.[148] On the surface, Matthew appears to make only a historical reference marking the time of Jesus' birth. But there is more to the story. The Gospel continues to mention the power of King Herod; he "summons" the wise men (2:7), sends them away (2:8), and "sent and killed all the male children" (2:16, RSV). The "king" has the power of life and death over his subjects. Herod does not merely have authority, though; he is evil as well. The authors of Matthew are also careful to use the word "king" often when referencing Herod (see 2:3, 9).

Matthew provides this seemingly harsh portrait of Herod for a specific reason. It shows the irony implicit in the persona of Jesus. Like Herod, Jesus is a "king" as well (2:2).[149] He is the Messiah (2:4), shepherds the people of Israel (2:6), and is the son of divinity (2:15). In contrast to Herod, though, Jesus is presented in a different light; he is a "child" ($\pi\alpha\iota\delta\iota\sigma\nu$). The term is used several times by Matthew within chapter 2 alone.

Why do the Matthean scribes do this? To begin, a child represents meekness, dependence, and innocence. This contrasts sharply with Herod's persona. Weaver states, "As the narrator [Matthew] portrays him on the lower level of the narrative, then, Jesus is a character who appears as powerless as Herod appears powerful. . . . He is depicted rather as a helpless, dependent 'child' who is acted upon, whether for good or evil, by all the other characters in the story."[150]

Matthew, then, is in reality setting Herod up for a great fall.[151] Already in 2:2 the author is emphasizing who the true "king" really is: Jesus. Furthermore, Herod becomes "terrified" or "troubled" when he hears that Jesus has been born (2:3). He feels "tricked" by the magi (2:16), although he himself had attempted to

---

148. Weaver, "Power and Powerless," 182–87. Unless otherwise noted, I am following Weaver in this example.
149. Ibid.
150. Ibid., 185.
151. Ibid., 186–87.

trick them (2:7). This is where the reader truly begins to see the irony. Although he has tried to trick and deceive others, Herod himself will be fooled.

Herod consistently fails to accomplish his goal of killing Jesus, although only the reader is privy to the reasons why. Obviously Herod does not know that the angel of God is helping Joseph. Herod is rendered "powerless" to stop Jesus. The ultimate irony, of course, is that Herod dies (2:19) and Jesus is able to go to Galilee as a healthy child (2:22). Therefore the reader sees Herod is not the true "king"; Jesus is. The Matthean scribes use irony concerning other leaders, such as Herod the tetrarch (14:1–2) and Pilate (chs. 27–28). Irony, then, serves as another means by which the Gospel illustrates literary excellence.

Matthew and Allusion

An allusion may be thought of as a reference to another text meant to spark similar themes in the mind of the audience. For example, consider the usage of Jer 31:15. Matthew 2:18 reads, "A voice was heard in Ramah, wailing and loud lamentation, Rachel weeping for her children; she refused to be consoled, because they are no more." This citation formula, concerning the slaughtering of the innocents, is used more than just to console the audience. It is placed at this point in the story to remind the readers of Moses and the exodus from Egypt.[152]

The Jesus/Moses allusion is quite prominent in this portion of the Gospel. Brown has provided a list of at least five allusions within chapter 2 alone.[153] First, both babies (Moses and Jesus) depart due to the threat of death from the king (Pharaoh and Herod). Second, the king demands the murder of all male infants. Josephus also records an account of this story.[154] Third, both kings die. Fourth, both children are told by God to return to their lands.

---

152. Richard J. Erickson, "Divine Injustice? Matthew's Narrative Strategy and the Slaughter of the Innocents (Matthew 2.13–23)," *Journal for the Study of the New Testament* 64 (1996): 13.

153. Brown, *Birth of the Messiah*, 113.

154. See Josephus, *Jewish Antiquities* 2:9:1–4.

Finally, each child returns home. Also, notice the emphasis on Egypt. Although Moses leaves Egypt and Joseph enters it, the significance of the country is worth noting.[155] Howard points out this Egyptian connection and believes that the Gospel intentionally provided the link between the Messiah (Jesus) and Israel.[156]

The allusion is quite clear. Exodus 2:15 in the LXX reads in part, δὲ Φαραω τὸ ῥῆμα τοῦτο, καὶ ἐζήτει ἀνελαῖν Μωυσῆν. Now compare this to Matt 2:13: μέλλει γὰρ Ἡρῴδης ζητεῖν τὸ παιδίον τοῦ ἀπολέσαι αὐτό. The texts are similar. Both plots involve rulers who wish to harm a child. Also, each story uses the same verb, "search." Finally, although not entirely revealed in these brief passages, both stories speak of the main character "departing" via the Greek word ἀνεχώρησεν.[157] This word appears in Matt 2:14 and Exod 2:15. These allusions are purposely inserted into the text. The authors use the technique to draw a typological inference between Moses and Jesus. Why is this done?

The Matthean scribes place "hints" in the text to signal the reader. The audience, as well as the authors of the Gospel, was for the most part a learned community. They would have been familiar with the Old Testament texts. Therefore, key words from the Old Testament were inserted into the Gospel to remind the readers of the Moses/Jesus typology. Both characters were vital to the Jewish Christians. For example, the Greek verb ἀναχωρέω ("goes away") is used in the LXX as well as the Gospel. Erickson remarks how the verb is used several times in the Gospel (2:13, 14; 12:15; 14:13; 15:21) in a similar manner to Exod 2:15.[158] This would remind the Matthean community of their continued link to Moses and the Torah. Hence, as argued in previous chapters, this group remained loyal Jews.

In addition to the individual Moses/Jesus typology, there is a collective typology as well. The authors seem to identify Jesus with the people of Israel. In fact, it is possible that the "son" referred to in

---

155. Erickson, "Divine Injustice?" 14.
156. Howard, "Use of Hosea 11:1," 321.
157. Erickson, "Divine Injustice?" 15.
158. Ibid., 17–18.

Matt 2:15 is in reality the people of Israel, as is indicated in Hos 11:1.[159] Howard argues that Matthew sought to link the history of Israel with the history of the Messiah.[160] The events of Israel parallel the life of the Messiah. Further support for the Jesus/Israel typology is found in Matt 2:18, in which the authors are presumably using Jer 31:15.[161] Why have the authors of Matthew done this?

The answer may be linked to a single word: "return." What is striking about Jesus is that although he "departs," he does something unusual: he returns.[162] As seen in Jer 31:16–17, although Rachel cries for her children, she is consoled by the fact that they will return. In Matt 2:19–23, Jesus "returns" to his land from Egypt. He already, as a child, is fulfilling Old Testament prophecies. Matthew 2:23 itself may be an allusion to Isa 11:1, in which the Hebrew term נצר, meaning "branch," or "stump," refers to a descendant of Jesse who will come as a "signal" to the people.

The phrase "branch of Jesse" refers to the messianic line of David, a prominent theme in the Matthean genealogy.[163] The Matthean scribes, following the MT, had two word choices if they wished to make a reference to the "stump," or to Messiah from the Davidic line: צמח or נצר.[164] The former term occurs at least three times in the MT to refer to the Davidic Messiah (Isa 4:2; Jer 23:5; 33:15). The latter term, however, is never used in the Old Testament. Curiously, Matt 2:23 contains the similar-sounding Greek word Ναζωραῖος to refer to Jesus. Why don't the authors choose צמח?

Gundry believes that Matthew selects Ναζωραῖος for at least two reasons. First, the obscurity of Nazareth fits with the theme of Jesus' rejection in Matthew (see Isa 14:19). Matthew, therefore, may have preferred the term.[165] Second, and more important to

---

159. Ibid., 18.
160. Howard, "Use of Hosea 11:1," 321.
161. Davies and Allison, *Gospel according to Saint Matthew*, 1:282.
162. Erickson, "Divine Injustice?" 19.
163. Davies and Allison, *Gospel according to Saint Matthew*, 1:277.
164. Robert H. Gundry, *Matthew: A Commentary on His Literary and Theological Art* (Grand Rapids: Eerdmans, 1982), 40.
165. Ibid.

this discussion, both terms sound quite similar. It is possible that Matthew's authors have placed Ναζωραῖος into the text as a signal for the audience. Of course, the authors of Matthew were writing in Greek, not Hebrew. Still, Gundry feels that Matthew incorporates an interlinguistic technique to flag his audience. I agree with his assertion. Matthew wishes to remind the readers of the Gospel of the hopeful passage from Isa 11 to show that Jesus is the fulfillment of Old Testament prophecy.[166] The authors use a play on words to alert their audience to the point.[167]

One final explanation for the use of Ναζωραῖος in 2:23 is also linked to the Old Testament. Some scholars claim that the term is borrowed from Judg 13:5,[168] which reads, ". . . for you shall conceive and bear a son. No razor is to come on his head, for the boy shall be a nazirite [in Greek, Ναζωραῖον] to God from birth. It is he who shall begin to deliver Israel from the hand of the Philistines." The immediate similarities to Jesus are noteworthy. Beyond the similar Greek terms, there is, of course, the reference to deliverance. According to this theory—and most relevant to this discussion—Matthew is utilizing the technique of the allusion.[169] The birth narratives of Jesus and Samson form the connection. Their stories are linked together.

Although this explanation varies slightly from Gundry's, it is tempting to accept this point of view. There are problems, however.[170] Linguistic difficulties cloud the theory. Matthew's plural usage of τῶν προφητῶν suggests a general reference instead of a specific citation of Judg 13:5. Second, the similar life situations found so often in the formula citations are absent here. Samson and Jesus have nothing in common in this example. Third, that Samson is to

---

166. Erickson, "Divine Injustice?" 20–21, discusses this in more detail. Davies and Allison also agree; see *Gospel according to Saint Matthew*, 1:276–78. See also Donald A. Hagner, *Matthew 1–13* (Dallas: Word Books, 1993), 41–42.

167. Gundry, *Matthew*, 40.

168. Goerge M. Soares Prabhu, *The Formula Quotations in the Infancy Narrative of Matthew: An Enquiry into the Tradition History of Mt 1–2* (Rome: Biblical Institute Press, 1976), 205–7.

169. Ibid., 205.

170. Ibid., 206–7. In fairness to Prabhu, he openly presents the following difficulties regarding his theory. Yet the theory remains compelling.

be a "nazir" has no real bearing on the fact that Jesus is from "Nazareth." Finally, this example would probably be useful to an audience well-versed in Greek; there is no Hebrew linguistic link. Therefore, the hypothesis is suggestive, but falls short due to a lack of evidence. In any event, one crucial point surfaces as a result of this theory: it again illustrates a deliberate attempt to incorporate an exegetical technique, while at the same time signaling the audience. Is it possible that the Matthean scribes were actually testing the community members? This indeed may be the case. Considering the level of education among the Jewish population in general (higher than most others), this is plausible.

In fact, Davies and Allison feel that the authors of Matthew have placed other clues in various locations throughout the text. For example, there is evidence of a Hebrew *gematria* (numerical analysis of letters) in chapter 1, as well as a Hebrew play on words in 1:21.[171] First, consider the usage of the *gematria*.[172] The Hebrew name of דוד (David) is often linked to the Jewish messianic line. Matthew's genealogy in chapter 1, taken in part from 1 Corinthians (see 1:34; 2:1–15), is broken down into clusters of fourteen generations. The Matthean scribes exclude various names to maintain this arrangement. Why have they done this? The answer may be contained in the Hebrew name דוד. When the letters are converted into numerals (as is the case with Hebrew), they add up to fourteen (4 + 6 + 4). Matthew intentionally did this to portray Jesus as the true fulfillment of messianic hope. This is another example of linguistic mastery.

The second example comes from Matt 1:21.[173] Matthew apparently is quoting Ps 130:8 in this verse. The Psalm reads, "It is he who will *redeem* Israel from all its iniquities." Matthew displays for the reader another play on words from Hebrew and Greek. Consider the line pronouncing the name of Jesus: "and you shall call his name Jesus, for he will *save* his people from their sins"

---

171. Davies and Allison, *Gospel according to Saint Matthew*, 1:278–79.

172. Gundry, *Matthew*, 18–19. My example of the *gematria* is taken from here. See also Davies and Allison, *Gospel according to Saint Matthew*, 1:278–79.

173. Gundry, *Matthew*, 22–23.

(RSV). Jesus, of course, is now the new "king," and the authors of the Gospel, using Ps 130, wished to stress this point. Yet the Matthean scribes insert the term "save" instead of the word "redeem." Why is this done?

According to the Old Testament, a king is one who indeed "saves" his people (see 1 Sam 10:25–27; 2 Sam 5:1–3).[174] Matthew's insertion of "save" maintains the theme of salvation. In fact, the name "Jesus" itself is intriguing, since its Greek translation from the Hebrew יהושע (Joshua) means "Yahweh is salvation."[175] Matthew replaces "redeem" with "save" in order to keep the theme alive throughout the text. It is a common Matthean tactic to substitute the Greek verb σώζω for other terms; in fact, it is repeated several more times in the Gospel.[176] Gundry states, "Matthew has assimilated the tradition to OT phraseology in order to show fulfillment."[177] In this case, the Matthean scribes take the theme of salvation and apply it to Jesus. He saves the people from their sins, as 1:21 states. In other words, the Gospel authors recognize the meaning and relevance of Hebrew terms and incorporate them into Greek to show how Jesus represents the fulfillment of Old Testament prophecy.

This evidence supports the theory that the Gospel contains an unmistakable Semitic texture. Numerous times the authors manipulate the MT in order to suit their purposes. C. F. D. Moule reenforces this thought by providing additional examples. For instance, he points to unique Matthean passages such as 7:28; 11:1; 13:53; 19:1; and 26:1, all of which begin with the characteristically Semitic phrase καὶ ἐγένετο ὅτε.[178] The Gospel remains true to its Jewish background.

---

174. Ibid., 23.

175. Gundry recognizes Noth's invaluable work here. See M. Noth, *Die israelitischen Personennamen* (Stuttgart: Kohlhammer, 1978), 106–7.

176. Gundry, *Matthew*, 23.

177. Ibid.

178. C. F. D. Moule, *The Birth of the New Testament* (Black's New Testament Commentaries 1; London: Adam & Charles Black, 1962), 217. Such phrases are to be distinguished from those "typically Greek" phrases. Moule provides other examples as well. See pp. 215–19.

The Audience of Matthew:
A Learned Group

For the Matthean scribes to have used all of these rhetorical techniques successfully, one thing must be true. The audience must have been educated enough to have understood the allusions, ironies, and other wordplays. By "educated," I mean that the scribes expected the community to be literate in Greek as well as Hebrew.[179] Therefore, members of the Matthean community would have been able to recognize intentional rhetorical devices. One cannot make the simple assumption that the community understood only Greek, especially if the group was located in Galilee, where Hebrew was the liturgical language. Hebrew would have been read in the synagogue on a regular basis. Davies and Allison state, "So Matthew was not above scattering items in the Greek text whose deeper meaning could only be appreciated by those with a knowledge of Hebrew. Indeed, it might even be that Matthew found authorial delight in hiding 'bonus points' for those willing and able to look a little beneath the gospel's surface."[180]

Consider those instances where Matthew may have intentionally omitted pieces of information. Did the Matthean scribes believe that their audience was so knowledgeable that they could skip certain introductory phrases without diminishing the importance of the point? The answer is yes. It is likely that the Matthean scribes' confidence in their own community's literary abilities led them to believe they could omit certain obligatory introductory phrases.

The citation formulas taken from the Old Testament are perfect examples of such instances. For instance, Matt 4:14 states, "that what was spoken by the prophet Isaiah might be fulfilled." Yet in 1:22 the text reads, "All this took place to fulfill what the Lord had spoken by the *prophet*" (RSV). Notice the obvious omission of the prophet's name in the second phrase. Why do the Matthean scribes do this? The Gospel authors probably felt no need to cite the name

---

179. Hagner, *Matthew 1–13*, 41–42. I agree with Hagner on this point.
180. Davies and Allison, *Gospel according to Saint Matthew*, 1:279.

of every prophet that was mentioned. The educated Matthean community would automatically recognize the citation. A prophet such as Isaiah certainly would invoke immediate audience recognition. Therefore, I conclude that the audience must have been literate as well.

Conclusion

In this chapter I discussed how Matthew's Gospel uses the Old Testament. Through textual analysis, it became clear that the Matthean scribes incorporated a number of versions of the Old Testament, including the LXX and the MT, as well as the Targums, into the Gospel. Krister Stendahl's groundbreaking work was instrumental. Regardless of whether one accepts all of his conclusions, he proves one vital point: the Matthean scribes carefully pieced together the Gospel with great precision. Old Testament texts are methodically interpreted to show how Jesus fulfilled Jewish prophecy. The Matthean treatment of the Old Testament may even be thought of as a midrash itself. Philip Alexander asserts, "Midrash was meant to stand beside Scripture: it left Scripture intact."[181] The scribes' usage of the Old Testament left the Torah intact; they remained true to Judaism.

The second portion of this chapter dealt with Matthew's usage of Jewish exegetical techniques. In particular, I examined the Gospel's incorporation of the *binyan av* and *kal vehomer*. Once again, the Matthean scribes proved their abilities by artfully using these techniques. Additionally, I showed how the Gospel upheld the authority of the Jewish halakah, especially pertaining to Sabbath and divorce laws. The authors of Matthew, in fact, appeared to enter into Jewish debates surrounding interpretation of the halakah.

---

181. Philip S. Alexander, "Midrash and the Gospels," in *Synoptic Studies: The Ampleforth Conferences of 1982 and 1983* (ed. C. M. Tuckett; Journal for the Study of the New Testament Supplement Series 7; Sheffield: JSOT Press, 1984), 13.

The last portion of the chapter discussed the incorporation of other literary and rhetorical devices. Some of the techniques cited were inclusion, allusion, allegory, *gematria*, typology, as well as plays on words. These examples further illustrate scribal ability. Although much of the Matthean material was based upon the earlier Gospel of Mark, this does not negate my argument. Alexander notes:

> Are we to suppose, then, that Matthew wanted his Gospel to be read alongside Mark? Surely not. It is much more likely that he aimed to replace Mark. . . . He has taken over into his own text whatever he thought was "good" and "useful," and added to it his own "improvements," but he has woven together his Markan and non-Markan materials so smoothly that it is only by diligent use of a . . . detailed comparison with the original Mark, that the Matthean plusses can be separated from the basic Markan source.[182]

The Matthean scribes showed themselves to be fine editors. In this chapter I argued, then, that learned Jewish scribes wrote this Gospel. They did not merely use numerous literary and rhetorical techniques, but intentionally inserted them into the text as "signals" or "markers" for the community. It is plausible that the Matthean audience was learned and familiar with Hebrew and Greek texts. Otherwise, there was no reason to display signal words so prominently throughout the Gospel. The citation formulas provide support for this argument. The Jewish Christian audience must have been quite familiar with the words of the prophets. On the strength of this evidence, therefore, I adduced that the Matthean community also was a learned group.

The Gospel exhibits an "accomplished Greek" style.[183] In addition, the community was familiar with the Torah and sought to uphold its laws. This includes the written and the oral Torah. Goulder supports this assertion: "No distinction is drawn between the written law and the oral. . . . All the Oral Torah delivered by the Pharisaic scribes comes from Moses' throne, and is valid."[184]

---

182. Alexander, "Midrash and the Gospels," 13.
183. Moule, *Birth of the New Testament*, 217.
184. Goulder, *Midrash and Lection in Matthew*, 16.

This remains true in spite of the emphasis upon Jesus as the fulfillment of Jewish prophecy. As Davies points out, "[D]espite his sense of the didactic significance of Jesus, the Messiah, Matthew, nevertheless, remains sensitive to the niceties of the expectations of Judaism."[185] Sigal even makes the case that Jesus himself is portrayed as a "proto-rabbi" in the Gospel.[186] Although I may not be prepared to go that far, I conclude that the Matthean scribes were thoroughly competent in the halakah as well as in the application of Jewish forms of argumentation and reasoning.

---

185. Davies, *Setting of the Sermon on the Mount*, 190.
186. Sigal, *Halakah of Jesus of Nazareth*, 159.

6

Conclusions

BEFORE SUMMARIZING, I RETURN TO ONE OF THE GOALS
mentioned in the introduction. As noted there, I have attempted to
provide a survey of contemporary Matthean scholarship. Therefore, I tried to incorporate diverse points of view. For example,
whenever possible, I used the latest strands of archaeological evidence, since this field has yielded much relevant data pertinent to
the study of ancient Judaism and Christianity. Again, I realize that
some fine sources may have been omitted due to space constraints,
and I apologize for any blatant errors in this regard.

Matthew: A Jewish Christian Community

The first major premise concerned the Jewish nature of the
Matthean community. The authors of the Matthean Gospel and
the corresponding community were conservative Jewish Christians
who remained loyal to the Torah. This is evident. I proved, for
instance, that the Gospel used a number of Jewish exegetical techniques. These techniques not only required literate authors but
scribes well-schooled in Jewish methods of argumentation. Only a
Jewish scribe could have used techniques such as the *kal vehomer*
and the *binyan av* so adeptly. The authors of the Gospel also
engaged the MT and the LXX in a skillful manner, which further
illustrated their knowledge regarding the laws of the Torah.

I also asserted that when they used Jewish exegetical techniques, the scribes presented a Jesus who upholds the Jewish laws. This contrasts with scholars who believe that the Gospel seeks to do away with the Torah. Passages such as Matt 5:17, 32; 12:1–8; and 19:9 were cited as evidence. There is no place in the Gospel where the scribes specifically abrogate the Torah. As 5:17–20 shows, Matthew's Gospel remains true to the Torah.

The Jewish background of the Gospel becomes more apparent when one examines the community's historical situation. At the end of the first century, formative Judaism was engaged in debates with Jewish Christians concerning the nature and scope of the halakah. Judging by the authors' interpretation of the legal code, it is clear that they stated their views regarding Jewish law. In other words, the scribes were concerned with how the Torah was observed, especially following the destruction of the Temple in Jerusalem. An example of this debate is Matt 12:1–8, in which Jesus engages in a dialogue regarding Sabbath observance. Here, in contrast to many other scholars, I argued that Jesus was in no way attempting to do away with the Jewish laws concerning the holiday. In reality, Jesus was arguing in a Jewish manner that hunger itself may allow one to "pluck" on the Sabbath legally. His disciples were not violating the Sabbath. They maintained the sanctity of the holiday by taking only what they needed to fend off their hunger. And recall that Matthew's Gospel inserts "because they were hungry" into the text. Jesus, again, uses the Old Testament in order to prove his point. Other examples from the text illustrated the community's loyalty to the Torah.

The Location of the Matthean Community

A second major conclusion dealt with the location of the Matthean community. I argued that the Matthean Gospel originated from a major city. Money in the ancient world flowed to the cities, and for a Gospel the magnitude of Matthew's to be produced, it is logical to place the community in an urban environment. The majority of scholars agree on this point. Yet I disagreed with many scholars' selection of the Syrian city of Antioch.

One of the main arguments for Antioch is based upon tradition. In other words, many scholars have concurred with their predecessors by stating that the Gospel originated from this city. A number of facts dispute this theory. For instance, the population in Antioch was Greek-speaking and contained a mixed population of Jews and Gentiles. This factor has often been cited as a prerequisite for the Gospel's authorship there. Yet, as evidence indicates, the city of Sepphoris also contained a Jewish population that was familiar with the Greek language. I also refuted other supposed reasons why the Gospel had to be written in Antioch, such as the fact that Peter was active there.

In contrast, I argued that Matthew's Gospel originated from a major city in Galilee, probably Sepphoris. Historically, this location is more plausible than Antioch. The Matthean community, judging by the contents of the Gospel, was in conflict with a nearby established, authoritative Jewish community. Sepphoris contained such a population. Ancient rabbinic texts were justified as legitimate sources for the purposes of this study. These texts indicate that many rabbis were active in Galilee and in Sepphoris at the same time as the Matthean community. Although texts such as the Mishnah also mention Syria, they do so more sparingly when compared to Galilee. This led to the conclusion that a major city in Galilee, such as Sepphoris, was the logical choice. Sepphoris was a Jewish, aristocratic city with many wealthy inhabitants. This is the same type of population that would have been in conflict with the group of Jewish Christians associated with the Gospel. In sum, modern scholarship is replacing traditional hypotheses that place the community in Syria.

The Wealth of the Matthean Community

Since I located Matthew's community in Sepphoris, it followed that the group itself was affluent. Sepphoris engaged in many economic activities, as recent archaeological evidence proves. The city was even granted the authority to mint its own coins, and the Matthean Gospel contains many references to coinage, especially those of higher denominations. Matthew's alteration or omission of many passages pertaining to the poor led me to hypothesize that like the residents of Sepphoris, Matthew's own community was wealthy.

Hence, I concluded that the Matthean community was affluent. This was important to another main hypothesis—the level of literacy of the group—in two ways. First, since only the wealthy had access to educational materials and teachers, the argument for literacy would be strengthened if the Matthean congregation were financially independent. Second, a wealthy community would have had the means to distribute the texts and to transport them to the various markets of the region. It was possible for books to be distributed quite liberally throughout the ancient world. The Gospel was known soon after its completion, having been mentioned by ancient writers as early as the second century.

Many other factors led to the conclusion that the Matthean community was wealthy. As alluded to above, Galilee was a hub of economic activity, with many agricultural and commercial pursuits. Archaeological evidence bears this out. Excavations have unearthed a large amount of pottery and other cookware items produced in the region. Also, non-Galilean coinage has been found throughout Galilee, suggesting a large amount of contact with neighboring regions.

Textual evidence supports the argument for a wealthy Galilean Gospel community. The Mishnah mentions Galilean manufacturing and trade. The Gospel refers to only large denominations of coinage. For example, only Matthew contains a story discussing a king who is owed ten thousand talents—a huge amount (see 18:23). The Matthean Gospel even mentions two forms of currency not found anywhere else in the New Testament. Small denominations are omitted from the text. Taxation did not seem to be a problem for the community members, and Jesus does not object to the payment of taxes. This is unusual, considering how unpopular such taxes were.

Other textual evidence confirms my hypothesis. For example, the authors of Matthew insert words like "rich" into the text, as in 19:23. Not surprisingly, then, they delete words like "poor" and "begging." The story of the wedding feast (22:9) is changed by the scribes, who remove the words "poor" and "blind" from the their version of the Markan story. Businessmen, homeowners, and landowners are also mentioned in the Gospel, suggesting an affinity for business ventures, in which the community members were probably involved. Considering the abundance of evidence, I concluded that the Matthean community was wealthy.

The Crux of the Debate:
Matthew as a Learned Community

Ultimately, I concluded that the authors of Matthew as well as the corresponding community members were an educated and learned group. The introduction listed some problems associated with a study of education and literacy in the ancient world. Hence, I attempted to approach the topic from a sociohistorical and literary perspective. These two methodologies allowed for a thorough examination of the Gospel.

First, I concluded that the authors of the Gospel were learned Jewish scribes. Old Testament references from three languages appear in the Gospel. Also, the authors of the text used a number of literary and exegetical techniques. The authors, throughout Matthew, skillfully manipulated the text, proving their prowess as Jewish scholars. I provided several examples of these scribal techniques. In particular, I showed how the scribes incorporated the Jewish techniques of the *kal vehomer* and the *binyan av* into the text. Only literate scholars could use such erudite techniques. In addition, the authors also used allusions, irony, chiastic arrangement, wordplay, and other literary devices.

Finally, I discussed the literacy of the community members. Even if one could prove that the authors of the Gospel were educated, does it necessarily follow that the members of the Matthean community were educated as well? I believe it does, for a number of reasons. First, the Jewish community emphasized education more than the general Roman population. The Matthean community was Jewish Christian. It would follow that the Gospel community placed more emphasis on education, especially Jewish education. This would have led to a high literacy rate among its members.

In the end, one other point supported the theory that the Matthean community members must have been literate. This can be stated in one simple question: why would the Matthean scribes incorporate so many Jewish exegetical techniques (and numerous other rhetorical techniques) if their own audience were not educated enough to understand them? In other words, why carefully edit a text that no one could comprehend? The authors of the Gospel must have been confident regarding the ability of their community to understand the plethora of literary techniques contained in the text.

I conclude, then, that the Matthean scribes and their community members were learned. They certainly exceeded traditional literacy levels of the time. The Gospel confirms this, if one examines the text carefully. I have demonstrated the scribes' careful arguments concerning the validity of the Torah. Both the leaders as well as the members of the community were still studying and following the Jewish laws. Hence, the authors of the Gospel interspersed Torah instruction with skillful textual editing, while remaining confident in their community's ability to benefit from these teachings. Therefore, both groups were learned.

Works Cited

Adan-Bayewitz, David. *Common Pottery in Roman Galilee: A Study of Local Trade*. Ramat-Gan, Israel: Bar-Ilan University Press, 1993.

Alexander, Loveday. "Ancient Book Production and the Gospels." Pages 71–111 in *The Gospels for All Christians: Rethinking the Gospel Audiences*. Edited by Richard Bauckham. Grand Rapids: Eerdmans, 1998.

Alexander, Philip S. "Midrash and the Gospels." Pages 1–18 in *Synoptic Studies: The Ampleforth Conferences of 1982 and 1983*. Edited by C. M. Tuckett. Journal for the Study of the New Testament. Sheffield: JSOT Press, 1984.

Allen, W. C. *The Gospel according to St. Matthew*. Edinburgh: T&T Clark International, 1912.

Allison, Dale C., Jr. "Two Notes on a Key Text: Matthew 11:25–30." *Journal of Theological Studies*, n.s., 39 (1988): 477–85.

Anderson, Janice Capel. *Matthew's Narrative Web Over, and Over, and Over Again*. Journal for the Study of the New Testatment Supplement Series 91. Sheffield: Sheffield Academic Press, 1994.

Anson, Peter F. *Christ and the Sailor: A Study of the Maritime Incidents in the New Testament*. Fresno, Calif.: Academy Library Guild, 1954.

Applebaum, Shimon. "Economic Life in Palestine." Pages 631–700 in *The Jewish People in the First Century*. Vol. 2. Edited by Samuel Safrai and M. Stern. Philadelphia: Fortress, 1976.

Banks, Robert. *Jesus and the Law in the Synoptic Tradition*. Society for New Testament Studies Monograph Series 28. London: Cambridge University Press, 1975.

Batey, Richard A. *Jesus and the Forgotten City*. Grand Rapids: Baker, 1991.

Bauckham, Richard. "For Whom Were Gospels Written?" Pages 9–48 in *The Gospels for All Christians: Rethinking the Gospel Audiences*. Edited by Richard Bauckham. Grand Rapids: Eerdmans, 1998.

——, ed. *The Gospels for All Christians: Rethinking the Gospel Audiences*. Grand Rapids: Eerdmans, 1998.

Bockmuehl, Markus. *Jewish Law in Gentile Churches*. Grand Rapids: Baker, 2000.

——. "Matthew 5:32; 19:9 in the Light of Pre-Rabbinic Halakah." *New Testament Studies* 35 (1989): 291–95.

Bonner, Stanley F. *Education in Ancient Rome from the Elder Cato to the Younger Pliny*. Berkeley: University of California Press, 1977.

Boring, M. Eugene, Klaus Berger, and Carsten Colpe, eds. *Hellenistic Commentary to the New Testament*. Nashville: Abingdon, 1995.

Bornkamm, Günther, Gerhard Barth, and Heinz Joachim Held, eds. *Tradition and Interpretation in Matthew*. Translated by Percy Scott. Philadelphia: Westminster, 1963.

Borowski, Oded. *Agriculture in Iron Age Israel*. Winona Lake, Ind.: Eisenbrauns, 1987.

Botha, P. J. J. "Mute Manuscripts: Analysing a Neglected Aspect of Ancient Communication." *Theologica Evangelica* 23 (1990): 35–47.

Bowker, John. *The Targums and Rabbinic Literature*. Cambridge: Cambridge University Press, 1969.

Brown, Raymond E. *The Birth of the Messiah*. New York: Doubleday, 1993.

Brown, Raymond E., and John P. Meier. *Antioch and Rome: New Testament Cradles of Catholic Christianity.* New York: Paulist Press, 1983.

Brownlee, William H. *The Midrash Pesher of Habakkuk.* Missoula, Mont.: Scholars Press, 1979.

Bruce, F. F. *The New Testament Development of Old Testament Themes.* Grand Rapids: Eerdmans, 1968.

Büchler, Adolph. "The Minim of Sepphoris and Tiberias in the Second and Third Centuries." Pages 245–74 in *Studies in Jewish History.* Edited by I. Brodie and J. Rabinowitz. London: Oxford University Press, 1956.

Budd, P. J. *Numbers.* Edited by David A. Hubbard and Glenn W. Barker. Word Biblical Commentary 5. Waco, Tex.: Word Books, 1984.

Carter, Warren. *Matthew and Empire: Initial Explorations.* Harrisburg, Pa.: Trinity Press International, 2001.

Chancey, Mark A. "The Cultural Milieu of Ancient Sepphoris," *New Testament Studies* 47 (2001): 133.

———. *The Myth of a Gentile Galilee.* Cambridge: Cambridge University Press, 2002.

Chancey, Mark, and Eric M. Meyers. "How Jewish Was Sepphoris in Jesus' Time?" *Biblical Archaeology Review* 26 (2000): 18–33.

Charles, J. Daryl. "The Greatest or the Least in the Kingdom? The Disciples' Relationship to the Law." *Trinity Journal* 13 (1992): 139–62.

———. "The Greatest or the Least in the Kingdom? The Disciples' Relationship to the Law (Matt. 5.17–20)." Paper delivered at the Annual Meeting of the Society of Biblical Literature, Nashville, Tennessee, 18 November 2000.

Cohen, Shaye J. D. *From the Maccabees to the Mishnah.* Philadelphia: Westminster, 1987.

———. *Josephus in Galilee and Rome: His Vita and Development as a Historian.* Leiden: Brill, 1979.

———. "The Significance of Yavneh: Pharisees, Rabbis, and the End of Jewish Sectarianism." *Hebrew Union College Annual* (1984): 27–53.

Cohn-Sherbok, Dan. *Rabbinic Perspectives on the New Testament.* Studies in the Bible and Early Christianity 28. Lewiston, N.Y.: Edwin Mellen, 1990.

Conzelmann, Hans. *Gentiles-Jews-Christians: Polemics and Apologetics in the Greco-Roman Era.* Translated by M. Eugene Boring. Tübingen: J. C. B. Mohr, 1981.

Cope, O. Lamar. *Matthew: A Scribe Trained for the Kingdom of Heaven.* Washington, D.C.: Catholic Biblical Association of America, 1976.

Crosby, Michael H. *House of Disciples.* New York: Orbis Books, 1988.

Daube, David. *The New Testament and Rabbinic Judaism.* New York: Arno Press, 1973.

Davies, W. D. *Christian Origins and Judaism.* Philadelphia: Westminster, 1961.

———. *The Setting of the Sermon on the Mount.* Cambridge: Cambridge University Press, 1964.

Davies, W. D., and Dale C. Allison Jr. *The Gospel according to Saint Matthew.* Edited by J. A. Merton et al. 3 vols. International Critical Commentary. Edinburgh: T&T Clark International, 1991.

Deutsch, Celia. "Christians and Jews in the First Century: The Gospel of Matthew." *Thought* 67 (1992): 399–409.

———. *Lady Wisdom, Jesus, and the Sages: Metaphor and Social Context in Matthew's Gospel.* Valley Forge, Pa.: Trinity Press International, 1996.

———. "The Transfiguration: Vision and Social Setting in Matthew's Gospel (Matthew 17:1–9)." Pages 124–37 in *Putting Body and Soul Together: Essays in Honor of Robin Scroggs.* Edited by Virginia Wiles et al. Valley Forge, Pa.: Trinity Press International, 1997.

Drijvers, Hans. "Syrian Christianity and Judaism." Pages 124–46 in *The Jews among Pagans and Christians in the Roman Empire.* Edited by Judith Lieu, John North, and Tessa Rajak. London: Routledge, 1992.

Duling, Dennis C. "The Jesus Movement and Network Analysis." Pages 301–32 in *The Social Setting of Jesus and the Gospels.*

Edited by Wolfgang Stegemann et al. Minneapolis: Augsburg, 2002.

———. "The Matthean Brotherhood and Marginal Scribal Leadership." Pages 159–82 in *Modeling Early Christianity: Social-Scientific Studies of the New Testament in Its Context*. Edited by Philip F. Esler. London: Routledge, 1995.

Duncan-Jones, Richard. *The Economy of the Roman Empire: Quantitative Studies*. Cambridge: Cambridge University Press, 1964.

———. *Structure and Scale in the Roman Economy*. Cambridge: Cambridge University Press, 1990.

Edwards, Douglas. "The Socio-economic and Cultural Ethos in the First Century." Pages 53–74 in *The Galilee in Late Antiquity*. Edited by Lee I. Levine. Cambridge: Harvard University Press, 1992.

Elliott-Binns, L. E. *Galilean Christianity*. London: SCM Press, 1956.

Erickson, Richard J. "Divine Injustice? Matthew's Narrative Strategy and the Slaughter of the Innocents (Matthew 2.13–23)." *Journal for the Study of the New Testament* 64 (1996): 5–27.

Evans, Craig A. "Faith and Polemic: The New Testament and First-Century Judaism." Pages 1–20 in *Anti-Semitism and Early Christianity*. Edited by Craig A. Evans and Donald A. Hagner. Minneapolis: Fortress, 1993.

Ferguson, Everett. *Backgrounds of Early Christianity*. Grand Rapids: Eerdmans, 1987.

Finegan, Jack. *The Archeology of the New Testament: The Life of Jesus and the Beginning of the Early Church*. Princeton: Princeton University Press, 1969.

Finley, M. I. *The Ancient Economy*. Updated ed. Berkeley: University of California Press, 1999.

Fitzmyer, Joseph A. "The Aramaic Language and the Study of the New Testament." *Journal of Biblical Literature* 99 (1980): 5–21.

———. *A Wandering Aramean: Collected Aramaic Essays*. Society of Biblical Literature Monograph Series 25. Missoula, Mont.: Scholars Press, 1979.

Flusser, David. "The Jewish Religion in the Second Temple Period." Pages 3–40 in *Society and Religion in the Second Temple Period.* Edited by Michael Avi-Yonah and Zvi Baras. World History of the Jewish People 8. Jerusalem: Massada, 1977.

Foster, Paul. "Why Did Matthew Get the Shema Wrong? A Study of Matthew 22:37." *Journal of Biblical Literature* 122 (2003): 309–33.

Fowler, Henry Thatcher. *The History and Literature of the New Testament.* New York: Macmillan, 1925.

Fradkin, Arlene. "Long-Distance Trade in the Lower Galilee: New Evidence from Sepphoris." Pages 107–16 in *Archaeology and the Galilee: Texts and Contexts in the Graeco-Roman and Byzantine Periods.* Edited by Douglas R. Edwards and C. Thomas McCollough. Atlanta: Scholars Press, 1997.

France, R. T. *Matthew: Evangelist and Teacher.* Grand Rapids: Academie Books, 1989.

Freyne, Seán. "Bandits in Galilee: A Contribution to the Study of Social Conditions in First-Century Palestine." Pages 50–68 in *The Social World of Formative Christianity and Judaism: Essays in Tribute to Howard Clark Kee.* Edited by Jacob Neusner et al. Philadelphia: Fortress, 1988.

———. "Christianity in Sepphoris and Galilee." Pages 299–307 in *Galilee and Gospel: Collected Essays.* Edited by Seán Freyne. Wissenschaftliche Untersuchungen zum Neuen Testament 125. Tübingen: Mohr, 1997.

———. *Galilee from Alexander the Great to Hadrian, 323 BCE to 135 CE: A Study of Second Temple Judaism.* Edinburgh: T&T Clark International, 1980.

———. *Galilee, Jesus, and the Gospels: Literary Approaches and Historical Investigations.* Philadelphia: Fortress, 1988.

Gafni, Isaiah. "Daily Life in Galilee and Sepphoris." Pages 51–57 in *Sepphoris in Galilee: Crosscurrents of Culture.* Edited by Rebecca Martin Nagy et al. Winona Lake, Ind.: Eisenbrauns, 1996.

Gamble, Harry Y. *Books and Readers in the Early Church: A History of Early Christian Texts.* New Haven: Yale University Press, 1995.

————. *The New Testament Canon: Its Making and Meaning.* Philadelphia: Fortress, 1985.

Garland, David E. "Matthew's Understanding of the Temple Tax (Matt 17:24–27)." Pages 190–209 in *SBL Seminar Papers, 1987.* Edited by Kent Harold Richards. Atlanta: Scholars Press, 1987.

————. *Reading Matthew: A Literary and Theological Commentary on the First Gospel.* New York: Crossroad, 1993.

Garnsey, Peter. *Famine and Food Supply in the Graeco-Roman World: Responses to Risk and Crisis.* New York: Cambridge University Press, 1988.

Garnsey, Peter, and Richard Saller. *The Early Principate: Augustus to Trajan.* Greece and Rome: New Surveys in the Classics 15. Oxford: Clarendon Press, 1982.

————. *The Roman Empire: Economy, Society, and Culture.* Berkeley: University of California Press, 1987.

Gerhardsson, Birger. *Memory and Manuscript: Oral Tradition and Written Transmission in Rabbinic Judaism and Early Christianity.* Translated by Eric J. Sharpe. Copenhagen: C. W. K. Gleerup, 1964.

Glancy, Jennifer A. "Slaves and Slavery in the Matthean Parables." *Journal of Biblical Literature* 119 (2000): 67–90.

Golomb, B., and Y. Kedar. "Ancient Agriculture in the Galilee Mountains." *Israel Exploration Journal* 21 (1971): 136–40.

Goodman, Martin. *State and Society in Roman Galilee, A.D. 132–212.* Totowa, N.J.: Rowman & Allanheld, 1983.

Goodspeed, Edgar J. *Matthew: Apostle and Evangelist.* Philadelphia: John C. Winston, 1959.

Goulder, M. D. *Midrash and Lection in Matthew: The Speaker's Lectures in Biblical Studies.* London: SPCK, 1974.

Grant, F. C. *The Economic Background of the Gospels.* Oxford: Oxford University Press, 1926.

Gundry, Robert H. *Matthew: A Commentary on His Literary and Theological Art.* Grand Rapids: Eerdmans, 1982.

————. *The Use of the Old Testament in St. Matthew's Gospel.* Leiden: Brill, 1967.

Guttmann, Alexander. *Rabbinic Judaism in the Making: A Chapter in the History of the Halakhah from Ezra to Judah I.* Detroit: Wayne State University Press, 1970.

Hadas, Moses, ed. *The Complete Works of Tacitus.* Translated by Alfred John Church and William Jackson Brodribb. New York: Random House, 1942.

Hagner, Donald A. *Matthew 1–13.* Dallas: Word Books, 1993.

———. "Matthew: Apostate, Reformer, Revolutionary?" *New Testament Studies* 49 (2003): 193–209.

Hare, Douglas R. A. "Current Trends in Matthean Scholarship." *Word and World* 18 (1998): 405–10.

———. "How Jewish Is the Gospel of Matthew?" *Catholic Biblical Quarterly* 62 (2000): 264–77.

Harrington, Daniel J. *God's People in Christ.* Philadelphia: Fortress, 1980.

———. *The Gospel of Matthew.* Sacra pagina 1. Collegeville, Minn.: Liturgical Press, 1991.

———. "Not to Abolish, but to Fulfill." *Bible Today* 27 (1989): 333–37.

Harris, William V. *Ancient Literacy.* Cambridge: Harvard University Press, 1989.

Harvey, John D. *Listening to the Text: Oral Patterning in Paul's Letters.* Grand Rapids: Baker, 1998.

Herford, R. Travers. *Christianity in Talmud and Midrash.* New York: Ktav, 1903.

Hershkovitz, M. "Miniature Ointment Vases." *Israel Exploration Journal* 36 (1986): 45–51.

Hezser, Catherine. *Jewish Literacy in Roman Palestine.* Texts and Studies in Ancient Judaism 81. Tübingen: Mohr-Siebeck, 2001.

Hoehner, Harold W. *Herod Antipas.* Cambridge: Cambridge University Press, 1972.

Horsley, Richard A. *Galilee: History, Politics, People.* Valley Forge, Pa.: Trinity Press International, 1995.

Howard, Tracy L. "The Use of Hosea 11:1 in Matthew 2:15: An Alternative Solution." *Bibliotheca sacra* 143 (1986): 314–28.

Jennings, Theodore W., Jr., and Tat-Siong Benny Liew. "Mistaken Identities but Model Faith: Rereading the Centurion, the Chap, and the Christ in Matthew 8:5–13." *Journal of Biblical Literature* 123 (2004): 467–94.

Johnston, Robert M. "'The Least of the Commandments': Deuteronomy 22:6–7 in Rabbinic Judaism and Early Christianity." *Andrews University Seminary Studies* 20 (1982): 205–15.

Jones, A. H. M. "The Urbanization of Palestine." *Journal of Roman Studies* 21 (1931): 79–85.

Josephus, Flavius. *The Complete Works of Josephus*. Translated by William Whiston. Grand Rapids: Kregel, 1981.

Katz, Steven T. "Issues in the Separation of Judaism and Christianity after 70 C.E.: A Reconsideration." *Journal of Biblical Literature* 103 (1984): 43–76.

Kee, Howard Clark. "The Transformation of the Synagogue after 70 C.E.: Its Importance for Early Christianity." *New Testament Studies* 36 (1990): 1–24.

Keener, Craig S. *A Commentary on the Gospel of Matthew*. Grand Rapids: Eerdmans, 1999.

Kenney, E. J. "Books and Readers in the Roman World." Pages 3–32 in *The Cambridge History of Classical Literature*. Edited by E. J. Kenney. Cambridge: Cambridge University Press, 1982.

Kilpatrick, G. D. *The Origins of the Gospel according to St. Matthew*. Oxford: Clarendon Press, 1946.

Kimball, Charles A. *Jesus' Exposition of the Old Testament in Luke's Gospel*. Sheffield: JSOT Press, 1994.

Kingsbury, Jack Dean. *Matthew as Story*. Philadelphia: Fortress, 1986.

———. "The Place, Structure, and Meaning of the Sermon on the Mount within Matthew." *Interpretation* 41 (1987): 131–43.

———. "The Verb *Akolouthein* ('to follow') as an Index of Matthew's View of His Community." *Journal of Biblical Literature* 97 (1978): 56–73.

Koester, Helmut. *Introduction to the New Testament: History and Literature of Early Christianity*. Vol. 2. Philadelphia: Fortress, 1982.

Kosowski, Chaim J., ed. *Thesaurus Talmudis*. Jerusalem: Israel Ministry of Education and Culture, 1971.

Krauss, S. "The Jews in the Works of the Church Fathers." *Jewish Quarterly Review* 5 (1892–1893): 122–57.

Krentz, Edgar. "Community and Character: Matthew's Vision of the Church." Pages 565–73 in *SBL Seminar Papers, 1987*. Edited by Kent Harold Richards. Atlanta: Scholars Press, 1987.

Kugel, James L., and Rowan A. Greer, eds. *Early Biblical Interpretation*. Philadelphia: Westminster, 1986.

Lampe, W. H. "A.D. 70 in Christian Reflection." Pages 153–72 in *Jesus and the Politics of His Day*. Edited by Ernst Bammel and C. F. D. Moule. Cambridge: Cambridge University Press, 1984.

Lauterbach, Jacob Zellel. "Talmud Hermeneutics." *The Jewish Encyclopedia*. Volume 12. Edited by Cyrus Adler. Translated by Isidore Singer. New York: Funk and Wagnalls, 1904.

Leaney, A. R. C. *The Jewish and Christian World, 200 BC to AD 200*. Vol. 7. Cambridge: Cambridge University Press, 1984.

Lieu, Judith. "History and Theology in Christian Views of Judaism." Pages 79–96 in *The Jews among Pagans and Christians in the Roman Empire*. Edited by Judith Lieu et al. London: Routledge, 1992.

Longenecker, Richard N. *Biblical Exegesis in the Apostolic Period*. Grand Rapids: Eerdmans, 1975.

Luz, Ulrich. *Matthew 1–7: A Commentary*. Translated by Wilhelm C. Linss. Minneapolis: Augsburg, 1985.

Malherbe, Abraham J. *Social Aspects of Early Christianity*. 2nd ed. Philadelphia: Fortress, 1983.

Manns, Frederic. *John and Jamnia: How the Break Occurred between Jews and Christians, c. 80–100 A.D.* Jerusalem: Franciscan Printing Press, 1988.

Marrou, H. I. *A History of Education in Antiquity*. Translated by George Lamb. New York: Mentor Books, 1956.

Marx, Werner G. "Money Matters in Matthew." *Bibliotheca sacra* 136 (1979): 148–57.

Mattingly, Harold. *Roman Coins from the Earliest Times to the Fall of the Western Empire*. London: Spink & Son, 1977

McDonald, Lee Martin. "Anti-Judaism in the Early Church Fathers." Pages 215–52 in *Anti-Semitism and Early Christianity: Issues of Polemic and Faith.* Edited by Craig A. Evans and Donald A. Hagner. Minneapolis: Fortress, 1993.

McKitterick, Rosamond. *The Uses of Literacy in Early Mediaeval Europe.* Cambridge: Cambridge University Press, 1990.

Meeks, Wayne A. *The First Urban Christians: The Social World of the Apostle Paul.* New Haven: Yale University Press, 1983.

Meier, John P. "The Antiochene Church of the Second Christian Generation." Pages 45–72 in *Antioch and Rome: New Testament Cradles of Christianity.* Edited by Raymond E. Brown and John P. Meier. New York: Paulist, 1983.

———. *Law and History in Matthew's Gospel: A Redactional Study of Mt. 5:17–48.* Analecta biblica 71. Rome: Biblical Institute Press, 1976.

———. "Locating Matthew's Church in Space and Time." Pages 15–27 in *Antioch and Rome: New Testament Cradles of Christianity.* Edited by Raymond E. Brown and John P. Meier. New York: Paulist, 1983.

———. *A Marginal Jew: Rethinking the Historical Jesus.* Vol. 1. New York: Doubleday, 1991.

———. *Matthew.* New Testament Message 3. Collegeville, Minn.: Liturgical Press, 1980.

———. *The Vision of Matthew: Christ, Church, and Morality in the First Gospel.* New York: Paulist, 1979.

Merrill, Selah. *Galilee in the Time of Christ.* Oxford: Oxford University Press, 1898.

Meshorer, Ya'akov. *City-Coins of Eretz-Israel and the Decapolis in the Roman Period.* Jerusalem: Israel Museum, 1985.

Metzger, Bruce M. *Historical and Literary Studies: Pagan, Jewish, and Christian.* New Testament Tools and Studies 8. Edited by Bruce M. Metzger. Grand Rapids: Eerdmans, 1968.

Meyers, Eric M. "Jesus and His Galilean Context." Pages 57–66 in *Archaeology and the Galilee: Texts and Context in the Graeco-Roman and Byzantine Periods.* Edited by Douglas R. Edwards and C. Thomas McCollough. Atlanta: Scholars Press, 1997.

———. "Roman Sepphoris in Light of New Archaeological Evidence and Recent Research." Pages 325–38 in *The Galilee in Late Antiquity*. Edited by Lee I. Levine. Cambridge: Harvard University Press, 1992.

Meyers, Eric M., and James F. Strange. *Archaeology, the Rabbis, and Early Christianity*. Nashville: Abingdon, 1981.

Miller, Stuart S. *Studies in the History and Traditions of Sepphoris*. Leiden: Brill, 1984.

Montefiore, C. G. *Rabbinic Literature and Gospel Teachings*. New York: Ktav, 1970.

Moore, George Foot. *Judaism in the First Centuries of the Christian Era: The Age of the Tannaim*. Vol. 1. Cambridge: Harvard University Press, 1962.

Moule, C. F. D. *The Birth of the New Testament*. Black's New Testament Commentaries 1. London: Adam & Charles Black, 1962.

Muecke, D. C. *The Compass of Irony*. London: Methuen, 1969.

Mussies, G. "Greek in Palestine and the Diaspora." Pages 1040–64 in *The Jewish People in the First Century*. Edited by Samuel Safrai and M. Stern. Vol. 2. Philadelphia: Fortress, 1976.

Neusner, Jacob. "Beyond Myth, after Apocalypse: The Mishnaic Conception of History." Pages 91–106 in *The Social World of Formative Christianity and Judaism: Essays in Tribute to Howard Clark Kee*. Edited by Jacob Neusner et al. Philadelphia: Fortress, 1988.

———. *First-Century Judaism in Crisis*. Nashville: Abingdon, 1975.

———. *Judaism in the Beginning of Christianity*. Philadelphia: Fortress, 1984.

———. *Judaism: The Evidence of the Mishnah*. Atlanta: Scholars Press, 1988.

———. *The Rabbinic Traditions about the Pharisees before 70*. Leiden: Brill, 1971.

Nickelsburg, George. *Jewish Literature between the Bible and the Mishnah*. Philadelphia: Fortress, 1981.

Noth, M. *Die israelitischen Personennamen*. Stuttgart: Kohlhammer, 1978.

Oakman, Douglas E. "Jesus and Agrarian Palestine: The Factor of Debt." Pages 57–73 in *SBL Seminar Papers, 1985*. Edited by Kent Harold Richards. Atlanta: Scholars Press, 1985.

———. "Money in the Moral Universe of the New Testament." Pages 335–48 in *The Social Setting of Jesus and the Gospels*. Edited by Wolfgang Stegemann et al. Minneapolis: Augsburg Fortress, 2002.

Oppenheimer, Aharon. *The 'Am Ha-Aretz: A Study in the Social History of the Jewish People in the Hellenistic-Roman Period*. Edited by K. H. Rengstorf. Translated by I. H. Levine. Arbeiten zur Literatur und Geschichte des hellenistischen Judentums 8. Leiden: Brill, 1977.

Orton, David E. *The Understanding Scribe: Matthew and the Apocalyptic Ideal*. Journal for the Study of the New Testament Supplement Series 25. Sheffield: Sheffield Academic, 1989.

Osiek, Carolyn, and David L. Balch. *Families in the New Testament World: Households and House Churches*. Louisville: Westminster John Knox, 1997.

Overman, J. Andrew. *Church and Community in Crisis: The Gospel according to Matthew*. Valley Forge, Pa.: Trinity Press International, 1996.

———. *Matthew's Gospel and Formative Judaism: The Social World of the Matthean Community*. Minneapolis: Fortress, 1990.

———. "Matthew's Parables and Roman Politics: The Imperial Setting of Matthew's Narrative with Special Reference to His Parables." Pages 425–39 in *SBL Seminar Papers, 1995*. Edited by Eugene H. Lovering Jr. Atlanta: Scholars Press, 1995.

Patte, Daniel. *Early Jewish Hermeneutic in Palestine*. Society of Biblical Literature Dissertation Series 22. Missoula, Mont.: Scholars Press, 1975.

Pesch, Rudolf. "'Wo zwei oder drei versammelt sind auf meinen Namen hin . . .' (Mt 18,20): Zur Ekklesiologie eines Wortes Jesu." Pages 229–43 in *Studien zum Matthäusevangelium: Festschrift für Wilhelm Pesch*. Edited by Ludger Schenke. Stuttgart: Verlag Katholisches Bibelwerk, 1988.

Phillips, Gary A. "Training Scribes for a World Divided: Discourse and Division in the Religious System of Matthew's Gospel." Pages 51–74 in *Religious Writings and Religious Systems: Systemic Analysis of Holy Books in Christianity, Islam, Buddhism, Greco-Roman Religions, Ancient Israel, and Judaism*. Vol. 2: *Christianity*. Edited by Jacob Neusner et al. Atlanta: Scholars Press, 1989.

Powell, Mark Allan. "Do and Keep What Moses Says (Matthew 23:2–7)." *Journal of Biblical Literature* 114 (1995): 419–35.

———. "Matthew's Beatitudes: Reversals and Rewards of the Kingdom." *Catholic Biblical Quarterly* 58 (1996): 460–479.

Prabhu, George M. Soares. *The Formula Quotations in the Infancy Narrative of Matthew: An Enquiry into the Tradition History of Mt 1–2*. Rome: Biblical Institute Press, 1976.

Prokter, Lewis J. "The Blind Spot: New Testament Scholarship's Ignorance of Rabbinic Judaism." *Scriptura* 48 (1994): 1–12.

Radice, Betty. *The Letters of the Younger Pliny*. Translated by Betty Radice. Baltimore: Penguin Books, 1963.

Reed, Jonathan L. *Archaeology and the Galilean Jesus: A Reexamination of the Evidence*. Harrisburg, Pa.: Trinity Press International, 2000.

Reicke, Bo Ivar. *The New Testament Era*. Translated by David E. Green. Philadelphia: Fortress, 1964.

———. "Synoptic Prophecies on the Destruction of Jerusalem." Pages 121–34 in *Studies in New Testament and Early Christian Literature: Essays in Honor of Allen P. Wikgren*. Edited by David Edward Aune. Supplements to Novum Testamentum 33. Leiden: Brill, 1972.

Robbins, Vernon K. "Progymnastic Rhetorical Composition and Pre-Gospel Traditions: A New Approach." Pages 111–47 in *The Synoptic Gospels: Source Criticism and the New Literary Criticism*. Edited by C. Focant. Bibliotheca ephemeridum theologicarum lovaniensium 110. Louvain: Louvain University Press, 1993.

Roberts, Colin H. "Early Christianity in Egypt: Three Notes." *Journal of Egyptian Archaeology* 40 (1954): 92–96.

———. *Manuscript, Society, and Belief in Early Christian Egypt*. London: Oxford University Press, 1979.

Roll, Israel. "Survey of Roman Roads in Lower Galilee." Pages 38–40 in *Excavations and Surveys in Israel*. Edited by Inna Pommerantz and Ann Roshwalb. Vol. 14. Jerusalem: Israel Antiquities Authority, 1994.

Safrai, Samuel. "Education and the Study of the Torah." Pages 945–70 in *The Jewish People of the First Century*. Edited by Samuel Safrai and M. Stern. Vol. 2. Philadelphia: Fortress, 1976.

Saldarini, Anthony J. "Comparing the Traditions: New Testament and Rabbinic Literature." *Bulletin for Biblical Research* 7 (1997): 195–203.

———. "Delegitimation of Leaders in Matthew 23." *Catholic Biblical Quarterly* 54 (1992): 659–80.

———. "The Gospel of Matthew and Jewish-Christian Conflict in the Galilee." Pages 23–38 in *The Galilee in Late Antiquity*. Edited by Lee I. Levine. Cambridge: Harvard University Press, 1992.

———. *Matthew's Christian-Jewish Community*. Chicago: University of Chicago Press, 1994.

———. *Pharisees, Scribes, and Sadducees in Palestinian Society: A Sociological Approach*. Wilmington, Del.: Michael Glazier, 1988.

Saller, Richard P. *Personal Patronage under the Early Empire*. Cambridge: Cambridge University Press, 1982.

Sanders, E. P. "Jesus' Galilee." Pages 3–41 in *Fair Play: Diversity and Conflicts in Early Christianity. Essays in Honor of Heikki Räisänen*. Edited by Ismo Dunderberg et al. Leiden: Brill, 2002.

———. *Jewish Law from Jesus to the Mishnah*. Philadelphia: Trinity Press International, 1990.

Sandmel, Samuel. *A Jewish Understanding of the New Testament*. Cincinnati, Ohio: Hebrew Union College Press, 1956.

Sawicki, Marianne. *Crossing Galilee*. Harrisburg, Pa.: Trinity Press International, 2000.

Schäfer, P. "Die Flucht Johanan b. Zakkais aus Jerusalem und die Gründung des 'Lehrhauses' in Jabne." Pages 43–101 in *Principat* 19/2. Edited by Wolfgang Hasse. Berlin: Walter de Gruyter, 1979.

Schams, Christine. *Jewish Scribes in the Second Temple Period.* Journal for the Study of the Old Testament Supplement Series 291. Sheffield: Sheffield Academic, 1998.

Schiffman, Lawrence H. *From Text to Tradition: A History of Second Temple and Rabbinic Judaism.* Hoboken, N.J.: Ktav, 1991.

———. "Was There a Galilean Halakah?" Pages 143–56 in *The Galilee in Late Antiquity.* Edited by Lee I. Levine. Cambridge: Harvard University Press, 1992.

Schnackenburg, Rudolf. *The Church in the New Testament.* New York: Herder and Herder, 1965.

Schroedel, William M. "Ignatius and the Reception of the Gospel of Matthew in Antioch." Pages 154–77 in *Social History of the Matthean Community: Cross-Disciplinary Approaches.* Edited by David L. Balch. Minneapolis: Fortress, 1991.

Schürer, Emil. *The History of the Jewish People in the Age of Jesus Christ.* Edited and translated by Geza Vermes and Fergus Millar. Vol. 1. Edinburgh: T&T Clark International, 1973.

Schüssler Fiorenza, Elisabeth. "Miracles, Mission, and Apologetics: An Introduction." Pages 1–25 in *Aspects of Religious Propaganda in Judaism and Early Christianity.* Edited by Elisabeth Schüssler Fiorenza. Notre Dame, Ind.: University of Notre Dame Press, 1976.

Schwabe, Moshe, and Baruch Lifshitz. *Beth She'arim,* vol. 2. *The Greek Inscriptions.* New Brunswick, N.J.: Rutgers University Press, 1974.

Schweizer, Eduard. *The Good News according to Matthew.* Translated by David E. Green. Atlanta: John Knox, 1975.

———. *Matthäus und seine Gemeinde.* SBS 71. Stuttgart: KBW Verlag, 1974.

———. "Matthew's Church." Pages 129–55 in *The Interpretation of Matthew.* Edited by Graham Stanton. Issues in Religion and Theology 3. Philadelphia: Fortress, 1983.

Segal, Alan F. *Rebecca's Children: Judaism and Christianity in the Roman World.* Cambridge: Harvard University Press, 1986.

Senior, Donald. "Between Two Worlds: Gentiles and Jewish Christians in Matthew's Gospel." *Catholic Biblical Quarterly* 61 (1999): 1–23.

————. "Directions in Matthean Studies." Pages 5–21 in *The Gospel of Matthew in Current Study*. Edited by David E. Aune. Grand Rapids: Eerdmans, 2001.

Setzer, Claudia. *Jewish Responses to Early Christians: History and Polemics, 30–150 C.E.* Minneapolis: Fortress, 1994.

Sevenster, J. N. *Do You Know Greek? How Much Greek Could the First Jewish Christians Have Known?* Leiden: Brill, 1968.

Shedinger, Robert F. "Must the Greek Text Always Be Preferred? Versional and Patristic Witnesses to the Text of Matthew 4:16." *Journal of Biblical Literature* 123 (2004): 449–66.

Sigal, Phillip. *The Halakah of Jesus of Nazareth according to the Gospel of Matthew*. Lanham, Md.: University Press of America, 1986.

Sim, David C. *The Gospel of Matthew and Christian Judaism: The History and Social Setting of the Matthean Community*. Edinburgh: T&T Clark International, 1998.

Smith, D. Moody. "When Did the Gospels Become Scripture?" *Journal of Biblical Literature* 119 (2000): 3–20.

Smith, Robert H. "'Blessed Are the Poor in (Holy) Spirit'? (Matthew 5:3)." *Word and World* 18 (1998): 389–96.

————. "Were the Early Christians Middle-Class? A Sociological Analysis of the New Testament." *Currents in Theology and Mission* 7 (1980): 260–76.

Soulen, Richard. *Handbook of Biblical Criticism*. Atlanta: John Knox, 1976.

Stanton, Graham N. *A Gospel for a New People*. Louisville: Westminster, 1993.

————. "'Pray That Your Flight May Not Be in Winter or on a Sabbath' (Matthew 24:20)." *Journal for the Study of the New Testament* 37 (1989): 17–30.

Starr, Raymond J. "The Circulation of Literary Texts in the Roman World." *Classical Quarterly* 37 (1987): 213–23.

Stegner, William Richard. "Breaking Away: The Conflict with Formative Judaism." *Biblical Research* 40 (1995): 7–36.

————. "Leadership and Governance in the Matthean Community." Pages 147–57 in *Common Life in the Early Church:*

Essays Honoring Graydon F. Snyder. Edited by Julian V. Hills. Harrisburg, Pa.: Trinity Press International, 1998.

Stendahl, Krister. *The School of St. Matthew and Its Use of the Old Testament.* Uppsala, Sweden: C. W. K. Gleerup, 1954.

Strack, H. L., and G. Stremberger. *Introduction to the Talmud and Midrash.* Translated by Markus Bockmuehl. Minneapolis: Fortress, 1992.

Strecker, G. *Der Weg der Gerechtigkeit: Untersuchung zur Theologie des Matthäus.* Göttingen: Vandenhoeck & Ruprecht, 1962.

Streeter, Burntett Hillman. *The Four Gospels: A Study of Origins. Treating the Manuscript Tradition, Sources, Authorship, and Dates.* London: Macmillan, 1964.

Tcherikover, Victor. *Palestine under the Ptolemies: A Contribution to the Study of the Zenon Papyri.* Mizraim 4–5. New York: Hebrew University Press, 1937.

Theissen, Gerd. *Social Reality and the Early Christians.* Translated by Margaret Kohl. Minneapolis: Fortress, 1992.

———. *Sociology of Early Palestinian Christianity.* Translated by John Bowden. Minneapolis: Fortress, 1978.

Thompson, William G. *Matthew's Advice to a Divided Community: Mt 17,22–18,35.* Rome: Biblical Institute Press, 1970.

Tilborg, Sjef van. *The Jewish Leaders in Matthew.* Leiden: Brill, 1972.

Vermes, Geza. *Jesus and the World of Judaism.* Philadelphia: Fortress, 1984.

———. *Jesus the Jew: A Historian's Reading of the Gospels.* Philadelphia: Fortress, 1973.

———. *The Religion of Jesus the Jew.* Minneapolis: Fortress, 1993.

Viviano, Benedict T. "Social World and Community Leadership: The Case of Matthew 23.1–12, 34." *Journal for the Study of the New Testament* 39 (1990): 3–21.

Votaw, C. W. *The Gospels and Contemporary Biographies in the Graeco-Roman World.* Philadelphia: Fortress, 1970.

Weaver, Dorothy Jean. "Power and Powerless: Matthew's Use of Irony in the Portrayal of Political Leaders." Pages 173–96 in

Treasures New and Old: Recent Contributions to Matthean Studies. Edited by David R. Bauer and Mark Allan Powell. Atlanta: Scholars Press, 1996.

Weiss, Johannes. *Earliest Christianity: A History of the Period A.D. 30–150*. Translated by Frederick C. Grant. Vol. 2. Gloucester, Mass.: Peter Smith, 1970.

White, L. Michael. "Crisis Management and Boundary Maintenance: The Social Location of the Matthean Community." Pages 211–47 in *Social History of the Matthean Community: Cross-Disciplinary Approaches*. Edited by David L. Balch. Minneapolis: Fortress, 1991.

Whittaker, Molly. *Jews and Christians: Graeco-Roman Views*. Cambridge: Cambridge University Press, 1984.

Wilken, Robert L. *Judaism and the Early Christian Mind: A Study of Cyril of Alexandria's Exegesis and Theology*. New Haven: Yale University Press, 1971.

Wilson, Stephen G. *Related Strangers: Jews and Christians, 70–170 C.E.* Minneapolis: Fortress, 1995.

Wong, Eric Kun-Chun. "The Matthean Understanding of the Sabbath: A Response to G. N. Stanton." *Journal for the Study of the New Testament* 44 (1991): 3–18.

Wright, N. T. "The Divinity of Jesus." Pages 157–68 in *The Meaning of Jesus: Two Visions*. Edited by Marcus Borg and N. T. Wright. San Francisco: Harper, 1999.

Index

187